C000039481

DICTIONARY

MIND, BODY AND SPIRIT

Ideas, People and Places

DICTIONARY OF

MIND, BODY AND SPIRIT

Ideas, People and Places

COMPILED BY

Eileen Campbell and
J. H. Brennan

The Aquarian Press
An Imprint of HarperCollins*Publishers*

The Aquarian Press
An Imprint of HarperCollins*Publishers*
77–85 Fulham Palace Road,
Hammersmith, London W6 8JB

First published as *The Aquarian Guide to the New Age*
by The Aquarian Press 1990

This revised edition 1994
1 3 5 7 9 10 8 6 4 2

© Eileen Campbell and J.H. Brennan 1990, 1994

Eileen Campbell and J.H. Brennan assert the moral right to
be identified as the authors of this work

A catalogue record for this book
is available from the British Library

ISBN 1 85538 328 4

Typeset by Harper Phototypesetters Limited,
Northampton, England
Printed in Great Britain by
HarperCollinsManufacturing Glasgow

All rights reserved. No part of this publication may be
reproduced, stored in a retrieval system, or transmitted,
in any form or by any means, electronic, mechanical,
photocopying, recording or otherwise, without the prior
permission of the publishers.

Preface

In our fast-changing world, many people are now exploring ideas that seem to point in directions different from what our materialist, reductionist, scientific world-view offers. In a sense people are seeking, looking for answers to life's seemingly unanswerable questions. We recognize that we are Mind, Body and Spirit, and that, as Hamlet knew all too well:

> There are more things in heaven and earth, Horatio,
> Than are dreamt of in your philosophy.

Men and women have grappled with life's meaning and purpose throughout history, but today's world, for all its 'apparent' progress, seems unable to provide any real answers or, indeed, lasting satisfaction. Where does truth lie? Does each of us have to discover it for ourselves? What is it we seek? What makes for peace of mind?

Hopefully, this dictionary, which covers a whole range of different subjects – different spiritual and esoteric traditions, para-normal phenomena, people, places – will prove a useful starting-point for those embarking on a voyage of self-discovery.

A

Acupressure

A variation on Chinese **acupuncture** in which finger pressure replaces needles for stimulation of various acupuncture points. Serious illnesses are not normally treated by acupressure, but the system is useful as a means of first aid and/or pain relief. Acupressure is also called *G-Jo*, which is Chinese for first aid. The Japanese form is called *Shiatsu*.

Acupuncture

The world's oldest known medical system, first outlined in *The Yellow Emperor's Classic of Internal Medicine* (*see* **Nei Ching**) and attributed to China's semi-legendary Huang Ti (2697–2597 BC). Acupuncture postulates a flow of subtle energy, called *ch'i*, through 14 clearly-defined channels (*meridians*) in the human body. Thin needles inserted at specific points control the flow of this energy for therapeutic effect.

Although seventeenth-century Jesuits carried home news of the system, acupuncture was not taken seriously in the West until the 1930s when a number of French physicians began to experiment with its techniques. Even then, the Western world as a whole waited until US President Richard Nixon's historic China visit before any really widespread examination of acupuncture began.

The main stimulus was a movie of a major abdominal surgery operation carried out under acupuncture anaesthesia. The patient was shown eating orange segments and chatting to surgeons while the operation proceeded – something impossible to dismiss as suggestion or superstition.

For Western practitioners, the problem has always been the development of a satisfactory theory of acupuncture. The scientific establishment finds great difficulty in accepting Chinese ideas of *ch'i* even though, empirically, it is now widely accepted that acupuncture techniques can achieve spectacular medical results.

Adept

One skilled in the esoteric arts. (*See also* **Inner Plane Adepti**.)

Adi Granath

The central holy book of the Sikh religion. The name derives from a Punjabi expression meaning 'Original (or First) Book' and it is revered as a living **guru**. It was compiled by a succession of Sikh gurus and contains hymns and devotional songs.

The *Adi Granath* begins with a **mantra** declaring the nature of God and contains the *Japji* (or recital) written by the founder of the religion, Guru Nanak, which is believed to be the most sacred and important item in the entire work. The book is opened ritually each morning, closed and wrapped each evening. On special occasions continuous readings are given, lasting from 2 to 15 days. On martyrs' and saints' days, it is carried out in procession.

Advaita

See **Vedanta**.

A.E.

See **Russell, George**.

Aetherius Society

See **King, George**.

Agrippa, Cornelius

Legend records that when Cornelius Agrippa (real name Heinrich Cornelis) went out one day, he left the key of a secret room with his wife, who foolishly lent it to their lodger.

This worthy, a student, discovered a spell book in the room and while reading it accidentally called up a demon which strangled him.

When Agrippa came home he feared the authorities might charge him with murder, so he forced the demon to reanimate the corpse. Thus the student was witnessed walking in the street and although he collapsed when the magic wore off, the assumption was he had died of natural causes.

The legend is interesting not because it was true (for it most certainly was not) but because it gives some indication of Agrippa's fearsome reputation in his time.

Born in Cologne in 1486, he grew up to be one of the most colourful characters of his age. He spent much of his life on the move throughout Europe where his books on the occult earned him fame (or at least notoriety) in royal courts and universities alike. He functioned as a lawyer, doctor, historian, theologian and financial adviser, along with following less respectable pursuits such as alchemist, astrologer, demonologist and spy. He even took to forming secret societies, largely, it seems, in order to exploit their members.

Agrippa's real importance lies in his philosophy, expressed in two major works, *De Occulta Philosophia* (Occult Philosophy) and *De Incertitudine et Vanitate Scientiarum et Artum* (Uncertainty and Vanity of Science and the Arts), of which the former, first published in 1531, is by far the better known. Agrippa held that the individual contains God and the Universe within himself, that everything in existence has a spiritual component and that the fundamental essence of the Universe is unity.

Ahriman
Persian god of evil, the not-quite-eternal opponent of the beneficent Ohrmazd. (*See* **Ahura Mazda**, **Anthroposophy**; **Zoroastrianism**.)

Ahura Mazda
A variation on the name Ohrmazd, the benign deity of **Zoroastrianism**, a religion of Ancient Persia. Like many religions, Zoroastrianism taught of a cosmic duality in which Good, represented by Ahura Mazda, battled Evil, personified in the god's twin brother Ahriman.

Followers of the religion accepted that Ahriman ruled the world – a convenient explanation of death, disease, poverty, war and other ills – but insisted that his term of office would be limited to 9,000 years, after which Ahura Mazda would overthrow him.

Aikido
As with other Japanese **martial arts**, *aikido* is both a method of self-defence and a spiritual discipline. Its literal meaning is 'road'

(*do*) to 'union' (*ai*) with the 'life force' (*ki*). It was developed by Morihei Oyeshiba in the 1920s. As a discipline it aims to develop the ability to flow with events by developing *ki* (*see also Ch'i*) and working with it without attachment either to victory or defeat.

Akashic Record

Sometimes called the 'world memory', the akashic record is reputed to be an area of the **astral plane** which carries the imprint of everything that has ever happened. Certain **psychics** are reputed to be able to 'read' this record and thus obtain information about humanity's past unavailable from any other source.

Some occultists believe the akashic record to be of use in determining an individual's **past lives**.

Al-Ghazzali

The brilliant eleventh-century Persian philosopher, Abu Hamid Mohammed ibn Ghazzali, abandoned his university position in Baghdad to go into seclusion, seeking peace through **meditation**. He taught that although reason was higher than sense experience, **intuition** was higher than reason.

Al-Hallaj

The Sufi mystic Abu al-Mughith al-Husayn ibn Mansur al-Hallaj was born about AD 658 in the southern Iranian town of Tur, his grandfather reputedly a **Zoroastrian** and his father a convert to **Islam**. It is thought his father earned his living as a wool carder, hence Abu's adoption of the name al-Hallaj (which means 'wool carder'), following a common Sufi practice.

From an early age he showed a mystical bent, elected to follow the aesthetic path and had the three finest Sufi teachers of his age, al-Tustari, al-Makki and al-Junayd. In adult life he became an inveterate traveller, covering a large part of the Islamic Empire and constantly teaching, preaching and drawing students to him. He was, however, unpopular with many of the Sufi Masters of his time, who considered him far too willing to impart esoteric information to his followers.

Al-Hallaj was prone to mystic ecstasies – what the Sufis call 'an intoxicated man' – during which he experienced union with God. In one of these somewhere between AD 911 and 922 (the exact date is uncertain), he was so lost to the world that he called out, *'Ana al-Haqq'* ('I am the Truth') which in Islam was tantamount to claiming to be God. As a result he was jailed as a heretic, tortured and eventually, on 26 March 922, crucified, drawn and quartered.

In historical perspective, it appears Islam itself was on trial since al-Hallaj's mystical experiences are now generally accepted as genuine and he has been accorded the status of saint and martyr.

Albertus Magnus

The thirteenth-century alchemist and magician was a teacher of Thomas Aquinas and attributed author of various *grimoires* which sought to take advantage of his considerable reputation.

Albertus was born in 1205 in Larvigen and died in 1280. In between, inspired by the Virgin Mary, he learned to control the weather, change lead into gold and discovered the **Philosopher's Stone** . . . or so he claimed.

Alchemy

The term 'alchemy' derives from the Arabic *Khem*, an ancient word for Egypt, thus making it the 'Art of Egypt' or **magic**. It is also known as 'the royal art'. Superficially, however, alchemy has always appeared more a primitive form of chemistry than a branch of the magical arts, although medieval European alchemists dedicated much of their time to fabulous pursuits like the search for a **Philosopher's Stone** which would transform lead into gold, cure all diseases and bestow immortality. (*See also* **Taoist Alchemy**.)

The philosophical foundation for alchemy derives from classical Greek and Gnostic influences.

The psychologist **Carl Jung**, among others, has suggested that the obscure and often coded accounts of alchemical experiments actually conceal a profound system of spiritual development, a theory that has attracted widespread interest.

However a literal interpretation of alchemical claims has not completely died out. Idries Shah has recorded how Mrs Morag Murray Abdullah, a Scotswoman married to an Afghan, was introduced to a Pathan alchemist named Aquil Khan who demonstrated the creation of alchemical gold, not from lead, but from a mixture of stone and silver baked in clay over a special fire. The British Museum still exhibits a medallion reputed to

11

have been cast from alchemical gold by the Elizabethan magus, **John Dee**.

There has recently been renewed interest in vegetable alchemy, an obscure art-cum-science showing similarities with anthroposophical medicine. (*See* **Anthroposophy.**)

Alexander Technique

This technique is usually associated with good posture and relaxation and is popular with dancers, musicians and actors. However, it is also a good preventative technique, since it promotes healthy functioning of the body and has proved enormously helpful for people suffering from rheumatic and breathing disorders.

F. Matthias Alexander developed his technique as a result of studying his own poor use of his body which produced a disorder of the throat (in his case loss of voice, which for an actor in mid-performance was fairly devastating!)

The method he went on to develop is about re-educating people in the correct use of their bodies and giving up the acquired bad habits of a lifetime. This is achieved working with a teacher, by self-observation and conscious correction, together with a mental image of healthy functioning.

Altered States of Consciousness
See **Consciousness**.

Amulet

Amulets are used for defence – they protect against disease, the evil eye, bad luck, etc. Common amulets are gems and semi-precious stones, animal replicas, statues of gods and goddesses. Natural amulets include nuts, plants, berries and even garlic. (**Dion Fortune** recommended keeping some in a vase to ward off unwelcome visitors!) Amulets can also be symbols or inscriptions which are engraved in buildings and tombs. (*See also* **Talisman**.)

Andreae, Johann Valentin
See **Rosicrucians**.

Andrews, Lynn
Very much a female **Castaneda**, Lynn Andrews is a somewhat controversial teacher of the Medicine Way and author of several

best-selling books on the subject – *Medicine Woman*, *Flights of the Seventh Moon*, *Star Woman*, *Crystal Woman* and *Windhorse Woman*, as well as a set of **divination** cards called *The Power Deck*. Her books describe how her teacher of Native American ways of living, seeing and **dreaming**, Cree medicine woman Agnes Whistling Elk, has guided her through sometimes hazardous pathways to self-knowledge.

In spite of the controversy about her work, there is no denying that Lynn Andrews has helped many women to nourish and fulfil themselves and find their power.

Angels

Although the word 'angel' comes from the Latin *angelus*, denoting a supernatural entity of benign instincts, its strict Biblical meaning is 'messenger'. The first angel mentioned in the Bible appears in Genesis 16 as a messenger sent by the Lord to Hagar to announce she would give birth to Ishmael.

Early reports of angels, possibly drawn from, or at least influenced by, the supernatural messengers of Hittite and Canaanite gods, did not match the concept of winged beings so popular today. Old and New Testament angels were usually indistinguishable from human beings, with whom they were often confused. Even Gabriel, the messenger sent to Daniel to help him interpret his dreams, is referred to as a man despite the fact he was seen 'in swift flight'. Sometimes a particular glow around the angel betrayed its supernatural origin, but sometimes its essential nature was only realized after a visitation was complete.

It has been estimated that an 11-stone angel would require a wing-span of around 14 feet (and pectoral muscles weighing more than 20 pounds) to achieve lift-off, but the calculation has little relevance to the modern esoteric concept of angels as inhabitants of a different order of reality.

It is thought that certain angels are somehow 'in charge' of different countries, races, geographical areas and the planet as a whole. (*See also* **Guardian Angel**.)

Animism

One of the most ancient of all human belief systems, animism holds that all of nature is essentially alive with **spirits** or divinities inhabiting trees, streams, mountains, natural rock formations and even certain tools or weapons.

Animistic beliefs remain widespread among primitive societies, particularly those in which many different spiritual beings are believed to control various aspects of the natural and social environment.

The concept of animism was developed in the late nineteenth century by the British anthropologist Sir Edward B. Tylor, who regarded such beliefs as the earliest stage in the evolution of religion. He theorized that dreams, trances and the observation of death led primitive peoples to belief in a soul, and that these beliefs were then projected onto the natural world. Tylor further considered that a belief in animism led to the definition of more generalized deities and, eventually, to the worship of a single god.

Although this evolutionary view of religion has largely been discredited, modern psychologists have tended to support aspects of Tylor's theory by concluding that animism arises out of the projection of unconscious contents. According to this viewpoint, when a primitive communicates with, for example, a tree spirit, he is actually experiencing the reality of an inner voice. However, with such concepts as **Gaia** and the vigorous rise of neo-**shaman**ism, a new lease of life has been given to the spiritist theories of animism.

Anthroposophy

A system of spiritual science propounded by the Austrian scientist/mystic **Rudolf Steiner**. After a decade of association with the Theosophical Society, he broke away in 1909 to found his own Anthroposophical Society. The name is derived from the Greek – *anthropos* meaning 'man' and *sophia* 'wisdom'.

Anthroposophy taught of the evolution of the Earth through seven epochs and seven civilizations, with **Ahriman** and Lucifer standing as the eternal opponents of human progress.

On the more personal scale, Anthroposophy dealt with the individual's four 'bodies', **reincarnation** and life in the **spirit** worlds between incarnations.

Steiner also developed a system of anthroposophical medicine which combined **herbalism** and **homoeopathy**, and included counselling to deal with psychological and emotional problems.

Apparition

Little is known about the nature of apparitions, which manifest as people (living and dead), animals, objects and **spirits**. A large proportion of the apparitions studied seem to manifest in order to communicate a crisis or death, comfort the grieving or provide information which is needed.

An important class of apparitions are Marian apparitions. Throughout the centuries apparitions of the Blessed Virgin Mary have been reported and many have been pronounced authentic by the Catholic Church. The apparitions at Guadalupe, Lourdes and Fatima are the most famous. Pilgrims visit in the hope of miraculous cures. One of the more recent, but still unauthenticated Marian apparitions is in the village of Medjugorje in Bosnia-Herzegovina.

Applied Kinesiology
See **Kinesiology**.

Apport
An object materializing apparently out of thin air in the presence of a **medium** or an **adept**. Apports can be anything from flowers and perfumes to sweets, jewellery or *vibuti* (holy ash). One of the best-known producers of apports alive today is the holy man **Sai Baba**.

Aquarian Conspiracy
The idea, put forward by Marilyn Ferguson in her book *The Aquarian Conspiracy* (Routledge, 1981), that an underground network is working to bring about radical change in the world, not in the sense of destroying the existing order, but in the sense of a gradual shift towards a new order. The radical change is nothing less than a transformation of **consciousness**, an idea which is fundamental to **New Age** thinking and which, perhaps, the current ecological disaster threatening the planet has now brought home to us.

Arabi, Muhyiddin Ibn
A very ancient **Islam**ic tale states that Jafar, son of Yahya of Lisbon, was determined to find the greatest Sufi teacher of the age. He travelled to Mecca where a man in a green robe told him he had been seeking his teacher in the East when all the time he was in the West . . . and his name was Ibn'Arabi.

Returning to Lisbon where Ibn'Arabi was supposed to be, Jafar discovered the sage had gone to Seville. He followed and there found a boy who was pointed out to him as the Ibn'Arabi he sought. He established this was the same individual he had been sent to find, but could not believe the boy to be a sage. When Jafar asked the young Ibn'Arabi if he was the greatest Sufi teacher of the age, the boy answered that he needed time to reply. Jafar, disappointed in his quest, retorted that in that case he had no need of him, and left.

Thirty years later, still searching for the greatest teacher of the age, Jafar entered a hall in Aleppo where a great sage was supposed to be giving a talk. There he found the same boy, now grown to manhood, who recognized him at once.

'Now that I am ready to answer your question, there is no need for me to do so,' said Ibn'Arabi. 'Thirty years ago, Jafar, you had no need of me . . . do you still have no need? In Mecca, the Green One told you there were two things wrong with your search. The first was the wrong place . . . the second, the wrong time!'

Muhyiddin Ibn'Arabi, sometimes known as 'the Sheikh al-Akbar' ('the Greatest Sheik', 'Doctor Maximus' to the West), was born in Murcia, Spain, in 1165. From the age of 32 he travelled extensively throughout the Islamic world, meeting with the greatest mystics, divines and philosophers of the day. He wrote over 400 books and considered most important the *Fusus al-Hikam* (the 'Bezels of Wisdom'). Its theme is the Infinite Wisdom which is at once unique in itself and many-faceted in its representation in the line of prophets from Adam to Mohammed. His influence extended to Dante Alighieri, Thierry of Chartres and to the whole tradition of Courtly Love amongst the troubadours of Provence. It is, however, his correlation of the theory of *wahdat-i-wujud* (the oneness of being), of which he is celebrated as the originator and most complete propounder of all time, that has led to the recent revival of interest in his writings and teachings in the West. He died in Damascus in AD 1240.

The Muhyiddin Ibn'Arabi Society has offices in Oxford and San Francisco.

Archetype

In his psychiatric practice, one of the founding fathers of modern psychology, **Carl Gustav Jung**, was surprised to discover identical primordial images manifesting in the dreams of patients of differing sex, religion and culture.

Further investigation showed these images (The Spirit, The Mother, The Old Wise Woman, The Trickster, etc) also appeared in world mythology, leading Jung to conclude they represented absolutes in the human psyche. (*See also* **Collective Unconscious.**)

ARE
See **Association for Research and Enlightenment**.

Arhat
One who has attained **nirvana** in **Buddhism**.

Arica
An organization founded to propagate the ideas and methods of **Oscar Ichazo**. It was founded in the United States in 1972, following a visit by some 50 Americans to Chile. The organization teaches various breathing and meditational techniques, backed by claims of a scientific approach to **meditation** and alternate states of **consciousness**.

Aromatherapy
Traditionally, aromatherapy was a broadly-based therapeutic system concerned with the **healing** effects of pleasant smells found in flowers, fruit, spices, herbs, perfumes and other aromatic substances. The therapeutic value of aromas was widely studied in ancient times and a variety of crushed herbs, tree barks and spices were inhaled for their curative value.

The children's nursery rhyme *Ring-a-Roses* has links with aromatherapy in that it is the remnant of an old plague song. The phrase 'A-tishoo, a-tishoo, all fall down' refers to the sneezing which preceded death of the plague. The aromatherapy connection arises from the 'pocket full of posies' mentioned earlier in the rhyme. Posies of sweet-smelling flowers were carried during plague times and held over the mouth and nose as a prophylactic against the 'noxious fume' of the disease. Interestingly, sniffing tobacco was also believed to guard against plague.

The ancient classifications of curative scents has largely been lost and the current practice of aromatherapy is somewhat different from its traditional roots. Today, the art makes extensive use of essential oils extracted from aromatic plants and used in massage, rather than simply sniffed by the patient.

Arthurian Legend

The real King Arthur, if he existed at all, was probably a war chieftain of the Romanized Britons who fought against invading Saxons sometime from AD 450 onwards. But the importance of Arthur has never been his historical reality, but rather his power as a myth.

In Celtic legend, Arthur was a Herculean hero who killed the Demon Cat of Losanne, drove the boar Twrch Trwyth into the sea and even raided the Land of the Dead to steal the **magic** cauldron of Annwn, from which only the brave and true could eat.

The more familiar Arthur dates from AD 1135 with the publication of Geoffrey of Monmouth's *History of the Kings of Britain*.

Geoffrey seems to have invented Arthur's father, Uther Pendragon, by mistranslating the Welsh phrase *Arthur mab Uthr* as 'Arthur, son of Uther'. (It actually means 'Arthur the Terrible'.) Having done so, he proceeded to create a life history for Uther that would have done justice to Professor Tolkien.

Geoffrey's tale told how Uther, having fallen in love with Igerna, wife of the Duke of Cornwall, led an army against her husband at Tintagel. In the course of this action, Uther called on **Merlin** the magician to give him the exact physical appearance of the Duke. Merlin did so and, in this magical disguise, Uther entered Tintagel Castle, presented himself at Igerna's bedroom and there aided the confused woman to conceive the child who was to become the great King Arthur.

Fifteen years later, Pendragon died and was buried at Stonehenge. The young Arthur was crowned king at Silchester and proceeded to devote his time to warring with the Saxons. He went on to subdue the Scots, marry Guinevere, conquer Ireland, Iceland, Norway, Denmark and, with some difficulty, France. He even managed to rout a 40,000-strong Roman army and was planning to march on Rome itself when treachery at home forced him to return to Britain.

The traitor, Mordred, was defeated in a great battle, but Arthur himself was so severely wounded that he had to be carried for **healing** to the Isle of **Avalon** where he gave up the crown to his kinsman Constantine.

Many elements of this early account will be familiar to readers of Sir Thomas Malory's *Morte d'Arthur*, where the Arthurian legend achieved its fullest and finest expression. Malory drew on French sources to elaborate the concept of knightly chivalry and introduced the fabled Table Round at which Arthur's greatest knights would meet as equals.

By the time Malory came to write his great romance in the fifteenth century, mystical, magical and supernatural aspects of the Arthurian legend had multiplied and a central aspect had become the Quest for the **Holy Grail**. Malory identified the Isle of Avalon as **Glastonbury** where, in 1191, monks claimed to have found the oak coffin of Arthur and Guinevere. (The same identification was made in the modern esoteric romance, *Mists of Avalon*, with the interesting suggestion by its author, Marion Zimmer Bradley, that the Isle actually existed on a different plane and was inhabited by priestesses of the old pre-Christian matriarchy.)

A persistent aspect of the Arthurian legend insists that the epitaph on Arthur's tomb read, *Hic jacet Arthurus, rex quondam, rexque futurus* – 'Here lies Arthur, the once and future King.' This quotation, more than anything else, has become the foundation of a belief (current to the present day) that Arthur will rise again to lead Britain back to glory.

Since the power of any legend is derived from its ability to influence the human mind, it is not altogether surprising to discover Arthurian myths – and in particular the Grail Cycle – intermixed with modern esoteric practice.

A number of esoteric organizations in Britain and the United States are concerned with the **Matter of Britain** and draw on Arthurian and/or Grail elements in their training methods and **ritual** practice. (*See also* **Camelot**.)

Artificial Reincarnation

A curious technique developed in the early 1960s by Soviet psychiatrists Dr Milan Ryzl of Prague and Dr Vladimir L. Raikov of Moscow by which deeply hypnotized subjects are persuaded they are living incarnations of historical personages.

It was discovered that such subjects, who often remained convinced of their new identities for weeks, sometimes months, on end, would develop talents associated with their alter egos. A subject told she was the artist Raphael took only a month to develop drawing skills up to the standard of a good graphic designer. Other subjects developed musical and literary talents under similar circumstances. In no case did the talent equal that of the historical 'incarnation', but in all cases they were a substantial improvement on the natural talent of the subject.

Dr Ryzl went further and used artificial reincarnation as a therapy. On one occasion he cured an alcoholic by 'reincarnating' in him the personality of his own mother so that he could experience for himself her worry and sorrow about his drinking.

Asanas

Special postures of hatha **yoga**. When Westerners were first exposed to yoga techniques, it was assumed that the purpose of the postures – which often appear bizarre to European eyes – was to stretch ligaments and exercise muscles.

Although asanas do indeed do this, further investigation soon showed they went further. In the cross-legged *lotus* and *perfect* postures, for example, the lower body gradually loses sensation and ceases to exercise a disruptive influence on the mind, making these asanas ideal for meditation.

With the development of more open-minded viewpoints in the West, further subtleties have emerged and it now appears that the majority of yoga asanas are designed to influence currents of subtle energy within the human body. (*See* **Prana** and *Ch'i*.)

ASC

Common abbreviation for 'altered states of consciousness'. (*See* **Consciousness**.)

Ashcroft-Nowicki, Dolores

As a 10-year-old child in 1940 Dolores Ashcroft was evacuated from her native Jersey in face of the Nazi invasion threat and resettled in the north-west town of Wallasey. There, as the Luftwaffe pounded Liverpool and its surrounding towns, she spent most of her nights in the air-raid shelter, her head buried in her mother's lap.

One night, during a particularly bad raid, she became so frightened that it produced a trance-like state. Without warning she found herself in a small valley among high mountains. In front of her, huddled round a large fire, were seven monks wrapped in what appeared to be dark red woollen blankets. One of them beckoned her to join them.

After spending some time in the company of the monks, she

found herself abruptly back in the shelter, with the air-raid over. For more than a year Dolores found herself returning periodically to the circle of monks, but only during the worst of the air-raids. Then the family moved into the country, raids became a rarity and eventually the war finished.

Many years later, now married with children of her own, Dolores Ashcroft-Nowicki began esoteric training under the late **W.E. Butler**. During a collective meditation session, she suddenly found herself back among the monks, this time accompanied by Ernest Butler, who seemed to be known to them. When they returned to normal consciousness, Butler explained that such cases occurred when a person had past ties with an Inner Plane Order and the kind of **pathworking** she had experienced was used in times of stress by the Brethren to reach those with the ability to use the inner pathways of their minds.

Psychical experiences of this type were by no means rare in Dolores' life. When Ernest Butler died, he required her to take control of the **Servants of the Light**, the magical organization he had founded, and today she is its Director of Studies.

Recently described as 'a towering figure in the **Western Esoteric Tradition**', she spends much of her time on an international lecture circuit and has published several books on pathworking and other esoteric subjects, including her classic *The Ritual Magic Workbook*, which stands as one of the best introductions to the subject available today.

Ashram
A Hindu term for a spiritual centre or a retreat where disciples of a **guru** spend their time meditating and studying spiritual teachings.

Assagioli, Roberto
Born in 1888, Assagioli was a psychiatrist who developed his own theory of psychotherapy and personal development which he called **psychosynthesis**.

Association for Research and Enlightenment
A thriving organization operating out of Virginia Beach, USA, dedicated to the investigation and dissemination of the teachings of **Edgar Cayce**, America's famous 'Sleeping Prophet'.

Astral Body

Africa's Azande tribe believe that everyone has two souls, one of which, the *imbisimo*, leaves the body during sleep. In Burma, there is also a belief in a second soul which is likened to a butterfly. The Bacairis of South America talk of a *shadow* which travels out of the body when we fall asleep.

These examples are only the tip of an iceberg. A survey has shown no fewer than 57 cultures hold a firm belief in some sort of second body. The figure would be substantially higher if ancient cultures were included.

In ancient Egypt, for example, it was commonly believed that humanity had three souls. These were known as the *Ba*, the *Ka* and the *Ib*. The Ba was the bird-soul, the Ib was the heart, but the Ka, interestingly, was known as the *Double*. Egyptians believed it to be a mirror image of the physical body, composed of finer matter.

This Ka, under a variety of different names, would be recognized instantly by **yoga** initiates of India, Tibet and China . . . and by occultists. Many esoteric systems actually postulate a whole series of subtle bodies, one within the other, like a set of Russian dolls. This notion, carried into Europe and America by **Madame Blavatsky** and her Theosophists, has taken firm root in Western **New Age** thought.

How many bodies you are actually believed to have depends on the particular sub-system you are studying. Most authorities include an *astral*, a *mental* and a *spiritual*. Each has its own characteristics, function and sphere of operation, and each is composed of progressively finer material.

This multiplicity has led to difficulties in terminology. The name *astral* is frequently applied to different subtle bodies which some authorities argue should be considered as separate and distinct. In particular, the **etheric body** is often referred to as astral. (*See also* **Astral Projection**; **Body of Light**.)

Astral Doorways

Astral doorways are essentially symbols or pictures which can be used in a certain way to aid individuals in **astral projection** to the **astral plane**.

The **Tarot** trumps, the *I Ching* **hexagrams**, and even some forms of fantasy art can all be used in this way, but the definitive doorways, researched by members of the **Golden Dawn** and used by generations of magicians ever since, are undoubtedly the *Tattwas* of the Eastern Esoteric Tradition.

The major *Tattwa* symbols look like this:

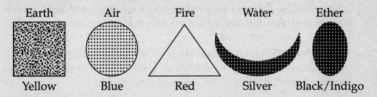

Earth	Air	Fire	Water	Ether
Yellow	Blue	Red	Silver	Black/Indigo

Each one gives access to a specific area of the astral plane, but many other elemental doorways may be constructed through the use of composite symbols.

To use the *Tattwas*, you will need to make special *Tattwa* cards. Use squares of white cardboard sufficiently large to allow a symbol two to two-and-a-half inches in height.

Leave the back of the cards plain white and blank. The diagram shows the five primary symbols and the colour associated with each of them. These should be painted on the front, one to a card. (The symbol for Ether should be coloured *either* indigo or black, but not both.) In each case, the colour should be as strong and brilliant as possible.

When you have made your symbol cards, cover them with transparent artist's film or, better still, give them a coat of clear gloss varnish to enhance the colours and preserve the symbols.

There are two ways to use the cards. One involves holding a specific card to your forehead and allowing images to arise in the visual imagination, a technique mentioned by **W.B. Yeats** in his autobiography.

Using the cards to trigger projection is more complicated. The technique is as follows:

Find a quiet room and a comfortable chair. Select your symbol card, sit back and relax as deeply as possible. Gaze intently at the coloured symbol for about half a minute, then turn the card over and gaze at its blank back. As you do so, an optical reflex will cause the symbol to appear on the back of the card in the complementary colour of the original.

Once you have seen your complementary-coloured symbol, close your eyes and interiorize it. What you are trying to do is

23

visualize what you have just seen, but the visualization works best if you imagine yourself drawing in the glowing symbol until it is established inside your head.

At this point, you should mentally enlarge the symbol until it is big enough for you to pass through. Then imagine yourself stepping through the enlarged symbol as if it were an actual door.

Once you have reached this stage, you should strongly imagine the doorway *behind* you, hanging luminous in the air. Then look around and take note of your surroundings.

Astral Plane

The eighteenth-century mystic, **Emmanuel Swedenborg**, recorded this account of what he believed to be a descent into hell:

> I once heard loud shouts which sounded as if they were bubbling up through water from lower regions; and from the left came the shout, 'Oh, how just!', from the right, 'Oh, how learned!', and from behind, 'Oh, how wise!'
>
> And as I wondered whether there could be any just, learned or wise persons in hell, I strongly desired to see the truth of the matter. A voice from heaven then said to me, 'You shall see and hear.'
>
> So I departed in the spirit and saw before me an opening which I approached and examined; and behold! there was a ladder, and by this I descended.
>
> When I had got down, I saw a plain covered with shrubs intermixed with thorns and nettles. I inquired whether this was hell, and was told that it was the lower earth which is immediately above hell.

More recently, the controversial anthropologist **Carlos Castaneda** published details of an extensive series of trips through what he called 'the crack between the worlds'. **William Blake**, the poet, visited heavenly spheres. **Carl Jung**, the psychologist, found himself transported to a phantasmagoric region of outer space. Every competent **shaman** has travelled to 'spirit worlds' and brought back power. In rural Ireland, it is still possible to collect second (and occasionally first) hand reports of visits to a faery underworld.

Many – indeed most – modern psychologists believe that accounts of visits to strange and alien dimensions are actually subjective visions, waking dreams, conditioned by the individual's personal concerns and cultural milieu. Some visionaries would concur. Blake claimed his own visions sprang from his imagination. They were, he said, tapping his forehead, 'in there'.

But occultists insist there is another explanation. They believe in the existence of an alternate dimension of reality known as the astral plane (or sometimes, in the older sources, astral light). According to occult theory, the astral plane is an environment so plastic that an individual's thoughts will actually impinge on it so that if, like Swedenborg, we imagine ourselves in hell, the external astral surroundings will immediately take on the appearance of hell. Alternatively, thoughts of a forest will create a forest, thoughts of a desert a barren wasteland.

Since the astral plane is believed to overlay the physical world, certain features of physical reality are mirrored in the astral as well, as are **thought-forms** made permanent by intense concentration and/or repetition (as in, for example, religious **ritual**).

There is at least some empirical scientific evidence that the occultists might be right about the objective existence of an astral plane. Anthropologist **Michael Harner**, whilst at the School for Social Research in New York, ingested a sacred drink made from the 'soul vine' *ayahuasca* during his work with the Peruvian Amazon Conibo people. Ayahuasca is a woody vine which contains a number of alkaloids with hallucinogenic próperties – one of which has been called 'telepatin' because it seems to turn those around you to glass, so that you can see through their bodies and read their minds. But Harner experienced something rather different. He had visions of soul boats, crocodile demons and bird-headed humans.

While the experience was vivid and disturbing, Harner had no doubt it was subjective. He concluded the action of the drug had unlocked strata of his own unconscious and released a string of associations related to his own background and culture.

It was an inaccurate assumption. For subsequently Harner met an old, blind, Amazonian shaman who was able to tell him exactly what he had seen – from the shaman's own experience. They had both visited the same visionary territory, a clear indication of its objective nature.

Astral Projection

Astral projection is a term which, though widely used, actually means different things to different people.

To some it suggests stepping out of the physical body to function like a ghost, passing through walls and doors while generally invisible to those still in their physical bodies. To others, it is the projection of consciousness into another world altogether, the fabled **astral plane**.

Although carrying the same label and frequently confused in occult literature, these two experiences are quite distinct. The 'astral projection' during which one functions like a ghost is more properly called **etheric projection** (and is dealt with in some detail under that heading).

True astral projection, by contrast, comes closer to visionary experience and is believed by many occultists to be experienced nightly, by everyone, during dreams. A number of techniques have been developed to stimulate conscious projection of the **astral body**, including the use of a specially created **body of light** which can also be used to simulate etheric projection.

Trance states, including **hypnosis**, are a considerable aid to astral projection, but one of the most popular approaches involves the use of so-called **astral doorways**.

Astrology

Astrology is one of the most ancient of the esoteric arts. It was practised in Sumeria, the world's oldest civilization, in 4300 BC and may actually have had its beginnings in the depths of prehistory, since there is some evidence of a study of the night sky by people of the Old Stone Age. It is also one of the most widespread of the esoteric arts today, albeit in a corrupt form disowned by most serious astrologers. Almost every popular newspaper and magazine features an astrological column offering predictions and advice to those born under one of 12 sun signs.

Although often referred to as '*star*-gazing', astrology is concerned with interpreting the influence of the *planets* on human affairs. To do so, astrologers adopt two convenient devices which they know to be untrue. They classify the sun and moon as planets and they make their calculations as if the Earth were the centre of the solar system.

In popular astrology – the sort that appears in the magazine columns – the term 'horoscope' is used loosely and generally refers to an interpretation based only on the zodiacal position of the individual's sun. When somebody says they were 'born under Taurus' they actually mean they were born when the sun was passing through that portion of the zodiac named after the constellation Taurus – something it does each year between 21 April and 22 May.

Since sun sign astrology, as this form of horoscope is sometimes called, divides the entire population of the planet into only 12 different categories, it is difficult to take seriously as a basis for either prediction or character analysis.

For professional astrologers, however, a horoscope is strictly a map of planetary positions as they appeared at the moment of an individual's birth from the geographical location where that birth occurred. The fundamental calculations are astronomical, but astrologers not only seek to find planetary positions in relation to the zodiac (that belt of the sky defined by the sun's passage against the background of fixed stars) but also in relation to specialist sub-divisions known as *Houses*.

The precise definition of Houses is speculative, even within astrology, and there are several systems in use to calculate them, each with its own adherents, each giving a totally different structure to the horoscope. A complete horoscope will, however, contain both zodiacal and House positions of the planets, however the latter may have been calculated. When the horoscope has been set up – a purely mechanical process anyone with a smattering of mathematical talent can quickly learn – the astrologer will attempt to make interpretations on the basis of these planetary positions and certain angular relationships between them.

When carried out using accurate and precise birth information, this approach creates an analysis which is at least (almost) unique to the individual concerned. For this reason, it has been taken seriously by some researchers with impeccable scientific credentials. **Jung**, for example, frequently cast the horoscopes of his patients, believing they gave insights into personality and **psychic** processes which would otherwise have remained hidden.

For most scientists, however, astrology's postulated link between planetary position and human destiny is at best unproven and at worst nonsensical. Even far more cautious

27

theories, such as that which suggested a gravitational linkage between the position of Jupiter and the occurrence of earthquakes, have generally been derided.

Several large-scale statistical analyses of personality characteristics and predictions vis-à-vis planetary horoscope positions have shown no correlation whatsoever. Surveys of this type have been seen, quite reasonably, as positive proof that astrology cannot work. Yet the plain fact is that in the hands of certain practitioners, astrology *does* work – and works very well indeed.

The empirical experience of astrological validity has led to the suggestion that there is an intuitive or psychic aspect to the art. According to this theory, competent astrologers merely use the traditional associations as a rough foundation for their interpretations, which are then modified in relation to their personal instincts so that the finished reading can differ profoundly from a mechanical assessment based on traditional associations.

Then, in the early 1970s, Professor Alan Smithers of Manchester University created substantial complications when he extracted data from the British Population Census for a total of 1,461,874 men and 842,799 women which showed clearly that architects tended to be born in the spring, secretaries in the summer, miners in the autumn and electricians in the winter.

Unable to leave well enough alone, Professor Smithers then asked members of the British Astrological Association to indicate which professions ought to be associated with the various sun signs. Without knowing the results of his massive survey, the astrologers correctly predicted the statistical connections. One member of the Association broke new ground by suggesting there should be a statistical bias towards nurses being born under the signs of Taurus, Cancer, Virgo, Scorpio, Capricorn and Pisces, while trade union officials should be born under one or other of the remaining six signs. Sure enough, when the graphs of 35,781 nurses and trade union officials were checked, the predicted correlation showed up loud and clear.

Further complications arose from the work of **Michel Gauquelin** whose analysis of 27,000 birth charts produced no evidence for traditional astrological associations, but threw up a whole new series of statistically valid links between career choice (possibly arising from personality characteristics) and the rise or culmination of certain planets.

Atlanteans

Members of a British philosophical society dedicated to a belief in the importance of the individual and inspired from an Inner Plane source. **Healing**, **meditation** and a new approach to the occult all form part of the society's activities.

Atlantis

About the year 590 BC, the Greek politician Solon completed a series of political and economic reforms in Athens. Then, to give them time to take root, he left for a protracted holiday in Egypt. Details of his journey have not been handed down to us, but we do know that Solon visited the Egyptian administrative capital Sais, only 16 kilometres from Naucratis, the country's only Greek trading port.

Solon's business in Sais was historical. He was deeply interested in times past and made a point of talking to antiquarians, archivists, historians and, eventually, with priests of the goddess Neith. One of the latter told him a very odd story about a primeval war and a continent that sank.

It appears Solon was intrigued by the tale, which was offered to him as fact and as proof that Egypt's historical records reached further back than those of Greece. There is a suggestion that he took notes, perhaps intending to compose an epic on the theme when he returned home. If so, he never managed it. But he did tell the story to his close friend and relative Dropides.

Dropides relayed the tale to his son Critias, who, as an old man in his late eighties, passed it on to another Critias, his grandson. The younger Critias was a cousin of Plato, a man destined to become one of the greatest of all Greek philosophers.

From this source, Plato heard the story as a youth, just possibly backed up by the original manuscript notes of Solon. In later years he decided to give it to the world and did so in two works, *Timaeus* and *Critias*. The account, sketchy though it was, founded an industry which thrives to this day. It became our earliest written reference to Atlantis.

The more complete *Timaeus* fragment begins with Egyptian ideas about recurring catastrophes. The priest of Neith refers to the Greek myth of Phaethon, who destroyed everything on Earth by fire because he could not control the chariot of his father Helios. While expressed in mythological form, the priest insisted the tale really signified 'a declination of the bodies moving in the heavens around the Earth and a great conflagration of things on the Earth, which recurs after long intervals'.

The priest then went on to speak about the ancient history of Solon's own people, the Athenians, of which Egypt claimed to have records dating back 9,000 years. At that time, he claimed, there existed in the Atlantic, beyond the Straits of Gibraltar, an island 'larger than Libya and Asia put together'. It was ruled, along with several smaller islands, by a vast military empire with territories stretching as far afield as northern Italy.

This empire, 9,000 years before the time of Solon, was poised to invade both Egypt and Greece. When war broke out, Egypt fell, but the city-state of Athens held out against almost unimaginable odds and actually managed eventually to turn the tide, liberating subdued countries in the process.

These proved hard times for Atlantis. Following the military defeat, the home island was struck by such violent earthquakes and floods that 'all your warlike men in a body sank into the earth and the island of Atlantis in like manner disappeared in the depths of the sea'.

According to Solon's account as quoted by Plato, the catastrophe occurred in a single day and night and left vast areas of the Atlantic impassable due to the residue of mud.

In his *Critias*, Plato gives a mythological outline of the origins of Atlantis, telling how the gods divided the Earth into allotments in order to establish humanity. But his description of the actual continent and its inhabitants reads more like history.

Running halfway along the entire length of the island was a fertile coastal plain. Some miles away, in the centre of the island, was a low mountain, possibly little more than a hill, on which developed the island's most ancient city. This city was surrounded by three moats, traditionally built by the god Poseidon. There was abundant vegetation and animal life, much of which seems to have been tropical in Nature. There was mining for a now unknown ore, orichalcum, described as 'more precious than anything but gold'.

The hilltop city became the nation's capital. A canal was cut from the sea to the outermost ring moat, making it a sort of inland port. The moats themselves were bridged in several places and further smaller canals cut between them, with their entrance and exit points guarded by towers. Walls surrounded each moat. The outer was coated in brass, the middle in tin and the inner in orichalcum. There were public and private baths, artificial fountains, running water – some of it apparently artificially heated – and even a race-course. Locally-quarried stone, black, red and white, was used for virtually all building work.

Beyond the city, transport and irrigation were provided by a massive network of canals, some of them so large that Plato had obvious difficulty in crediting that they were man-made.

Politically, Atlantis was a confederation of ten kingdoms, each an autonomous state which was, none the less, bound by an alliance to provide military men for the defence of the realm as a whole. A majority vote of the ten kings was required before the death sentence could be passed on any Atlantean citizen.

Plato's account seized the imagination of both the reading and the writing public. A recent estimate that more than 1,000 books have now been published on the subject of Atlantis is probably conservative. These works generally fall into three broad categories: those which seek to establish proof of the reality of Atlantis, those (often derived from inspirational sources) which purport to describe the lifestyle and history of the Atlantean civilization and those which deny the literal truth of the Atlantis legend, but look for genuine historical events on which it may have been based.

One of the most interesting examples of the first category is also one of the older publications in the field: *Atlantis: the Antediluvian World* by Ignatius Donnelly. Donnelly, who published his book in 1882, was intrigued by cultural and linguistic similarities between (in particular) ancient Egypt and the ancient peoples of South America. He pointed out that both built pyramids, both embalmed their dead, both had a highly-developed astronomy. Folk myths on both sides of the Atlantic often told similar tales and even place-names showed remarkable likenesses. To explain these similarities, Donnelly postulated an Atlantean culture which spread simultaneously east and west when the island continent sank.

Into the second category of works about Atlantis fall those of **Madame Blavatsky**, who saw Atlantis as part of an 18,000,000-year human history, and **Edgar Cayce**, America's famous 'Sleeping Prophet', who painted a picture of Atlantis that was, in many respects, like a science-fiction epic.

Cayce believed, with a number of other esoteric writers, that there were actually three sinkings of Atlantis and the one reported by Plato was only the last in a series which saw the gradual breaking up of a very considerable land mass. He placed Atlantis between the Gulf of Mexico on the one hand and the Mediterranean on the other. Portions of it now form parts of the Americas, the British West Indies and the Bahamas.

In its geographical structure, Cayce saw the later Atlantis as a series of islands, rather than a single undifferentiated continent. He taught that it supported a high technological civilization based on an understanding of **crystals** now lost to science. There are clear suggestions in his readings that at least one of the catastrophes which sank Atlantis was man-made, the result of heavy weaponry in a war which sought to free a slave race of artificially-created mutants.

The third category of book (typified by Professor Luce's *End of Atlantis*) is based on the discovery that Plato's account of the lost continent bears striking similarities with the High Bronze Age civilization of the Aegean. This civilization flourished in much more recent times than the ancient Egyptian records testified, but modern experts began to wonder if Plato had simply confused or mistranslated 900 years as 9,000. If so, the disaster which destroyed Atlantis would have occurred around 1500 BC rather than 9600 BC.

Oddly enough, the 1500 BC dating is fairly close to that of a vast natural disaster which did indeed destroy a mighty empire – that of Minoan Crete. The disaster was caused by the violent eruption of the island volcano Santorin, 70 miles north of Crete itself. This eruption was estimated to be five times greater than the explosion of Krakatoa which sent tidal waves across the entire Pacific. Santorin's waves certainly swept across Crete, causing devastation and loss of life from which the ancient empire never recovered.

Atman

In Hindu religion and philosophy, *atman* is the essential self of a human being and as such is the one part of the individual which is eternal. Interestingly, atman is closely identified with *Brahman*, the unchanging reality behind surface appearances. This identification creates an even more interesting double linkage with certain aspects of Western esoteric thought. The first is the Qabalistic belief in *Yesod*, an astral world of the imagination which forms the foundation of reality. The second is the insight by, among others, the visionary **William Blake** that the world of imagination is the world of eternity.

Aura
If you stand upright with both arms fully outstretched in a cruciform position parallel to the ground, your fingertips mark the outer edges of your aura . . . or so occultists will assure you.

Sometimes referred to as the 'human atmosphere', the aura in both oriental and occidental **occultism** is believed to be an envelope of subtle energy which exists like a giant egg around human (and other living animal) bodies, plants, magnets and **crystals**.

Generally speaking, auras are visible only to **psychics**, although in 1911 a London doctor named W.R. Kilner developed a series of screens based on a dicyanin dye which he claimed could be used to train the eye to see auras.

Kilner distinguished several layers in the aura and, like the industrial chemist Baron Karl von Reichenbach half a century before him, insisted his screens showed auras emanating from magnets.

A particularly interesting aspect of Kilner's work was his conviction that changes in the appearance of the aura could be used as a diagnostic tool – a belief shared by many psychics. There seems to be a direct link between the aura and the artistic convention of painting a halo or aureole around the heads of saintly personages. The theory is that sanctity so strengthens the human aura that parts of it at least become visible to normal sight. (*See also* **Kirlian Photography.**)

Aura Soma Therapy
A unique form of colour therapy which also uses herbal extracts and essential oils. It was devised by Vicky Wall, who was born in London at the end of the First World War, the seventh child of a seventh child. Her father was a deeply religious man who had an extensive knowledge of the medicinal use of herbs and natural methods of **healing**.

Gradually, Vicky became aware of her own healing abilities, auric sight and **clairvoyance**, but it was following three **near death experiences** and the loss of her physical sight that her inner vision and auric sight really developed and she was inspired to create Aura Soma therapy.

Aura is the electromagnetic field which surrounds the body, *soma* the being which resides in the body. Aura Soma therapy is about revitalizing and rebalancing the human aura. This is done by using Aura Soma Balance, which is based on beauty oils, healing herbs and aroma essences. Aura Soma Balance is designed to make a perfect emulsion, capable of allowing the dynamic healing energies of the specific colour vibrations to be absorbed through the skin and the lymphatic system along with the healing extracts and essential oils.

A wide range of colour bottles is used, each having a colour division in the middle, both for diagnostic and treatment purposes. Each colour has a sympathetic resonance with a particular part of the body as listed below:

Colour	Chakra/Physical area	Other Influences
Violet	Crown/Top of head	For and of the spirit, cooling.
Indigo	Brow/Pineal	For inspiration and intuition, also cooling.
Blue	Throat/Base of skull	Specific healer, strengthens potential and instinct, also cooling and gaining weight.
Green	Heart/Chest & shoulders etc.	Harmonizing, higher mind sympathy, compassion and understanding, relaxing and warming.
Yellow	Solar plexus/middle of back/kidney	Wisdom ray, affects psychological and lower mental as well as emotional bodies, cleansing and heating.
Orange	Navel/Spleen/ Abdomen and small of back	Imparts vitality, strengthens etheric body, heating.
Red	Base of spine/ Reproductive organs	Physical, wilful and assertive, heating and for losing weight.

Aurobindo, Sri

Sri Aurobindo Ghose (1872–1950), a young Bengali poet, studied classics at King's College, Cambridge, and seemed set for an academic career. On his return to India he became embroiled in nationalist politics and was jailed by the Raj authorities. While in prison, like **Arthur Koestler**, he underwent a mystical experience which was to change his entire outlook and personality.

On his release he fled to the French enclave, Pondicherry. He studied **yoga**, combining the traditional system with a new philosophy of his own, an evolutionary philosophy of individual and collective evolution towards God and 'The Life Divine', title of his most famous book. He founded a community called Auroville, meaning 'The City of Dawn', devoted to harmonious living on Earth. After his death, this was run by a Frenchwoman called 'The Mother', his spiritual collaborator, but she died in 1974. This was followed by many legal battles over the ownership of the land belonging to the community, but these have now been resolved, allowing Auroville to develop further in accordance with The Mother's 'Charter' of 1968.

Autogenic Training

If you have ever imagined yourself succeeding in a venture where previously you might have failed, you have been engaging in a primitive, simplistic form of 'autogenic training'.

The more sophisticated version of the art involves the use of very specific **visualization**s to achieve a particular end. The goal could be anything from increased self-confidence to better sports performance.

Much of the recent scientific work on autogenic training was done in the USSR where the interesting discovery was made that autogenics work better if carried out against a background of baroque music.

Baroque is a musical style dating back to the time of Johann Sebastian Bach, who himself discovered one of its more peculiar properties when he was called in by the Russian envoy, Count Kayserling, to help with Kayserling's insomnia.

Kayserling had decided that a little light music might be of benefit and asked Bach to compose something bright and interesting, but calm. Bach did so. On the next night he suffered from insomnia, Kayserling called in Johann Goldberg, a harpsichord player, and ordered him to play the new Bach composition. Goldberg did so and in minutes Kayserling was fast asleep. The music that did the trick is now known as the Goldberg Variations. Bach himself received a substantial sum of money for composing it.

During the early 1970s, the Bulgarian scientist, Dr Georgi Lozanov, began a laboratory study of the Goldberg Variations and discovered that the aria with which they began and ended had the effect of *slowing down certain body processes*. He also found it brought on what he called a 'meditative state'.

This was an interesting discovery with far-reaching implications. For the exhausted Count Kayserling, the effect was enough to help him get to sleep, because sleep was what he desperately wanted. But for those engaged in autogenic training, it helps the clarity and reality tone of the visualizations.

Bach was not the only composer to produce music of this sort. Vivaldi, Telemann, Corelli, Handel – sixteenth to eighteenth-century composers of the baroque school – all created something similar, according to Dr Lozanov's investigations, which concentrated on the largo (slow) movements of their concertos.

In these movements a particular rhythm – approximately 60 beats to the minute – arose again and again. Dr Lozanov and his Soviet colleague, the psychologist Dr I.K. Platonov, both theorized that it might be the rhythm rather than the music that was having the effect. Whether this theory is correct has not yet been confirmed, but it is possible to experiment with the effects of baroque music for yourself. Any one or more of the following works by Bach have the correct tempo:

Largo from the Concerto in G Minor for Flute and Strings
Aria to The Goldberg Variations
Largo from the Harpsichord Concerto in F Minor
Largo from the Solo Harpsichord Concerto in G Minor
Largo from the Solo Harpsichord Concerto in C Major
Largo from the Solo Harpsichord Concerto in F Major

Avalon

One of the early visions of Paradise, the Avalon of Celtic legend was supposed to be an island of apple trees far to the West. According to Geoffrey of Monmouth, it was the island where **King Arthur** died when taken for **healing** after he was wounded in his final battle. In *Mists of Avalon*, Marion Zimmer Bradley depicts Avalon as an island essentially existing on another dimension of reality. In this she mirrored the earlier tradition that the fairy queen Morgan ruled there. Many believe that the location of Avalon is at or near **Glastonbury**.

Automatic Writing

Writing produced whilst in an altered state ·of **consciousness**, often attributed to supernatural guidance. One of the best known **medium**s who practised automatic writing was Geraldine Cummins.

Avatar

In the great Hindu religious epic, the *Bhagavad Gita*, the god Vishnu promises, 'For the rescue of the pious and for the destruction of the evil-doers, for the establishment of the Law, I am born in every age.'

Ten divine incarnations of Vishnu, known as avatars, are recognized in popular **Hinduism**, including lives as a tortoise and a boar, as the heroes Krishna and Rama and even as Gautama, the founder of **Buddhism**.

Belief in avatars carried through strongly into Buddhist thought where the *Bodhisattva*, or ultimate essence of enlightenment, is perceived as a divine saviour which reincarnates periodically to rescue humanity. Thus Prince Gautama was only the most recent in a long line of Buddhas, and statues have already been erected to Maitreya, the Buddha-to-come.

Avebury

Larger than Stonehenge, Avebury is the oldest megalithic site in Britain, in use between 2600 BC and 1600 BC. According to Dr William Stukeley, who first documented the site in the eighteenth century, it was built in the shape of the Solar Serpent. The Sanctuary circle (on nearby Overton Hill) represents the head; the Kennet and Beckhampton avenues formed the body. Parts of the Kennet avenue still exist, but the Beckhampton avenue, which formed a double curve indicating the tail, was destroyed by farmers and builders who were clearing the land. Fortunately, this occurred after Stukeley had mapped out the area. In the centre of the snake's body was the real power house, the Sun Symbol, which is the main circle complex.

Avicenna

An Arab physician of the eleventh century noted for, among other things, the interesting theory that the brain is actually a sort of 'cooling system' for psychic processes that take place elsewhere. Although framed within the medical knowledge of his time, the notion mirrors the view popularized by **Aldous Huxley** of Mind-at-large.

This concept suggests that the human mind is a thing in itself with the potential for far more widely-reaching perceptions than we imagine. But as an aid to survival, the brain acts as a sort of reducing valve, filtering out those perceptions that are not immediately useful to physical survival. Huxley argued that psychedelic drugs like mescaline and LSD acted to reduce the brain's efficiency as a filter, allowing the direct perceptions of Mind-at-large to flood through.

Ayurveda

A system of medicine peculiar to India, long thought of by Western practitioners as a collection of superstitions, but now attracting some attention as a valid therapy. *Ayurveda* is from the Sanskrit, *ayur* meaning 'life' and *veda* meaning 'knowledge'. It is a holistic system of medicine involving fasting, baths, enemas, blood-letting, diet, drugs and herbs.

Ayurveda is one of the very few medical systems claiming a cure for the common cold. In a short, sharp treatment patients are strapped to a device similar in appearance to an upright iron bedstead. A lever is then pulled which causes the device to crash down into a horizontal position. The shock mobilizes the immune system to such an extent that, so it is claimed, the cold virus is burned out almost instantly.

B

Babaji

Babaji, or Shri Haidakhan Wale Baba, lived in the village of Haidakhan, in the Kumaon foothills of the Himalayas, between 1970 and 1984. His whereabouts before this date are unknown. He is reputed to be the latest manifestation of The Divine who, according to ancient mythology, has incarnated in remote places throughout history, especially when humanity is undergoing major changes, to help humankind understand, experience and achieve its relationship to The Divine. Babaji's teaching is not sectarian, but is supportive of all religions which guide people towards a life of harmony with The Divine.

Babaji was brought to the attention of the West by **Paramahansa Yogananda** in his book *Autobiography of a Yogi*. Although the basis of his teaching is to bring a renewed understanding to ancient traditions, he focused mainly on present-day problems through individual guidance. Babaji never travelled outside India, but was visited by thousands of people from all over the world at the **ashram** which was built at Haidakhan. Today the ashram is supervised by Shri Muniraj who was appointed by Babaji as his successor, and there are now ashrams dedicated to him in many countries.

Bach, Dr Edward

Edward Bach was born in 1886 in the Warwickshire village of Moseley, some three miles outside Birmingham. He left school at the age of 16 and went to work for three years in his father's brass foundry, but went on to qualify in medicine in 1912.

He became increasingly dissatisfied with orthodox medicine, particularly its persistent failure in the face of chronic ailments, and in 1919 took a post in the London Homoeopathic Hospital where he studied **homoeopathy** for the first time and soon began to relate the discipline to his work on vaccination and immunology. Later he added research on the curative properties of herbs to his other interests.

Nine years later, while attending a banquet, Bach was struck by the inspiration which was to help create a whole new branch of alternative medicine. He noted how various people at the dinner resembled one another even though there was no family relationship between them. It occurred to him that people in the same similarity grouping might well react in the same way to disease.

By 1930 he was still amplifying and extending this fundamental idea when he was taken by a sudden impulse to visit Wales. He returned to London with supplies of Impatiens and Mimulus which he had found growing near a mountain stream. As an experiment, he 'potentised' the plants in accordance with homoeopathic practice and began to prescribe them to his patients, based on the particular similarity grouping to which they belonged. Results were encouraging.

In May of the same year, he was taking an early morning walk when the thought occurred to him that the dew, under the influence of sunlight, must extract some of the essence of the plant on which it rested. On the basis of this insight he developed a range of **Bach Flower Remedies** which soon became his exclusive method of treatment.

Bach died in November 1936.

Bach Flower Remedies

A range of 38 herbal remedies discovered by the British physician **Dr Edward Bach** in the 1930s and today experiencing something of a popular revival.

Bach's lifelong ambition was to develop a natural curative system of such safety and simplicity that it could be used in the home without the necessity of a prescribing physician. He believed he had found such a system in the Flower Remedies which were, he felt, particularly effective for chronic illnesses and ailments which did not lend themselves to ready diagnosis.

Examples of the remedies themselves range from preparations of Rock Rose (for terror) through Mimulus, Aspen, Cherry Plum and Sweet Chestnut to Scleranthus and Agrimony, the latter usually prescribed for restlessness.

Bacheldor, Kenneth

In September 1966 *The Journal of the Society for Psychical Research* published an article entitled 'Report on a Case of Table Levitation and Associated Phenomena' which, despite its modest title, contained allegations as startling as any published by the society in its lengthy history. The author of the report was a professional psychologist named Kenneth Bacheldor.

In the opening paragraph of the article, Bacheldor drily observed, 'As the writer has had the good fortune to witness and experiment on total levitation of tables and allied phenomena, he offers here an account of his experiences.'

His experiences included a series of 200 experimental sittings in which a group he headed up attempted to duplicate a paranormal phenomenon which had virtually ceased to be investigated since the heyday of its popularity in Victorian times: table-turning. Of the sittings, 120 produced no worthwhile results. In the remaining 80, the table moved.

Since these early experiments, Bacheldor has become Britain's leading investigator of **psychokinesis** (PK) and associated **levitation** and **poltergeist** phenomena. His sessions, often carefully monitored by infra-red photography, audio and video recordings and sensitive touch pads, have produced violent movements of heavy tables, rappings and even brief total levitations.

One of his most interesting theories involves the importance of 'artefacts', by which he means the use of loosely-controlled procedures producing natural, but unusual, phenomena which then encourage their **paranormal** counterparts.

Baha'i

The Baha'i faith was founded by Mirza Husayn Ali, or Baha'u'allah, Glory of God, in Iran in the nineteenth century. Baha'u'allah attracted a large number of followers in his lifetime and the faith has now spread all over the world. It is a peace-loving and humanitarian religion with no clergy, **initiation** rites or sacraments. Its main teaching is the oneness of mankind and the unity of all religions.

Bailey, Alice

Author of several books presenting a comprehensive esoteric **cosmology** as revealed to her by an entity she refers to as 'The

Tibetan', Djwhal Khul. (*See* **Hidden Masters**.) This took place over a period of 30 years.

Alice Bailey was born in 1880 and during her lifetime believed herself in contact with several Inner Planes beings, including Koot Hoomi, one of **Blavatsky**'s Hidden Masters. She produced an enormous body of work and managed to bring up a family on a shoestring and run an international correspondence school as well as carrying out public lecture work and other activities. To further her received teachings, she founded the Arcane School. Alice Bailey died in 1949.

Always presented with Alice Bailey's writings is what is known as 'The Great Invocation':

The Great Invocation

From the point of Light
   within the Mind of God
Let the light stream forth into
   the minds of men.
Let Light descend on Earth.

From the point of Love
   within the Heart of God
Let love stream forth into
   the hearts of men.
May Christ return to Earth.

From the centre where the
   Will of God is known
Let purpose guide the little
   wills of men –
The purpose which the
   Masters know and serve.

From the centre which we
   call the race of man
Let the Plan of Love and
   Light work out
And may it seal the door
   where evil dwells.

Let Light and Love and
   Power restore the Plan
   on Earth.

Baker-Eddy, Mary

The woman who was to become the founder of **Christian Science** was born Mary Baker in New Hampshire in 1821, the youngest of six children. Her education seems to have been limited and in any case, what she learned from school-books 'vanished like a dream' (her own words) in later life.

For much of her early life, Mary Baker suffered a chronic illness (the precise nature of which is uncertain) which left her a semi-invalid. In 1862, she presented herself for treatment at the hands of Phineas P. Quimby, a highly unorthodox healer influenced by **Mesmer**. While she became increasingly reticent to admit it, there seems little doubt that Quimby's ideas profoundly influenced Mary Baker's own view on the **healing** process.

In 1875, two years after her divorce from her second husband, she published her first Christian Science textbook, *Science and Health*. Two years later she married one of her own students, Asa G. Eddy. It was an unusual example of harmony between teacher and pupil, for Mary Baker's early relationships with her students were marked by difficulties and quarrels. Only when she moved to Boston and ceased to have so much direct contact with her followers did Christian Science begin to achieve its real potential as a movement.

Mary Baker-Eddy died in 1910. (*See* **Christian Science**.)

Bardo Plane

According to Tibetan **yoga** and Buddhist belief this is an illusory dimension in which the soul finds itself after death. The concept of the *Bardo* is virtually identical to that of the **astral plane** of Western **occultism**.

Bardo Thodol

See Tibetan Book of the Dead.

Bates Method

A system of 'visual re-education' developed by Dr William Bates, a leading eye physician in New York, early in the twentieth century. His innovatory eye exercises, including palming (covering the closed eyes with the palm of the hand), swinging the body, and blinking, have been known to cure chronic eye

43

conditions. **Aldous Huxley** experimented successfully with the Bates Method and wrote about it in *The Art of Seeing*.

Bennett, J.G.

English pupil and biographer of **G.I. Gurdjieff**, noted, among other things, for his definition of Gurdjieff's work as evolving from the single question: *What is the sense and significance of life on earth in general and of human life in particular?*

Bennett produced a large body of work and founded the Institute for the Comparative Study of History, Philosophy and the Sciences to popularize Gurdjieff's work and offer training based on the Gurdjieff methods.

Benson, Herbert

A Harvard Medical School scientist, Dr Herbert Benson has for some time been in the forefront of scientific investigation into **yoga** phenomena such as the conscious control of what are normally autonomous body functions.

In 1981, following an invitation from the **Dalai Lama**, he led a group of scientists in an investigation of **tumo**, a yogic system whereby Tibetan initiates are reputed to generate exceptional body heat. During the investigation, which involved attaching sensors to various parts of the monks' bodies, he discovered all were able to increase the temperature of fingers and toes by as much as 15°F. Dr Benson theorized that the yoga practice of these Buddhists enabled them to dilate surface blood vessels, thus increasing blood flow and raising the temperature.

Bermuda Triangle

The term 'Bermuda Triangle', coined in a magazine article by Vincent Gaddis, refers to a geographical area of the Atlantic Ocean off south-east Florida, formed by drawing an imaginary line from Melbourne, Florida, to Bermuda, to Puerto Rico, and back to Florida.

Also called 'the Devil's Triangle', it is an area where the disappearance of ships and planes on a number of occasions has led to speculation on causes ranging from atmospheric disturbances to the intervention of **UFOs**.

Some investigators have linked the area with lost **Atlantis**, notably the version of Atlantis depicted in the readings of the psychic **Edgar Cayce** – a high-tech civilization based on the use of **crystals**. According to these theorists, planes and ships have been influenced by submarine crystal generators, still operative following the Atlantis sinking.

Since little or no wreckage has been found following some of the accidents in the area, other speculators postulate that the Triangle contains a gateway into an alien dimension.

Those who find such explanations difficult to swallow have pointed out that violent storms and downward air currents frequently occur within the Bermuda Triangle and studies have failed to reveal any significant peculiarities about the area. At the same time, radio broadcasts from at least one stricken plane suggests some sort of magnetic anomaly, possibly intermittent in its manifestation: the pilot found his flight instruments refusing to function and was soon hopelessly lost. Eventually radio contact was broken and both pilot and transport disappeared forever.

Besant, Annie

Annie Besant was one of those extraordinary Victorians who was both an adventurer and a feminist. Born Annie Wood, the second of three children in London in 1847, she devoted herself to a succession of causes ranging from such practical issues as free thought and birth control all the way through to the heady heights of **Theosophy**.

By the age of 14 she had become a devout Anglo-Catholic, immersing herself in the religion to the point of fanaticism. By the time she was 20 she had, in her own words, 'drifted into an engagement with a man I did not pretend to love'. The man was the Reverend Frank Besant, an Anglican cleric. In 1867 she married him.

The marriage did not last. In 1873, the couple separated and Annie, in revolt against her former values, plunged into the propagation of atheism and free thought. By 1875, she had become the vice-president of the National Secular Society. Two years later she had published a book called *The Gospel of Atheism* and was being prosecuted for obscenity because of another of her works, *The Fruits of Philosophy*. (It advocated birth control.) In 1878, her estranged husband successfully sued for custody of their daughter Mabel on the grounds that Annie was an unfit mother.

The period was typical enough of the frantic life she led. During the next decade she was a tireless feminist, leading the match-girls' strike of 1888 and becoming one of the first women ever to enrol at London University. Her willingness to embrace new ideas seems almost compulsive. In 1885 she had become an Executive Committee member of the Fabian Society, having met George Bernard Shaw the year before. In 1889, following what must have seemed one of the most remarkable U-turns of the age, she joined the Theosophical Society.

Theosophy proved a ladder for Annie Besant. By the summer of 1889 she had already entered the inner sanctum, the Esoteric Section of the Blavatsky Lodge, and, according to **H.P. Blavatsky** herself, formed her own link with one of the **Hidden Masters**, the Master Moyra.

When Blavatsky died in 1891, it was Annie Besant who emerged as leader of all but a smallish faction of American Theosophists. In this capacity she attended the World Parliament of Religions in Chicago in 1893. Later that year she took herself off to the spiritual home of Theosophy, India. She was promptly approached by a group of Brahmins who wanted her to lead a national Hindu movement. For once in her life, she refused.

By this stage of her career, Annie Besant had fallen under the influence of a former Anglican cleric, **C.W. Leadbeater**. She was appointed President of the Theosophical Society by the Hidden Masters in 1907 and confirmed in office by a majority vote of members. The following year, caught up in the Hindu notion of **avatar**s and convinced a new one was due, she and Leadbeater formally adopted a Brahmin boy named Jiddu **Krishnamurti**, who they believed would be the next Messiah.

The couple made intensive efforts to prepare Krishnamurti for his supposed destiny, but the boy proved wiser than his mentors and eventually renounced all claim to high spiritual office. The affair affected the Theosophical Society itself, which, under Besant's influence, had sponsored Krishnamurti: it was one of the main reasons for the departure of arguably its most brilliant member, **Rudolf Steiner**.

In 1913, once again reversing a former position, Annie Besant became involved in the national politics of India. Her entry into the arena was marked by a series of lectures (entitled 'Wake up, India!') which she delivered in Madras. Before long – and predictably – she was recognized as a nationalist leader. She formed the Home Rule for India League in 1916 and was interned for her pains the following year. On her release she became President of the Indian National Congress. Only the emergence of Mahatma Gandhi and a shift of influence towards the common people removed her latest power base.

But Annie Besant was destined to remain at the centre of controversy until the end of her days. Her friend Leadbeater was consecrated Bishop of the Old Catholic Church, but disowned by the movement soon after. Nothing daunted, in the early 1920s he formed his own Church, the Liberal Catholic, and took with him many former Theosophists in the process. Still shocked by this development, Annie Besant had, in 1929, to face Krishnamurti's dramatic announcement that he was not, after all, an avatar. She died four years later at the age of 86.

Bhagavad Gita

Many scholars consider the *Bhagavad Gita* to be the most important mystical treatise ever written. It is certainly the best known, loved and widest-read of all the Hindu scriptures. Yet paradoxically, it forms no part of the *vedas*, the Hindu sacred canon. Instead, it is a fragment – albeit lengthy – of an enormous epic poem, the *Mahabharata*, which describes a long and fratricidal war between two branches of the Kuru family.

The *Gita*'s mystical elements arise from the fact that the principal ally of one side in the war is the god Krishna. When Arjuna, the leader of the faction, decides he will not fight, Krishna attempts to persuade him in a long philosophical and mystical discussion which eventually extends to embrace such subjects as **reincarnation**, the essence of the self, the practice of **yoga**, the road to enlightenment and the nature of the universe.

With this discussion, the *Gita* added love and devotion to the ancient virtues of **Hinduism** and, for the first time, insisted salvation was open to all, regardless of caste or sex. It taught that the self's realization of its own changeless and indestructible nature, acquired in **meditation**, should be supplemented by the love of a personal god.

Biodynamic Massage

The originator of this **bodywork** technique is Gerda Boyeson, the Norwegian psychologist and physiotherapist. Going on from **Wilhelm Reich**'s work, Gerda Boyeson discovered that energy that is blocked builds up in the form of fluids, which get trapped between muscles and nerves. With massage, this fluid is dispersed and the intestine is activated in a spontaneous peristaltic movement, releasing emotion. In addition to massage and touch stimuli, deep breathing and relaxation techniques are employed.

Bioenergetics

A therapeutic technique, developed out of **Reichian therapy**, which is designed to help an individual regain real awareness of his/her body and to enjoy to the fullest degree possible the life of the body. This emphasis includes sexuality which, predictably, has become closely identified with the system in the public perception. But sexuality has its place in bioenergetics as a basic physical function, and the system also concentrates on even more basic functions like breathing, moving, feeling and self-expression.

Exponents of bioenergetics believe that cultural conditioning has created a situation in which most people go through life on a limited budget of energy and feeling. The goal of the system is to help patients regain their primary nature, defined as the condition of being free, the state of being graceful and the quality of being beautiful – these attributes believed to be natural to every animal organism.

Biofeedback

Feedback was defined by the mathematician Norbert Werner as 'a method of controlling a system by inserting into it the results of its past performance'.

At first, the systems under review were purely mechanical, but by the 1960s, the principles of feedback were being applied to living organisms with startling and exciting results. This process, known as *biofeedback*, is essentially the mechanical monitoring of bodily functions in order to gain control over them.

A simple, but useful, example of biofeedback is the monitoring of galvanic skin response (GSR) as an aid to relaxation. While tension is one of the most widespread ailments of the present age, many people maintain their tension at an unconscious (hence uncontrollable) level. Research has, however, shown a direct relationship between galvanic skin response – the ease with which an electrical current passes along the surface of the skin – and the degree of muscular tension present in the body.

Biofeedback devices have been constructed which measure any variation in GSR and signal them via an audible tone. The person listening to this tone can thus determine by its pitch his current level of tension and, more importantly, can note what thoughts, positions or actions lower it.

Biofeedback training has enabled ordinary individuals to emulate several of the more advanced feats of **yoga**, notably slowing the heart rate via electro-cardiac feedback and achieving altered states of **consciousness** through the monitoring of brain-wave patterns.

The technique has shown considerable promise in the field of medicine, where it is now used quite widely. Patients trained to create a temperature differential between hands and forehead can, for example, halt migraine attacks. Substantial strides have been made in pain control, particularly where the problem is of muscular origin and conditions like high blood-pressure can also be normalized via biofeedback training.

One of the most interesting developments in the field of biofeedback training and research is the fact that much of the electronic equipment necessary has so far dropped in price as to have come within reach of the average individual. It is still not cheap, but many biofeedback devices now cost less than, for example, a bicycle and in some cases substantially less.

Biorhythms

At the beginning of the twentieth century, Dr Hermann Swoboda, a Professor of Psychology, made the discovery that there were specific 23 and 28-day rhythms which influenced the mental processes of humanity – ideas would repeat in the mind at periodic intervals, as would dream patterns and so on. The rhythms, he concluded, began at birth and could consequently be calculated for anyone whose birth date was known. He published several books on his theory and even invented a slide rule to calculate the basic rhythms.

At much the same time as Professor Swoboda was investigating periodic recurrence in the realm of psychology, the Berlin physician, Dr Wilhelm Fliess, was accumulating substantial research material which seemed to point towards the same 23 and 28-day rhythms in the field of human biology. These, he thought, influenced such things as an individual's immunity to disease.

This pioneering work on what was later to be called biorhythms was taken up by other scientists, and during the 1920s a teacher of engineering, Dr Alfred Teltscher, added a third (33-day) cycle to the original two, based on his observations of student performance.

In recent years there has been renewed interest in the subject of biorhythms, which are usually defined as follows:

23-day Physical Rhythm

This rhythm, believed to be rooted in the action of muscle fibres, influences physical strength, endurance, energy levels, resistance to infection and (as a consequence) self-confidence. As with the remaining two biorhythms, the physical rhythm follows a predictable rise and fall waveform:

During the first half of the cycle – 11½ days – the individual will typically feel more vigorous, physical work will seem easier and vitality and endurance will be at their peak. During the second half, there will be noticeably fewer reserves of power, energy and endurance.

28-day Emotional Rhythm

This rhythm appears to derive from the nervous system and manifests as emotional changes and degrees of sensitivity. During the rising period of the cycle, creativity is heightened, the individual is typically more optimistic and cheerful. On the downswing, there is a tendency towards negativity and irritation.

33-day Intellectual Rhythm

This rhythm is believed to originate in the brain cells, although some experts have postulated a glandular reaction. The first half of the cycle brings an ability to think more quickly and clearly, while memory functions more efficiently. During the second half, learning becomes more difficult, thinking less clear and precise.

In all three cycles, experts believe the changeover periods (i.e.

from upswing to downswing and back) represent critical, often especially difficult, days for the individual concerned. More difficult still are those periods when two or more of the cycles reach a coincident changeover. Such days often make the individual accident-prone.

With increased interest in the whole subject of biorhythms, electronic and mechanical biorhythm calculators are fairly easily available, as are biorhythm calculation programs for most of the popular home computers. But even without these, the calculation of your current biorhythms is quite straightforward, if tedious. The method is as follows:

1) Add the total number of days in your life from the day of your birth to the first day of the month for which the calculations are being made.
2) Divide this total by 23 and note the remainder. This remainder will indicate the position of your physical cycle on the first day of the month.
3) Divide the total by 28 and note the remainder. This gives you the position of your emotional cycle on the first day of the month.
4) Finally, divide the total by 33 and note the remainder in order to determine the position of your intellectual cycle for the first day of the month.

There is still some controversy about the validity of the Swoboda/Fliess system of biorhythms, but no argument at all about the postulation that humanity is a cyclical species. Studies have shown conclusively that there is a distinct statistical tendency for fights, arson, accidents, kleptomania and even murder to occur more frequently at full moon. Humans show an annual, cyclical, fluctuation in body weight and, in the northern hemisphere, a tendency to be born more often in May and June than in November and December.

Black Elk

Black Elk was a warrior and medicine man of the Oglala Sioux. A remarkable document entitled *Black Elk Speaks* was written down by John Neihardt in the early 1930s from his extended conversations with him. It tells of a spontaneous numinous vision which came to Black Elk as a nine-year-old boy. This vision was of great power but he was afraid to tell anyone of it. He became consumed with fear and ill, and it was not until six years later that he finally told an old medicine man, Black Road. The medicine man understood that the vision was not just for Black Elk alone. What was necessary was for it to be performed and the fear would then depart. A public enactment of Black Elk's great vision then took place, accompanied by celebrations and **healing**.

Black Madonnas

Some of the most famous statues of the Madonna in Western Europe are black – Chartres, Le Puy, Rocamadour, Montserrat, Einsiedeln, for example. According to Robert Graves, they derive from an ancient tradition of Wisdom as Blackness. It is likely that the images represent a continuation of **pagan Goddess**-worship. In his book *The Cult of the Black Virgin*, Ean Begg explores the history and meaning of the Black Madonnas.

Blake, William

> To me, the world is all one continued vision of fancy or imagination.

The quote is from the works of William Blake, perhaps the most extraordinary visionary Britain has ever produced and a man who believed, again in his own words, that 'the world of imagination is the world of Eternity'.

Blake, who lived from 1757 to 1827, was primarily a creator of myths. In his verse and paintings he produced a potent pantheon based on the four 'Zoas', Urizen, Luvah, Urthona and Tharmas, manifesting as reason, feeling, **intuition** and sense. Each Zoa has a negative counterpart, sons, daughters and an emanation.

As a Christian, Blake accepted such religious absolutes as the Fall, the Adversary Satan and the divinity of Christ, but interpreted them in a highly unorthodox manner. He believed, for instance, that the Fall was an entirely inward affair, that Satan equated with 'the Selfhood' and that Christ should be more properly seen as the 'Jesus of the Imagination'.

'All deities,' said Blake, 'reside in the human breast.' He insisted that all religions were one and that perceived differences arose from each nation's differing reception of the **spirit** of **prophecy**.

It seems quite evident that Blake spent much of his time in states of **consciousness** others experience only in the briefest glimpses. The nature of his perceptions in these states is caught in the immense power of his paintings, most dealing with religious themes. Perhaps his best known, *The Ancient of Days*, shows Urizen, a bearded god-like figure, reaching down from his own sphere to create the material world with the aid of callipers.

Much of Blake's poetry was, on his own admission, 'dictated' – that is to say, it arose from inward, unconscious sources. His works frequently lack structure and artistry, but never power. Typical of his poetic themes is that showing his perception of a tiger:

> Tyger, Tyger burning bright
> In the forests of the night
> What immortal hand or eye
> Dared frame thy fearful symmetry?
>
> When the stars threw down their spears
> And water'd heaven with their tears
> Dare he laugh his mark to see?
> Dare he who made the lamb make thee?

But perhaps the most powerful statement of all of his mystical philosophy is contained in just four short lines entitled *Auguries of Innocence*:

> To see a World in a Grain of Sand
> And a Heaven in a Wild Flower
> Hold Infinity in the palm of your hand
> And Eternity in an hour.

Blavatsky, H.P.

When the Russian novelist Helena Fadeyev lay dying at the early age of 27, she remarked, 'Perhaps it's all for the best – I shall at least be spared knowing what befalls Helena.' The Helena she was talking about was her daughter, Helena Petrovna Hahn, a rebellious child born (some say prematurely, at the stroke of midnight) on 30 July 1831.

What befell Helena was, in the long term, bizarre. She was educated, principally in languages and music, by a governess who remarked on her talent for science and literature as well. Despite the woman's admiration, the relationship between the two was strained. Sometime in 1847, the governess was sufficiently exasperated to scream at her pupil that no man would marry her not even the 'plumeless raven' Nikifor Blavatsky, then Vice Governor of the province of Erivan.

Helena set out to prove her governess wrong and succeeded on 7 July 1848 when she became Blavatsky's blushing bride. Blavatsky may indeed have been 'plumeless', for the marriage was never consummated – although in fairness, Helena did not give him much time to try. She ran away the day after the ceremony, apparently in an attempt to reach Persia, but was turned back by the Cossack Guard. Three months later, she ran away again, this time to the home of her grandparents.

Unable to handle the troublesome young woman, her grandfather decided to send her to her father in St Petersburg. Part of the journey was made by boat. Fearing she might be returned to her husband, Helena persuaded the Captain to send her servants ashore at Kerch and sailed away with him to Constantinople.

It is difficult to determine with any certainty what happened next. Helena Blavatsky's official biographer, A.P. Sinnett, claims she met a countess in Constantinople and travelled with her to Greece and Egypt. Her cousin, Count Witte, says she became a bareback rider in a circus and formed a relationship with the Hungarian singer Agardi Metrovitch.

Metrovitch brought her to Europe where she agreed to marry him, having apparently forgotten she was married already. Evidently it was a memory lapse which recurred, for a few years later her grandfather received a letter from an Englishman convinced he too was married to Helena. From this communication it is possible to deduce that she was in America in the summer of 1851 and witnessed **Voodoo** rites in New Orleans.

It seems to have been a good year for matters occult, for it was then she 'first met physically the Teacher, the Elder Brother or Adept, who had ever been her protector, guarding her from serious harm in her wildest childish escapades'.[1] This teacher was a Secret Master and his appearance profoundly changed Helena's life. With this powerful **guide** behind her, she gradually

---

1. Josephine Ranson, 'HPB: A Sketch of her Life' published as an introduction to *The Secret Doctrine*, Adyar edition, 1938.

learned to control and direct her **psychic** powers. She spent part of her time in the Himalayas, studying the Eastern Esoteric Tradition under learned lamas, then came to Europe to give piano lessons in Paris and London and meet the famous Spiritualist **medium, Daniel Dunglas Home**.

In 1858 she made peace with her grandfather and returned to Russia where she displayed her budding mediumistic powers in séances for the aristocracy. Then Metrovitch turned up again and carried her off first to Kiev, then Odessa, where they set up in business making artificial flowers. Tragedy struck. Metrovitch, who was still pursuing his career as a singer, accepted an engagement in Egypt. He and Madame Blavatsky set sail for Cairo in 1871. The ship sank and Metrovitch drowned.

Two years later, Helena Blavatsky was in America, which was at that time gripped by a sort of Spiritualist fever. She plunged into the growing movement with enthusiasm and was soon claiming séance-room phenomena were only a part of a much larger body of knowledge. There were deeper laws of life, virtually unsuspected in the West, but known in the East for centuries and carefully guarded by the Secret Masters.

In 1877, she committed many of her ideas to paper in a two-volume work entitled *Isis Unveiled*. It sold out within ten days of publication. In an attempt to catch the flavour of the work, one of Blavatsky's modern biographers, John Symonds, has written, 'If **Atlantis** had really existed, and if one person, a single Initiate, had been selected by the gods to give to the world the arcane knowledge which was swept away when Atlantis was submerged, then HPB was that Initiate, and *Isis Unveiled* a repository of that knowledge.'

The book, like her later (and even more massive) work *The Secret Doctrine*, was written against the background of Blavatsky's position as head of the Theosophical Society, established two years earlier. Interest in the society waned as the Spiritualist fad ran out of steam, but revived substantially when Blavatsky and her friend Colonel H.S. Olcott sold up everything and departed for India. There they launched a monthly magazine called *The Theosophist* and watched their society grow into a flourishing international organization.

In 1884, the society's founders returned in triumph to Europe where Blavatsky was entertained in Nice by Lady Caithness, who loaned her a flat in Paris. Shortly afterwards she sailed for

England where the **Society for Psychical Research** proposed to investigate her 'marvellous phenomena'. But before they could issue a report, Blavatsky found herself embroiled in allegations of fraud issued by her old friend Madame Coulomb. In the wake of the scandal, which attracted the attention of the world's Press, the Society for Psychical Research modified its initial (quite favourable) impressions and issued a report which described Blavatsky as 'one of the most accomplished, ingenious and interesting impostors in history'.

By now too ill with Bright's Disease to care, Blavatsky travelled to Italy, Switzerland and Germany before returning to England, where she wrote her masterpiece, *The Secret Doctrine*, a work she claimed to be inspired by the Secret Masters. It was the culmination of a fascinating career – she died in 1891 – and has proved to be a lasting memorial, for Blavatsky's **Theosophy** was more than strong enough to survive the disapproval of the Society for Psychical Research.

Bodhidharma

This semi-legendary Indian missionary established **Zen Buddhism** in China and Japan. Buddhism itself was already well rooted in China at the time of his arrival, during the reign of the Emperor Wu Ti (AD 502–550), but Bodhidarma claimed he had made the journey in order to restore to the religion its original directness and meaningful simplicity.

The Zen flavour of Bodhidharma's approach is evident in the tradition of his meeting with Wu Ti. The Emperor explained about the temples he had built, the scriptures he had caused to be copied and the special privileges he had extended to Buddhist monks in his kingdom. What merit, he asked, had accrued to him because of these activities. None, replied the missionary.

'What, then, is the first principle of Buddhism?' asked the Emperor.

'Emptiness,' said Bodhidharma.

'Who are you to speak to me like this?' Wu Ti demanded.

'I don't know,' said Bodhidharma, who then took himself off to engage in nine years **meditation** facing a cave wall.

Bodhisattva

The term *Bodhisattva* is used in one of two ways. To Buddhists, it simply means one who aspires to be like the **Buddha**, but who has not yet achieved **nirvana**. To Theosophists, however, it refers to an individual who will definitely achieve the status of Buddha in his/her next incarnation and has developed an awareness of his own divinity even in this life.

Body of Light

A term often considered synonymous with **astral body**, the body of light had a special usage in the Hermetic Order of the **Golden Dawn** where it referred to an *artificially-created* vehicle for **astral projection**. (*See also* **Tulpa Creation**.)

Bodywork

There are many different bodywork techniques, therapies for working on the body to produce better physical and psychological health. They range from **Alexander technique** to **bioenergetics**, from **Feldenkreis** to **Rolfing**, from **Hellerwork** to **polarity therapy**. The underlying idea, derived from the pioneering work of **Wilhelm Reich**, is that painful traumas cause blocks to the flow of energy in the body, so that the body does not function as it should. Through working on these blocks, energy is released and the well-being of the individual is improved.

Boehme, Jacob

Jacob Boehme was born in Silesia in 1575 and grew up to become a master cobbler, married with four children. At the age of 25 he was struck by a mystical experience which was 'like the resurrection of the dead'. It was the first of several and influenced the course of his entire life. His first book, *Aurora*, which described his mystical experience, so disturbed the town council of Görlitz, where he lived, that he was forbidden to write any more. Fortunately he ignored the instruction and by his death in 1624 had produced some 30 books and pamphlets.

History has judged him as 'by far the greatest and most original of Protestant mystics', but he was, in fact, as much an occultist as a Protestant. He was familiar with **alchemy** and **astrology** and had studied the arcane symbolism of the **Qabalah**. One of his dearest wishes was to reform **Christianity** and bring about a reunion between Protestants and Roman Catholics. The notion did not prove popular and the Görlitz council were not the only ones to attack him bitterly. Later generations proved more sympathetic and there are clear indications of his influence in the works of Hegel, Schopenhauer, Nietzsche and even **William Blake**.

Bohm, David

Respected physicist whose book *Wholeness and the Implicate Order* went a long way towards underwriting the ancient mystical insight of essential unity in the universe. To some extent this is not altogether surprising since he has, over the years, been profoundly influenced by **Krishnamurti**, whom he considers his spiritual mentor.

In formulating his more recent theories, Bohm took the notion of wholeness as his starting point with the aim of exploring what he believes to be the order inherent in relationships at a non-manifest level. He refers to this as **implicate order**, in the sense that it is, so to speak, 'enfolded' in matter.

Book of Changes
See I Ching.

Book of the Dead
See Egyptian Book of the Dead and *Tibetan Book of the Dead*.

Book of the Way
See Tao Te Ching.

Borley Rectory

When it was burned down in 1939 Borley Rectory had achieved an invidious record as the most haunted house in Britain. Although one of its most famous investigators, the psychical researcher Harry Price, has been seriously questioned in terms of his methodology and even honesty, there seems little doubt that the site was a major **poltergeist** focus for many years. Hauntings of one sort or another were witnessed by more than 200 people, making it impossible to dismiss Borley completely.

Borley Rectory was built on the site of Herringham Rectory in 1863 by the Reverend Henry Bull and was situated on the edge of Borley village less than three miles from Long Melford and Sudbury.

Boyeson, Gerda
See **Biodynamic Massage**.

Bruno, Giordano

Gervase of Canterbury, the medieval chronicler, recorded an account of something very peculiar which happened to the moon on 18 June 1178, when a group of observers saw its upper cusp actually split in two. From the midpoint of the division, flames sprang up, fountaining high into the air while the lower portion of the moon appeared to writhe.

'This phenomenon was repeated a dozen times or more,' Gervase wrote, 'the flame assuming various twisting shapes at random, then returning to normal.'

For centuries, the account was taken as a fiction. Then, in the 1970s, astronomer Jack Hartung made some calculations and discovered the account almost certainly referred to the violent meteor impact which created one of the moon's more striking features, a 12-mile-wide crater named for the sixteenth-century philosopher and mathematician, Giordano Bruno.

If Hartung was correct, the subsequent naming of the crater was singularly appropriate, for in his lifetime Bruno was seen to be heretical and was eventually burned at the stake.

Born near Naples in 1548, Bruno entered a Dominican monastery at the age of 17 and took up an enthusiastic study of astronomy. He also seems to have studied **magic**, including the occult memory system of **Raymon Lull**. This worked so well for him that he was actually summoned to Rome by Pope Pius V to discuss memory training.

Bruno's ideas about the workings of the universe proved too revolutionary for the religious establishment of his day and he began a wandering life peppered by constant disputes with those with whom he came into contact. He seems to have been a less than likeable man; certainly he was less than diplomatic. On one occasion he took pains to point out 20 mistakes he claimed to have been made in a single lecture by one of the most popular local professors.

Many of his ideas were well ahead of his time. He believed the sun to be the centre of the cosmos at a time when a geocentric universe was the accepted doctrine and was one of the first to postulate the notion that the universe itself must be infinite. He also hit on the fascinating notion that any living being on any planet must consider its home world to be the centre of the universe.

By 1592, Bruno's doctrines proved too much for the Roman

Church. He was imprisoned by the Inquisition and burned at the stake in 1600.

Brunton, Dr Paul

English author, traveller, occultist and yogi, perhaps noted not only as a spiritual teacher, but also as one of the last men to obtain permission, in the 1930s, to spend a night in the King's Chamber of the **Great Pyramid** at Giza. The stay triggered a mystical experience in which the chamber was filled with light, Brunton heard spectral voices and eventually left his body in an **astral projection**.

He described the onset of his experience in these words:

> . . . all my muscles became taut, after which a paralysing lethargy began to creep over my limbs. My entire body became heavy and numb . . . The feeling developed into a kind of iciness . . . All sensation in the lower limbs was numbed.
>
> I appeared next to pass into a semi-somnolent condition . . . I felt myself sinking inwards in consciousness to some central point within my brain, while my breathing became weaker and weaker . . . There was a final mad whirl within my brain. I had the sensation of being caught up in a tropical whirlwind and seemed to pass upwards through a narrow hole; then there was the momentary dread of being launched into infinite space . . . I had gone ghost-like out of my earthly body . . .

These experiences were described in *A Search in Secret Egypt*. He also travelled widely in India and met the great sage **Ramana Maharshi**. His spiritual quest in India is described in *A Search in Secret India*. In all he wrote some 28 books about the spiritual life.

Buddha

Although Westerners tend to think of the Buddha as the single founder of a specific religion rather like Jesus or Mohammed, Oriental esoteric thought postulates a series of Buddhas (the name means the 'Enlightened One') who have incarnated at intervals throughout history in order to assist humanity towards a valid perception of spiritual reality.

The individual generally referred to as 'the Buddha' is only the most recent of the line. Historically, he was born Prince Siddhartha Gautama in Nepal about 563 BC, the son of a Sakya clan chieftain. Legend has it that his coming was announced to his mother, Queen Maya, by the appearance of an elephant.

As a child he was closeted from the ills of the world, but one day while out hunting happened to see a diseased beggar on the side of the road and realized he had been living in a fool's paradise. He left home and became a wandering holy man, desperately seeking answers to the age-old spiritual questions. He gathered a small group of followers, but lost them when he concluded that the traditional religious discipline of fasting had brought him no nearer understanding and began to eat again.

Eventually, after years of effort, he achieved enlightenment while meditating under a bo-tree. His followers believe that having reached the blissful state of non-being referred to as **nirvana**, he was freed from the necessity of physical incarnation, but voluntarily renounced his ecstasy in order to guide others towards the same goal.

Siddartha Gautama died at the age of 80 around 483 BC.

Buddhism

The first Buddhist sermon was preached in Benares, India, about 530 BC. By the time Prince Siddhartha Gautama, the **Buddha** (or Enlightened One) died some 45 years later, the religion he founded had attracted hundreds of monks and thousands of lay followers. It continued to grow and spread, rooting in China, Tibet, Japan, Burma and much of South East Asia. For a time it flourished much more strongly abroad than it did in its native India, although it is currently enjoying a considerable revival on the sub-continent today and is generally accepted to have influenced **Hinduism** profoundly.

The fundamental pattern of Buddhism, which some consider to be far more of a philosophy than a religion, was set in the Benares sermon, when Gautama proclaimed the Middle Way between extremes of asceticism and thoughtless hedonism. The Middle Way comprised the Noble Eightfold Path of Right Views, Right Intent, Right Speech, Right Action, Right Livelihood, Right Effort, Right Mindfulness and Right Concentration. The Path was based on Four Noble Truths: that all life is suffering, that the cause of suffering is desire, that suffering will cease when desire ceases and that the Noble Eightfold Path will lead to the cessation of desire.

Any practice of Buddhism is inextricably linked with the doctrine of **reincarnation** and the concept of **karma**. Buddhists believe that all of humanity is caught on an eternal wheel of reincarnation after reincarnation, driven by karma, and the only way to break free is to achieve enlightenment, expressed in the ecstatic state of **nirvana**. This is reached by following the Noble Eightfold Path and engaging in the Three Trainings – morality, concentration and wisdom. The Trainings go beyond the expression of pious platitudes into the realms of **yoga**, making Buddhism perhaps the most esoteric of all the great Oriental religions.

It recognizes that **meditation** is likely to produce *siddhis* or **psychic** powers, usually broken down into six categories of which the first five are:

Magic powers such as **levitation**, walking on water, shape-shifting or projecting a mind-made body. (*See* **Body of Light**.)
Clairaudience, the ability to hear the voices of **spirits**.
Telepathy, the ability to read minds.
Far memory, the ability to recall **past lives**. (*See* **Regression**; **Reincarnation**.)
Clairvoyance, the ability to obtain information at a distance without the intermediary of mind-to-mind contact.

These five curious abilities are believed to be the natural outgrowth of trained concentration. The sixth, a type of suspended animation, in which all major physical functions come to a halt, is thought to come only from insight. All six are dismissed as distractions which should be ignored in order to achieve the central goal of nirvana.

But this dismissal is a relatively recent phenomenon. There seems little doubt that early Buddhism, including the life of the Buddha himself, had strong elements of **shamanism** with powers of the type listed exercised frequently in order to gain merit.

Budge, E.A. Wallis

Former Keeper of Egyptian and Assyrian Antiquities at the British Museum, best noted for his translation of the *Egyptian Book of the Dead* and several other works on Egyptian language and magical practice.

Butler, W.E.

An adept in both Eastern and **Western Esoteric Traditions**, W. Ernest Butler achieved public prominence with the publication in 1952 of his shortest book, *Magic: its Ritual, Power and Purpose*, which was responsible for generating an interest in occult subjects in an entire generation. He followed the work with perhaps his most important book, *The Magician: His Training and Work*, which described plainly for the first time the elements of esoteric training.

A former initiate of the Society of the Inner Light, Butler had throughout much of his life a contact with a **Hidden Master** who encouraged him to form the **Servants of the Light**, which he headed until ill health (he was diabetic and suffered from a heart condition) forced him to pass on both the organization and his contact to **Dolores Ashcroft-Nowicki** shortly before his death in 1978.

C

Caddy, Eileen

Co-founder of the **Findhorn** Foundation whose 'still small voice within' guided the early development of the community. Caddy's book *Foundations of Findhorn* tells how it all began in a caravan camped on a barren stretch of sand. Among her other books are *Footprints on the Path* and *Opening Doors Within*.

Caduceus

A universal symbol of spiritual enlightenment, wisdom and **healing**. Two snakes are entwined around a wand, with wings or a winged helmet on top.

Camelot

The oldest known stories of **Arthurian legend** never refer to Camelot, the supposed capital of Arthur's realm. It first appears in Chrestien de Troyes' twelfth-century romance *Lancelot* and was taken up by Malory, who seemed to equate it with Winchester and made it the seat of the Round Table.

There are several modern candidates for the site of the original Camelot – assuming it existed at all. One is the Roman city of Colchester, which in the original Latin was called *Camulodunum*. Another is an area around Tintagel in Cornwall, reputed to have been Arthur's birthplace. The River Camel flows through the area and there is also a town of Camelford.

Perhaps the hottest possibility is the Iron Age earthwork on Cadbury Hill overlooking the Vale of Avalon to **Glastonbury**. The fifteenth-century antiquary, John Leland, wrote that local people referred to the hill fort as 'Camalat'. The village of Queen Camel is close by . . . and was once known simply as Camel. The River Cam flows nearby as well. If local place-names are any indication, then the site is further supported by the fact that the plateau at the summit of the hill is named as 'King Arthur's Palace' while there is also a 'King Arthur's Well' within the earthwork itself.

Most recent scholarly theory places Camelot in the south of Scotland, however, with the famous Round Table relegated to a mistranslation of the Scottish Gaelic term for a circular corbelled building of polished stone. Such buildings were popular as moratoria for the bones of saints throughout the Roman Empire and the Middle East. It is postulated that the prototype Arthur, fighting in an early Crusade, became involved in a religious cult of Mary Magdalene which he imported into Britain on his return.

He caused the circular building to be erected as part of his religious observance and it became colloquially known as 'Arthur's O'on' (Arthur's Oven). The building actually stood until the early 1800s when it was demolished by a local landlord, who used the stones to build a dam. A replica was, however, built from the original plans.

Campbell, Joseph

The world's foremost authority on mythology died in Honolulu in 1987. Born in 1904 in New York City, from first seeing Buffalo Bill's Wild West Show at Madison Square Gardens and the Museum of Natural History, he developed a life-long interest in Native American Indians. He began his career in 1934 as an instructor at Sarah Lawrence College, where he taught for almost 40 years. In his spiritual and scholarly and cross-cultural exploration of the world's mythology he discovered remarkable parallels. As he saw it, 'Myths are clues to the spiritual potentialities of the human life.' *Hero with a Thousand Faces* is his famous analysis of the spiritual quest in the myths of the world. His other major work on mythology is *The Masks of God*. In 1988 a one-hour film production of 'The Hero's Journey: The World of Joseph Campbell', aired on national television in America, plus a six-part series of 'Joseph Campbell and the Power of Myth' resulted in an explosion of popular interest in Campbell.

Capra, Fritjof

Fritjof Capra received his Ph.D from the University of Vienna and engaged in research in the field of high-energy physics at several European and American universities.

But it was his work *The Tao of Physics* which catapulted him into international prominence. An immensely readable book on an extremely difficult subject, it sold more than half a million copies in a dozen translations and profoundly influenced a whole generation of physicists as well as attracting an enormous following of lay readers.

The book was based on an insight which dawned on Capra in 1969 when he experienced the movement of subatomic particles as the Dance of Shiva, believed by Hindu mystics to underlie the whole of manifestation. In April the following year, he received his last pay cheque for research in theoretical particle physics and began to devote his time to far more broadly based research. Capra himself described this in the following words:

> I spent many hours in intense discussions with some of the leading scientists of our time; I explored various altered states of consciousness, with and without teachers and guides; I spent time with philosophers and artists; I discussed and experienced a whole range of therapies, physical as well as psychological; and I participated in many meetings with social activists . . . throughout the past 15 years I have consistently pursued a single theme – the fundamental change of world view that is occurring in science and in society, the unfolding of a new vision of reality and the social implications of this cultural transformation.

The new view (as explained in *Tao of Physics*) was, in fact, a very old view. Capra showed how, in instance after instance, the work of modern physicists expressed, in different terms, precisely the same world view as that of the ancient mystics.

Carey, Ken

Ken Carey lives with his family on a remote forest farm in southern Missouri. In 1979 he began **channelling** via an entity named Raphael. Many find the resulting books – *The Starseed Transmissions, Terra Christa* and *Return of the Bird Tribes* – remarkable. Jean Houston has described *The Starseed Transmissions* as 'perhaps the finest example of "channelled knowledge" I ever encountered'.

Carezza

See Karezza.

Carnac

If **Glastonbury** is the magical capital of Britain, then Brittany – and more particularly the district of Carnac – must surely be the magical capital of France. Certainly it has one of the most dramatic collections of **megaliths** to be seen anywhere in the world, line upon line of menhirs marching across the countryside for miles. According to legend, these standing stones were formed when the Christian Saint Cornely was pursued by an army of **pagan**s until he reached the sea shore and could go no further. In desperation, he called on God to turn his pursuers into stones, which God obligingly did. Saint Cornely then made off in a bullock cart.

In fact the megaliths predate **Christianity** by about 2,000 years. Orthodox archaeologists look on the site as a huge burial ground which includes grave mounds, stone tombs and circles. Others point out that certain **leys** begun in Britain seem to continue in Carnac. Professor Alexander Thom investigated the area and found that, as in British sites, there were clear astronomical alignments in evidence among the stones. (*See also* **Geomancy**.)

Case, Paul Foster

An American occultist best known for his work on the **Tarot**, Paul Foster Case claimed to be the US head of the **Golden Dawn** and insisted he was in touch with the Secret Chiefs of that Order. (*See* **Hidden Masters**.)

He subscribed to the widespread esoteric notion that the Tarot pack came into being when Masters of Wisdom decided to synthesize the entire esoteric tradition into a series of symbols. But where the usual belief states that this took place before the Flood in order to preserve the wisdom, Case set the meeting around AD 1200 in Fez, Morocco.

During his most active years, he founded the *Builders of the Adytum*, an occult centre in Los Angeles, and wrote several excellent books on the Tarot. He died in 1954 at the age of 70.

Castaneda, Carlos

One of the most widely known investigators of shamanism is the anthropologist Carlos Castaneda, whose books about the Yaqui sorcerer, Don Juan Matus, have sold world-wide in their millions.

Castaneda began his career as Carlos Arana (or Aranha – the spelling is uncertain) but changed it when he acquired American citizenship in 1959. Between that year and 1973, he undertook a series of degree courses in anthropology at the University of California. For the first of these, he travelled in 1960 to the American South-west for the purpose of investigating the Indian use of medicinal plants. While there he met Don Juan.

Don Juan was a *brujo*, one who cures by means of magical techniques, and an expert on plant hallucinogenics, notably peyote, the psychedelic cactus. He had been born in Mexico in 1891 and spoke Spanish fluently.

Their first meeting was not easy. After being told of Don Juan by a friend, Castaneda spent a day searching for his house but could not find it. He suspected the Indians from whom he asked directions deliberately misled him. But then one scorching afternoon he was sitting in the bus depot of an Arizona border town when an elderly Indian strolled in. He was white-haired and very wrinkled, his brown skin burned even deeper by years of exposure to the sun, but he moved well and seemed fitter than any old man had a natural right to be. Someone told Castaneda this was the *yerbero* (seller of medicinal herbs) he was looking for.

Despite sticky beginnings, a strong bond developed between Don Juan and the young anthropology student. The brujo eventually invited Castaneda to become his apprentice and Castaneda agreed. It was, he felt, the only way to gain access to the body of traditional knowledge locked in the old Indian's brain.

Castaneda's first four books are largely the story of that apprenticeship, the experiences he underwent and the magical theories Don Juan put forward to explain them. While the first published, *The Teachings of Don Juan*, had some pretensions of academic style, the remainder have been far more popular in tone. All were immensely readable and the Flower Power culture of the sixties, fascinated by hallucinogenics, could hardly get enough of them.

At the centre of Don Juan's magical system lay three plants, all hallucinogenic. These plants were peyote, jimson weed and a species of psylocebic mushroom. The old brujo considered each a key to communication with a specific entity or force. To him, for example, peyote was the physical manifestation of a being he called Mescalito. To eat the cactus was to put yourself in a state in which Mescalito could reach you and in which you became gradually aware of the signs this entity wrote in the mundane world. Communication with Mescalito and other inward beings was the first step towards making them your allies.

Castaneda's apprenticeship involved frequent use of the hallucinogenics, notably the 'little smoke' as Matus called the psylocebic mushroom. The fungus was dried and finely powdered, then inhaled through a pipe. In the brujo's terms, the process allowed the ally to 'remove one's body'.

Over the years, Castaneda's adventures became increasingly bizarre. He was, for instance, the focus of a magical murder attempt by a woman named Catalina, who had the power to turn herself into a blackbird.

There was a problem with all this. Despite his academic credentials – he was awarded a PhD from UCLA for his third book, *Journey to Ixtlan* – some people with an expert knowledge of native Indian sorcery simply did not believe him. They pointed out that no one other than Castaneda had ever met Don Juan or, indeed, even seen a photograph of him. Castaneda failed to produce his field notes. No Yaqui had ever been known to use datura, as Castaneda claimed of Don Juan, and sacramental mushroom rites were unknown in the area where Castaneda claimed to have met him.

The writer Richard De Mille went into print to highlight internal inconsistencies in Castaneda's accounts . . . and there were many. They varied from linguistic questions to the common sense objection that some of the non-magical talents Castaneda claimed (like the ability to sew up a lizard's eyes with a thorn) were just plain impossible.

In his latest book, *The Art of Dreaming*, Castaneda turns his attention to the remarkable spiritual adventures that can be attained through dreams.

Cathars

Arthur Guirdham, formerly Chief Psychiatrist of the Bath District, unearthed substantial evidence that both he and a number of his friends and acquaintances were **reincarnation**s of thirteenth-century Cathars. The story of his discovery, told in his *The Cathars and Reincarnation*, is no more fantastic than the history of the Cathar sect itself.

Catharism was rooted in ancient **Gnosticism**, but had its immediate development as a western offshoot of the Bogomils. It appeared in Europe around AD 1140 and spread rapidly in southern France, northern Italy and, to a much lesser extent, Germany. By 1208, the religion had grown so strong that Pope Innocent III declared a Crusade against it, unleashing a war which lasted 20 years.

The war ended with the Treaty of Méaux in 1229, but the Cathars, largely driven underground, still suffered as heretics under the Inquisition established by Pope Gregory IX. In 1244, 200 members of the sect were massacred at Montségur, a tragedy from which the movement never really recovered, although a neo-Catharist sect appeared in Toulouse as late as the Second World War.

The central philosophy of the Cathars was a dualism in which the power of evil, known as the Monster of Chaos, was the weaker force, but the personification of good, God, was not all-powerful. Their ideas on Christ were equally unorthodox: they believed the crucifixion to be fictitious, that Jesus' real mission was carried through on another plane and that his work on Earth was to warn humanity that the God of the Old Testament was really a demon who had created the material world.

Cayce, Edgar

Today, many hundreds of healers and literally thousands of their patients world-wide are using curative techniques developed (if that is the word) by a man with no medical training whatsoever, who did his best work while unconscious. That man was Edgar Cayce, America's 'Sleeping Prophet', one of the most remarkable **psychic**s of the twentieth century.

Edgar Cayce was born on a farm near Hopkinsville, Kentucky, on 18 March 1877. First hints of psychism came early. At the age of seven, he told his parents of a meeting with his dead grandfather and there are some suggestions he may have had a vision of an **angel**.

Cayce did not get beyond seventh grade at school and by the age of 16 was working in a bookshop. Like most young Americans, he played baseball and during one game a blow to the back caused sufficient damage to necessitate a stay in bed. While suffering from the injury, he suddenly ordered his mother to apply a certain type of poultice to the damaged area. She did so and he arose next morning cured. He had no memory at all of the experience – a situation which was to be repeated frequently throughout his life.

By 1898, at the age of 21, Cayce had become a salesman for a wholesale stationery company, had developed an interest in photography and was teetering on the edge of becoming one of the most remarkable healers the world had ever known. The latter development arose out of an ailment of his own which he thought might be cured through the use of **hypnosis**. He presented himself to a local hypnotist, whose suggestions did little to relieve the problem. But during one session, while still deep in trance, Cayce suddenly prescribed his own cure. It was effective, and he began to wonder if he might perhaps be able to repeat the trick to the benefit of others. Before long, he was able to dispense with the services of the hypnotist altogether, sinking easily into a self-induced trance state.

Cayce's cures were far too numerous and well attested for any controversy to surround them now. But he was not a 'faith healer' in the accepted sense of the term. He did not engage in any laying on of hands and ran no therapy sessions. His real skill lay in diagnosis, which he carried out psychically, in many cases without even having to see the patient. Often his conclusions flatly contradicted orthodox medical opinion, but time and again, Cayce would be proven right and the doctors wrong.

His methods of treatment varied from perfectly orthodox prescriptions like castor oil through **homoeopathy** and osteopathic referrals to bizarre medicaments like bed-bug juice. The one thing they had in common was that they worked. By the time of his death in 1945, he had successfully treated many thousands of patients, often referred to him by medical practitioners.

The psychism which underpinned his **healing** activities led him into some peculiar pathways. On one occasion, for example, he discovered the identity of a murderer by psychic means. (And for his pains was briefly charged with the crime by an officer who did not believe in psychism and became convinced that the only way Cayce could know so much about the crime was by committing it.)

From medical 'readings' Cayce went on to 'life readings' – evaluations of the patient's destiny. An orthodox and somewhat fundamentalist Christian while in his waking state, Cayce was profoundly disturbed to discover that while in trance he delivered life readings which included **past lives** and evoked an aeons-long history of humanity dating to the fabled lost continent of **Atlantis**.

Chakras

Chakra is the Sanskrit word for wheel. When seen by clairvoyants, chakras appear as wheel-like vortices of energy within the human **aura**. In both Oriental **yoga** and Western magical thought, chakras are energy centres which exist for the purpose of absorbing from the cosmos, transforming and distributing the **universal life force**.

There are seven main chakras and many minor ones:

1) The root chakra (*muladhara*) is located at the base of the spine and it is here that the **kundalini** resides.
2) The sacral chakra (*svadhisthara*) is located near the genitals and governs sexuality and reproduction.
3) The solar plexus (*manipura*) is situated above the navel and affects the pancreas, stomach, liver and gall bladder. It is associated with the emotions.
4) The heart chakra (*anahata*) is located in the centre of the chest and governs the heart, the blood and the circulatory system. It is through this chakra that unconditional love is radiated.
5) The throat chakra (*vishuddha*) is concerned with speech, communication, the search for truth and creativity.
6) The brow chakra (*ajna*) is associated with both the pineal gland and the pituitary gland. It is in the centre of the head between the eyebrows and is also referred to as the **Third Eye**, responsible for increased psychic ability and imagination.
7) Above the top of the head is the crown chakra (*sahasrara*). It is only activated once all the other chakras are in balance, and brings spiritual illumination and cosmic consciousness.

Channelling

There is nothing new about channelling. It has been around since the beginning of human experience. At various times in history it has been either accepted or decried. Recently, it has been seen as something of a fad.

Channelling is similar to mediumship in that both seek to bring through to the physical world information originating from beings in another plane of existence. But where mediumship almost always involves trance, channelling may or may not do so. Furthermore, while mediumship is concerned, almost exclusively, with the **spirits** of the dead, channelling tends to make contact with entities professing an important message for humanity as a whole. Both the **Seth** material and *A Course in Miracles* are examples of channelled texts. Recent non-physical entities who have been channelled are **Lazaris**, **Ramtha** and **Emmanuel**.

Chanting

One of the oldest routes to changes in **consciousness**, chanting is believed to achieve its effect in three ways:

1) Prolonged chanting can lead to hyperventilation or, conversely, hypoventilation, both of which influence blood oxygen and blood carbon-dioxide levels, with consequent effects on the brain.
2) *Mantra*-like repetition has a direct effect on the mind, often leading to trance states if sufficiently prolonged.
3) Sound itself, properly directed through chanting, has a vibrationary influence on the **chakras** of the human body.

Charismatic

The word 'charismatic' comes from the Greek words *charismata* or *charisms*, meaning spiritual gifts, which might include speaking in tongues, **prophecy**, **healing** and the ability to perform miracles.

Chela

In Oriental terminology, the pupil of a **guru**.

Ch'i

Ch'i, in Chinese esoteric and medical thought, is a universal energy generated by the sun and utilized within the human body. Manipulation of this energy, which manifests in the negative/positive polarities of **yin/yang**, forms the basis of medical **acupuncture**. Control of the energy is also involved in Chinese **yoga** and some branches of the **martial arts**. (*See also* **Universal Life Force**.)

Ch'i Kung

Also spelled *Ch'i gung*, *Ch'i gong* and *Qi gong*, *Ch'i kung* is Chinese **yoga**, a system closely related to the more familiar Indian yoga, **meditation** and certain of the Oriental **martial arts** in background and philosophy.

Chinese medicine sees the body as a matrix of energy pathways (*see* **Acupuncture**) through which *ch'i*, the vital energy, flows. *Ch'i kung* seeks to manipulate this energy, focusing on the goal of health rather than muscular fitness. Benefits from the practice range from increased energy and stamina to a more centred disposition, and the system is extremely popular in a variety of forms in modern China.

In its more esoteric aspects, the meditation practices of Chinese yoga concentrate on arousing a *kundalini*-type energy through the **chakras** in order to achieve enlightened states and/or magical powers.

Chinese Hand Analysis

Western palmistry is concerned with the lines and mounds of the hand as related to traditional **astrology**. (The fleshy mound at the base of the thumb is known as the Mound of Venus; the pad at the tip of the index finger is related to Jupiter; and so on.) Chinese hand analysis, by contrast, relies on the Law of the Five Elements, which is also found in **acupuncture**. The Elements are not those of medieval Western **alchemy** (i.e. Earth, Air, Fire, Water and Ether) but rather a peculiarly Chinese subdivision of Fire, Earth, Metal, Water and Wood, each related to the other in accordance with clearly defined laws. In hand analysis, the Elements are used to determine how and why the individual life means what it does.

Chinmoy, Sri

Sri Chinmoy Kumar Ghose was born in Bengal in 1931 and spent 20 years on **Sri Aurobindo**'s **ashram**. An exponent of Bhakti (devotional) **yoga**, he travels all over the world. He has written over 50 books and also claims to paint the higher realms of **meditation** and composes music to take listeners to higher states of awareness.

Chiropractic

Devised by Dr Daniel David Palmer, chiropractic is similar to **osteopathy**, being based on the idea that the displacement of the vertebrae causes disease. The main difference is in the different styles of manipulation of the joints.

Christian Science

More properly referred to as the Church of Christ Scientist, Christian Science is the religion founded in the latter half of the nineteenth century by **Mary Baker-Eddy**.

The sect differs from orthodox **Christianity** in that central to its philosophy is the belief that neither evil nor matter exist in any ultimate sense, but the most dramatic statement of Christian Science beliefs undoubtedly lies in the realm of health and **healing**. Broadly speaking, Christian Scientists consider that disease is usually caused by fear and that healing occurs when Truth enters the sick individual. From this stems the fact that practising members of the Church will not take drugs and, in fact, tend to shy away from most orthodox forms of medicine, preferring to use their own spiritual resources. Interestingly, the movement's most definitive and authoritative sourcebook is still Mrs Eddy's *Science and Health with Key to the Scriptures*, which was originally published in 1875.

Christian Science grew very rapidly in America in its early years and, while it had little or no missionary impetus, it had crossed the Atlantic and taken root in England, Germany and Switzerland before the end of the nineteenth century. By 1936, there were some 238,000 recorded Christian Scientists in the United States, but it is believed the numbers have declined in most States and in Britain since then. It may, however, be fair to say that the influence of Christian Science has always outweighed its numerical strength.

Christianity

In spite of a wide variety of sects and denominations, Christians are at one in their common devotion to Jesus Christ as the founder of Christianity and in their reverence for the Bible. Through Jesus Christ – his birth, life, teaching, death, resurrection and ascension – Christians believe that God has been fully revealed to the world, and the Bible is the source of man's knowledge of God and God's message to mankind.

In the centuries after Christ's death, Christianity spread throughout the Roman Empire. It survived the fall of the Western Empire in AD 476 and converted the invading peoples. The Eastern Empire survived as the Christian state of Byzantium until its fall in AD 1453.

The two oldest divisions in the Christian Church are the

Western and Eastern Orthodox, which had come about by the eleventh century. The sixteenth-century Reformation and Counter-Reformation split the Western Church into Roman Catholic and Protestant. The Protestant Church then fragmented further.

Chuang Tzu
The 'hermit of Meng', Chuang Tzu, who lived in the fourth century BC, was one of the greatest of the early Taoists, and an advocate of getting back to Nature.

Clairaudience
The ability to hear **spirit** voices and other sounds from alien dimensions.

Clairsentience
An ability close to **intuition**, clairsentience permits an awareness of psychical manifestations which cannot be perceived in any other manner. A commonplace example of clairsentience is the 'sensing' of an 'atmosphere' in a haunted building.

Clairvoyance
Literally 'clear seeing', clairvoyance is the ability to obtain information at a distance by paranormal (**ESP**) means. It is distinguished from telepathy by the fact that no mind is involved other than that of the individual exercising the clairvoyance.

Cloud of Unknowing, The
One of the most famous of all Christian mystical works, *The Cloud of Unknowing* was written in the fourteenth century by an unknown author. The work teaches that a knowledge of God is impossible through the exercise of reason: only love will penetrate the 'cloud of unknowing' that stands between the individual and the divine.

Collective Unconscious
Following his experience of a vivid and impressive dream about an old house, the psychologist **Carl Jung** postulated the existence of a bed-rock level of the psyche common to all humanity. This 'Collective Unconscious', as he called it, was, he believed, a mental reflection of physical brain structure.

According to Jung's theories, the Collective Unconscious is the objective home of many mythic elements, including the **archetype**s.

Colour Therapy

Colour appears to have a real effect on us both psychologically and physiologically. At the most mundane level we are aware that different coloured decors can have an effect on our moods, but research also shows that blue light has a calming effect and lowers blood-pressure whereas red light has the opposite effect.

The Luscher Colour Test, devised in the 1940s by Dr Max Luscher, is a personality test which uses colour preferences to reveal psychological make-up.

Colour therapy is the use of colour or coloured light as an aid to **healing**.

Confucianism

It is difficult to be certain whether Confucianism should be classified as a religion, a philosophy or simply a social system. At various times, different scholars have emphasized one or other aspect of Confucianism in order to define it more exactly. To complicate things further, not all elements of Confucianism derive from the sage **Confucius**. What is really meant by Confucianism is a loose collection of ideas and beliefs given stature and coherence by being attributed to Kung Fu-tze.

In outline, the cosmology of Confucianism teaches that at the beginning of time there was a single cosmic cell containing *ch'i* which was made to pulsate by the creative force of **Tao**. The cell subsequently split to produce the **yin/yang** differentiation so pervasive in all branches of Chinese thought.

Where **Taoism** holds that the Tao represents the ultimate mystery, to Confucianism the nature of Tao is perfectly obvious – it is the rules of conduct, etiquette and ceremonial, the guide to all social action. Since Confucianism does not support any belief in the survival of a soul, its impact traditionally tended to be on the here rather than the hereafter. Within the family unit, the system taught respect for authority, veneration of the old by the young and loyalty as the supreme virtue. It was a short step to extrapolate these doctrines to the State which was seen – and sometimes even saw itself – as a macrocosm of the family.

Confucius

Anglicized version of the name of the most famous of all Chinese sages, Kung Fu-tze, who lived from 550 to 480 BC. His conservative philosophy, which strongly supported the State and family unit, became so influential that it is no exaggeration to say much of the traditional Chinese view of the universe, the gods and morality came to be based on his doctrines. After his death, a cult following developed with shrines to the sage in a great number of temples, notably those in the administrative centres.

Much Confucian wisdom is contained in the *Analects*, a collection of sayings attributed to the sage. Many are remarkably appropriate to our present culture, e.g. 'The superior man understands what is right. The inferior man understands what will sell.'

Consciousness

When Greek texts state that ancient heroes like Ulysses spoke with the gods or fought against the siren's song, they are not recording a myth, according to an intriguing theory. Rather, they are describing a literal experience, but one which has far more to do with the evolution of the human psyche than religious experience.

The theory suggests that consciousness, as we currently experience it, is a very recent development, a mutation occurring within historical times. Prior to its appearance, the common pattern of human mentation was very different from what it is today. The actions of individuals were often controlled not by conscious decisions, but by promptings of the unconscious which manifested not as a 'voice within' but rather as hallucinatory instructions apparently emanating from the outside world. Small wonder our ancestors believed so fervently in gods and **spirits**: they conversed with them daily.

But whatever the state of consciousness throughout history, one fact has remained constant: humanity's need to change it. The search for consciousness-altering drugs and techniques has been an obsession of the species for millennia. Almost certainly, the very earliest of these was alcohol, probably discovered as the result of natural fermentation. (The fruit of Africa's marula tree ferments so quickly and effectively when it drops that it forms a pulp sufficiently potent to get elephants drunk.)

Other narcotics quickly followed. Any hunter/gatherer

community must quickly sample hallucinogenic fungi, herbs, succulents and other plants which, when eaten, trigger profound changes in consciousness and open the door to new and exciting inner experience. It is even possible that such plants were originally responsible for the creation of the **shaman**, a ubiquitous figure in primitive cultures, although modern anthropologists have discovered the use of psychedelics is relatively rare in shamanism world-wide.

Shamanism itself is, however, vitally important in establishing an historical perspective on the phenomenon of consciousness. Its fundamental doctrine across a broad spectrum of cultures is that there is a second reality accessible through a change in conscious perception. While the change is sometimes brought about by drugs, it is far more often the result of rhythmic drumming or dancing. Experiences while in the altered state are usually interpreted within a religious context.

Aldous Huxley, who experimented with the mind-altering drug mescaline, made the intriguing suggestion that much more modern and sophisticated religious practice may have its consciousness-altering aspects. He pointed out that a variety of colour in daily life is very much a twentieth-century phenomenon and that the further back one goes in history, the more the average individual's experience of colour is confined to the dun browns and greens of Nature. Against this background, he argued that the use of candlelight, stained glass and richly-coloured vestments in church ceremonial would tend to stimulate a change of consciousness in the congregation. Other authorities have pointed to prolonged **chanting**, a commonplace monastic practice, as a consciousness changer due to its influence on blood carbon-dioxide levels.

Esoteric techniques such as **pathworking**s, the procedures of **yoga meditation** and the central visionary experience of **mysticism** all involve altered states of consciousness and have attracted the attention of many scientists, including **John Lilly**, who used a **flotation tank** in an attempt to understand his own mind better through sensory deprivation.

Sensory deprivation and its influence on consciousness was also of considerable interest to the United States Navy (because of its bearing on the work of submariners) which sponsored an extensive programme of isolation tank experiments.

Volunteer subjects, floating in darkness in lukewarm water and deprived of all sensory input, typically caught up on sleep for the first eight hours or so, talked to themselves for a period of time, then underwent a change of consciousness characterized by vivid hallucinations. (One reported watching a naked soldier dressed only in his steel helmet rowing a hip-bath across his field of vision.)

Interestingly, sensory deprivation of this type is mirrored in a far older technique, that of the so-called witch's cradle. The 'cradle' is in fact a sack in which the subject is suspended at night from a tree branch, having first been swung and spun to produce disorientation. Over a period of hours, sensory deprivation is supposed to create an altered state of consciousness inducive to **astral projection**.

Constant, Alphonse Louis
See **Eliphas Lévi**.

Cosmic Consciousness
A term coined by the psychologist R.M. Bucke in 1901 to describe the ecstatic experience of illumination which gives insight into the meaning of the universe.

Cosmology
Cosmology is a term used to denote a theory, usually esoteric or religious, of the nature of the universe and how it came into being. Given this definition, it is scarcely surprising to discover there are as many differing cosmologies as there are esoteric systems and religions.

The best-known Western cosmology is the orthodox Judaeo-Christian, which postulates a specific moment of creation by a pre-existent deity who stands outside his handiwork and a universe essentially maintained by hierarchies of celestial beings.

Qabalistic cosmology, by contrast, suggests a sort of condensation of the universe out of a pre-existent, eternal and essentially unknowable field of unmanifestation. This picture leaves God (or at least any God who can be known to humanity) immanent in creation and identified with the totality of the universe.

Oriental cosmologies tend to be cyclical in nature, like the Hindu concept of the 'Breath of Brahma' which sees the universe as emerging from the body of the divine, developing and changing through a series of ages or *yugas* then being reabsorbed in a final cataclysm, only to re-emerge to begin another cycle.

Several authors have remarked on the similarities between modern scientific theories of cosmic origins and structure and the ideas put forward within several ancient cosmologies. The Big Bang theory, for example, postulates a specific instant of 'creation' from which all else flowed, thus equating quite closely with the Genesis myth that 'God created the heaven and the earth and all that in them is.' The (largely discredited) Steady State theory, which considers that matter is continually emerging from nowhere to cause the expansion of the universe, obviously runs parallel to Qabalistic and Oriental notions of manifestation from an unknowable source.

Although similarities between ancient systems and modern thought are often eerily exact when one allows for the difference in terminology, psychologists tend to interpret this as indicative of the fact that the human mind works in essentially the same way whatever the time or culture.

A Course in Miracles

A self-study course designed to help change one's perceptions. The *Course* is a channelled text: i.e. it was heard as a kind of inner dictation. It came through Dr Helen Schucman, a respected research psychologist as Columbia University's School of Physicians and Surgeons in New York. She was helped in the transcription of the text over a period of seven years by Dr William N. Thetford, the head of the psychology department in which she worked.

The *Course* is summed up in the Introduction:

Nothing real can be threatened. Nothing unreal exists.

The distinction between truth and illusion is a major one. The *Course* teaches how to distinguish between the voice of the ego (fear) and the voice of inner wisdom (love). Although Christian in its language, the *Course* deals with universal spiritual themes and not with religious doctrines.

First published in 1975, many hundreds of thousands of people from all kinds of spiritual backgrounds have been profoundly affected by *A Course in Miracles*. Recently it has been popularized by Marianne Williamson in her best-selling book *A Return to Love*.

Creation Spirituality

A movement gathering momentum within **Christianity**. Matthew Fox, its controversial advocate, is a theologian, educator, founding director of the Institute in Culture and Creation Spirituality in Oakland, California, and was also a Dominican priest until excommunicated by the Vatican for his views.

Fundamental to Creation Spirituality is the idea of awe, or wonder, as a mystical response to creation and first step towards transformation. Awe results in appreciating the blessings of God's creation and, in experiencing our world in a deeper way, we are awakened to a new relationship to it. A new vision is possible, one through which we learn to honour the earth and the people who inhabit it as the gift of a good and just creator.

Creation spirituality is an ancient tradition – the basic spiritual heritage of native peoples everywhere. It is also the oldest tradition in the Bible. It was important for the prophets of the Old Testament, as well as for Jesus. It was at the centre of the teachings of the Greek fathers, of the Church and also for the medieval mystics like **Hildegard of Bingen**, **Meister Eckhart** and St Francis of Assissi.

Fox claims that as human beings we have lost touch with the transformative power of **mysticism**, which has led to our current impoverishment of the soul, our alienation and ecological suffering. Creation spirituality advocates the rebirth of a mysticism which we can all relate to, which reveres the feminine principle, which values social justice and environmentalism and celebrates sexuality, passion, creativity and the divine child within.

Matthew Fox's books include *Original Blessing, The Coming of the Cosmic Christ, A Spirit Named Compassion, Creation Spirituality* and *Sheer Joy*.

Creative Imagination

A technique developed by the psychologist **Carl Jung** which enabled certain of his patients to use their visual imagination in order to enter the archetypal realms of the **Collective Unconscious**. Jung's technique of guided reverie has distinct similarities to Qabalistic **pathworking**, an ancient form of occult practice, and to fantasy role play – a comparatively recent form of indoor game.

Crop Circles

A phenomenon of recent years, mostly in south-east England but also in other parts of the world, whereby large circles and other patterns appear in the middle of grain fields when the crop is several feet high. There are many theories as to their origin, ranging from natural forces like irregular weather patterns or the effects of irrigation to **UFOs** and other intelligent life forces. While some crop circles have been exposed as hoaxes, many others have not been explained.

Crowley, Aleister

'Crowley is more than a new-born Dionysus, he is more than a **Blake**, a Rabelais or a Heiné; for he stands before us as some priest of Apollo,' wrote J.F.C. Fuller about Aleister Crowley, 'hovering twixt the misty blue of the heavens and the more serious purple of the vast waters of the deep. It has taken 100,000,000 years to produce Aleister Crowley. The world has indeed laboured and it has at last brought forth a man.'

Some of Captain Fuller's hyperbole may be explained by the fact that he was writing the prize-winning (and only) entry in a competition set by Crowley for the best essay on his work. But there is no doubt Crowley impressed people who had no axe to grind. **Israel Regardie** described him as a 'great mystic, sincere, dedicated and hard-working'. Nina Hamnet found him 'extremely intelligent'. G.I. Gurdjieff admitted he had magnetism.

But in 1922, the *Sunday Express* stated baldly, 'This man Crowley is one of the most sinister figures of modern times. He is a drug fiend, an author of vile books, the spreader of obscene practices.' Sadly, it was almost all true and while history may have judged Crowley more kindly than the Press of his day (which named him 'The Wickedest Man in the World') it is difficult to see how pre-war society could have reacted other than it did to a man who claimed to be the Anti-Christ and encouraged several of his female followers to have sexual intercourse with goats.

The boy who was to become the Great Beast 666 (in his own and his mother's estimation) was born the son of a puritanical brewer who was to leave him a great deal of money in his Will. As a schoolboy, he was sexually precocious, masochistic and rebellious, traits which remained with him for the rest of his life. During his three years at Cambridge, he met George Cecil Jones, a chemist with an interest in the occult. Jones introduced him to the **Golden Dawn**.

Crowley had an enormous talent for **magic** and swarmed up the lower grades of the organization. He became friendly with the Order's head, **S. L. MacGregor Mathers**, and sided with him in a political battle with **W. B. Yeats** for control of the Order. (The disagreement was largely caused by Crowley himself.) The real loser in the battle was the Golden Dawn itself, which never really recovered from the schism.

It did not take Crowley long to make an enemy of Mathers as well as Yeats. But his departure from the Golden Dawn was less serious to his magical development than it might have been. In 1904, while in Cairo, Crowley had a visionary experience in which Aiwaz, his Holy Guardian Angel, dictated to him a work called *The Book of the Law*, which announced a new age, the 'Aeon of Horus' with Crowley himself as its prophet.

As if this was not enough for one man in one lifetime, Crowley, who believed himself to be a **reincarnation** of both the French magus **Eliphas Lévi** and the Irish scoundrel **Edward Kelley**, set up his own occult organization, the *Astrum Argentium*, or Order of the Silver Star. Many of its rites were drawn from Golden Dawn material – something which resulted in a copyright lawsuit mounted by Mathers.

Mathers was not the only adept to be concerned about Crowley revealing esoteric secrets. Crowley received a visit from two representatives of the German *Ordo Templo Orientis* (the Order of Eastern Templars) who accused him of publishing – in an interesting little work called *Book 4* – the central secret of their magical workings.

Crowley persuaded them he knew nothing of the OTO and any secrets in *Book 4* he had discovered for himself. (Which, since the central secret of the OTO was sex magic, may well have been true.) The OTO representatives decided they were better off with Crowley safely inside their organization than experimenting on his own behalf and were sufficiently impressed to make him head of the British Section of their Order. Before long, Crowley had swallowed the entire organization and used it, like the Silver Star, to propagate his *Word of the Aeon*, *Thelema* and *The Book of the Law*.

In anticipation of the hippie movement of the sixties, Crowley established a commune (complete with temple) in Cefalu in Sicily. His old friend and former lover Nina Hamnet wrote that it was supposed to be a centre for Black Magic. Crowley sued her for libel and lost. Mussolini threw him out of Sicily.

With the outbreak of the Second World War, there were very few people prepared to listen to Crowley – now a heroin addict preaching the arrival of the Aeon of Horus. He died in Hastings in 1947 and the reading of his *Hymn to Pan* at his cremation so incensed Brighton Corporation that they issued a statement promising, 'We shall take all the necessary steps to prevent such an incident occurring again.'

But if Crowley was dead, he certainly was not finished. Rather more than a decade after his death, John Symonds published a witty, urbane, irreverent and sympathetic biography of the magician entitled *The Great Beast*. It did more than sell well: it created a Crowley revival. Today, the OTO flourishes and virtually all of Crowley's books – which vary from the fascinating to the near unreadable – have found commercial publishers where once he was forced to finance their distribution himself.

There is no doubt Crowley was a skilled and learned **Qabalist**. Nor is there very much doubt that he was a rather nasty little boy who never really grew up. His philosophy, embodied in the two commandments 'Love is the Law; Love under Will' and 'Do what thou wilt shall be the whole of the Law', was not, he insisted, to be interpreted as a licence for self-centred hedonism. Unfortunately, the example of his life belied the warning.

Crystals

Aldous Huxley, in one of his essays, explored the mystery of why precious stones are precious and why crystalline structures have exercised such a fascination for humanity since prehistoric times. Huxley dismissed the common argument that certain stones are valuable simply because they are rare. He pointed out that there are much rarer substances which have no appeal at all. But having ingested the psychedelic drug mescaline and experienced vivid visions, he had his own theory. Precious stones are precious because they remind us of the glittering vistas of the inner worlds, pregnant with light and colour. Crystals – even commonplace crystals like ice or snowflakes – have essentially the same effect. To look across a landscape suddenly transformed by snow is literally to witness an act of **magic**.

In the depths of prehistory, our European ancestors bequeathed us a mystery when they constructed megalithic circles

85

and menhir avenues at enormous cost in time and effort (*see* **Megaliths**). We still do not know for certain why they did so, but we do know that certain of these ancient constructions generate a measurable field activity and some produce infrasound and ultrasound when struck by the rising sun. The reason they do so is that the stones used in their construction have a high content of mica and/or quartz crystal.

It is a curious fact that shamanic cultures as far apart as the Tlingit Eskimos and the Amazon Conibo all consider quartz crystals to have a special power. Shamanic theory holds that reality has an inner and outer aspect and **shaman**s are people trained to explore the inner worlds. Such explorations show that the thing we perceive as a physical tree may have an inner, spiritual aspect in the form of a human figure, an oddly-shaped stone or a pillar of mist. But quartz crystals are unique. Their inner and outer aspects are identical, the only known structures on our planet to exhibit this characteristic. This makes them ideal for the working of magic.

The notion of crystals as magic is not confined to primitive societies. When the Elizabethan magicians **John Dee** and **Edward Kelley** attempted to communicate with **angels**, they did so with the aid of a crystal shewstone. Such a device was by no means unusual. **Psychics** and fortune-tellers throughout the ages have used crystal balls in their attempts to divine the future. Today, as often as not, the instrument is made from moulded glass, but it is accepted that this is a poor imitation of the real thing. The real thing is a sphere of polished crystal.

Psychologists interested in such things have postulated that crystal balls work by providing a glittering eye fixation which encourages the user to pass into trance. This may be so, but there are occultists who are convinced that crystals have a much more direct physical influence on those who come into contact with them, generating effects which include **healing**.

If they are correct, Russian scientists may have found the reason why. During the 1960s, an article in *Khimiya i Zhizn*, the journal of the Soviet Academy of Sciences, explored the possibility that the Earth itself is a giant crystal.

According to this theory, a crystalline lattice, providing a matrix for cosmic energy, may have formed part of the original structure of our emerging planet. More exciting still, this structure can still be seen in twelve pentagonal slabs covering the surface of the globe.

The Soviets overlaid the resultant dodecahedron with 20 equilateral triangles and have claimed the entire geometric structure has influenced such diverse phenomena as magnetic anomalies, earth faults, volcanoes, mineral and oil deposits, bird migrations, cyclone centres, solar radiation and even the siting of ancient civilizations.

Cupping

A specialized form of therapy from China combining elements of **acupuncture** and **moxibustion**, largely used to treat back pain and muscular disorders.

Unlike acupuncture and **acupressure**, cupping can only be used on areas of the body – notably the back – which present a relatively flat surface. Traditionally, the cups are of wood, notably bamboo, although glass is sometimes used. They are heated, usually by inserting a burning taper or a piece of moxa inside, until a partial vacuum is created. The taper is then removed and the cup immediately placed on the relevant body part.

The partial vacuum creates suction, causing the cup to adhere. It is left in place for a few minutes, then gently prised off. Since the suction produced is quite strong, blood is drawn into the surface vessels, leaving a temporary reddish-pink mark and stimulating any acupuncture point in the area.

D

Da Avabhasa

Da Avabhasa was born in 1939 as Franklin Jones in Jamaica, New York. The story of his early life is told in his autobiography, *The Knee of Listening*. He became a devotee of **Muktananda** and in 1970 entered *samadhi* and changed his name to Bubba Free John. By 1979 he had dropped Bubba in favour of 'Da' (Giver of Life). In 1986 he reportedly died and claimed to have resurrected himself for the sake of humanity. He adopted new titles, including Da Love-Ananda. He lives almost as a recluse in Fiji. The Free Daist Communion, the present name of his religious organization, dedicates itself to spreading his teachings.

Da Free John

See **Da Avabhasa**.

Dalai Lama

In the Year of the Wood Hog, the Regent of Tibet travelled to the sacred lake of Lhamoi Latso, about 90 miles south-east of Lhasa and there saw a vision which, nearly two years later in 1936, guided a party of high lamas and officials to the region of Dokham, the village of Taktser and a house with turquoise tiles.

In the house was a two-year-old boy who, incredibly, identified both the disguised head of the party, the Lama Kewtsang Rinpoché of Sera monastery. and his servant, Amdo Kasang, who had pretended to be leader. The boy then went on to identify a series of items (such as a walking stick and a drum) which had belonged to Thupten Gyatso, the recently deceased God-king of Tibet.

Faced with this performance, the party concluded the boy was Thupten Gyatso's reincarnation. He was taken from his home and family to become the fourteenth Dalai Lama of Tibet.

Prior to the Chinese invasion in 1950, Tibet was the only

reincarnatory monarchy on Earth. It had for several centuries been ruled by a succession of Dalai Lamas, each believed to be the reincarnation of the last, with the first of the line believed to be the incarnation of Chenresig, the patron god of Tibet.

The current, fourteenth Dalai Lama fled Tibet in 1959, having failed to reach a lasting accommodation with the Chinese invaders, and set up a government in exile in India. Although the Chinese have made overtures on several occasions since then for his return, it is doubtful if he would do so for anything less than a Chinese withdrawal. Curiously enough, the old Tibetan state **oracle** predicted on several occasions that the fourteenth incarnation would be the last of Tibet's Dalai Lamas.

In 1989 the Dalai Lama was awarded the Nobel Prize for his efforts to achieve world peace.

Dark Night of the Soul
A stage in the road to spiritual development often noted in mystical literature. Typically, the Dark Night of the Soul is a state of mind characterized by depression, disbelief, uncertainty and a feeling of personal and universal worthlessness. Also typically, the experience tends to arise immediately in advance of a breakthrough to fresh understanding.

Darshan
The term is drawn from the Sanskrit and means literally 'vision' or 'sight'. But there is no connection with visionary experience. Rather, in Hindu belief, *darshan* is a type of energy or essence, carrying strong overtones of a spiritual blessing, which a saint may convey to a follower via his/her gaze. It also means being in the presence of the **guru**.

Dass, Baba Ram
An American academic, Richard Alpert, who was involved with Timothy Leary in the 1960s in experimentation with LSD. In India he met Neem Karoli Baba and underwent a conversion, changing his name to Baba Ram Dass.

Ram Dass has published a number of books including *Be Here Now,* which tells the story of his personal transformation.

David-Neel, Alexandra
Alexandra David-Neel was 101 when she died in 1969, having enjoyed a life as an acclaimed operatic soprano, political

anarchist, religious reformer and, above all, initiate of the esoteric mysteries of Tibet.

Madame David-Neel travelled freely throughout Tibet for 14 years and was distinguished as the only European woman ever to be made a lama. She had enormous sensitivity towards Tibet's secret doctrines and became a **yoga** adept in the discipline of **tumo**, the essentially Tibetan yoga of body heat.

In the course of her travels and later, she produced more than 40 books on **Buddhism** and introduced many Westerners to Tibetan occult concepts for the first time. Her works, which often deal openly with the technical details of the techniques involved, are still amongst the most reliable available, almost certainly because she was seldom satisfied simply to study occult methods, but insisted on practising them for herself.

To this end, she underwent the horrifying *chod* initiation, a visionary experience in which the adept offers her body to be eaten by demons and experiences total physical disintegration in the process. She also, on one occasion, successfully engaged in an act of **tulpa creation**, generating an imaginary figure so strongly that it was eventually seen by others in her camp.

Deathbed Visions

Deathbed visions have been recorded since ancient times. Most are of glowing beings of light, **apparitions** of the dead known to the dying or great religious or mythical figures such as Jesus, the Virgin Mary or other deities. They are significant because they provide some sort of evidence in support of survival of **consciousness** after death.

See also **Near Death Experience (NDE); Thanatology**.

Dee, John

Court astrologer to Queen Elizabeth I and Admiralty spy (with the code name 007), John Dee was one of the most learned, and in many ways remarkable, occultists of his time. Although he practised **astrology** with considerable skill, engaged in alchemical research (*see* **Alchemy**) and travelled widely throughout Europe, he remains best known for his relationship with the clairvoyant scoundrel **Edward Kelley**.

Dee was greatly interested in communicating with **spirits** and employed Kelley as a **psychic** or **medium** for the sum of £50 a year. The salary was not always paid, but they stayed together all the same. Their experiments in **crystal**-gazing, using a shewstone now in the care of the British Museum, began in 1582 and continued, despite various unconnected adventures, until 1587.

By June 1583, the experiments had taken a particularly weird turn. The two men believed themselves to be in contact with a number of entities including a rather sweet elfin girl named Madimi and an impatient **angel** called Ave. It was this latter entity who dictated, letter by letter and backwards, the text of an entirely new system of **magic** in a language called **Enochian**.

While Kelley seems to have had some genuine psychical ability, he was undoubtedly a confidence trickster as well. On one occasion he persuaded Dee that the spirits had instructed them to 'hold their wives in common', an arrangement that broke down within weeks when the women, less gullible than the doctor, could stand it no longer.

Dervish Dancing

The whirling dances of the Mevlevi dervishes – sometimes accompanied by howling – convinced many Victorian travellers that these Sufi mystics were little better than fanatical lunatics. For the dervishes themselves, however, the dances were (and are) a form of **yoga**, part of a rigorous training regime designed to produce the perfected man or woman, and often leading in the short term to trance experience.

Oddly enough, at least one secret monkish Order in Tibet recommended whirling as an aid to longevity, since the action was believed to stimulate the major **chakras**.

Dervish Order

Although dancing is firmly associated with the dervishes in the Western mind, only Mevlevi dervishes dance, just as howling – another widespread association – is largely typical of the Rufais.

Strictly speaking, the term 'Dervish Order' is inaccurate, since the dervish community comprises a series of Orders, monastic and lay, each independent and free to go its own way. The word 'dervish' is usually defined as an **Islam**ic holy man, probably (but not necessarily) associated with one of the Dervish Orders, who follows the Sufi way. Historically, the Sufis have generally appeared within Islam, but since the doctrine is held to be the inner reality of all religions, Christian Sufis have occasionally arisen.

All dervishes are believed to be linked by a mysterious force called *baraka*. Dervish schools are always temporary, a body of people working towards a common purpose with the school disbanded once the purpose is achieved.

Despite the image which persists in the West to this day, the central Asian picture of a dervish is more typically that of a cultured scientist with a grounding in literature and philosophy; and a scientist who would, moreover, combine the qualities of a saint, magician, healer and miracle-worker.

Desire Body
See **Astral Body**.

Devas

This term carries distinct meanings depending on whether it is used in the context of **Theosophy** or **Zoroastrianism**. In the latter, it refers to malevolent **spirits** ruled by the God of Darkness. In the former, by contrast, it denotes a hierarchy of spirits which help rule the universe. In the original Sanskrit, the word derives from 'celestial beings'.

Today the term is commonly used to describe Nature spirits, particularly those which encourage plant growth. (*See* **Findhorn**.)

Dhammapada

A lengthy work of verse which has become the central canon of Buddhist thought, since it contains many doctrines of the **Buddha**, including that of the Noble Eightfold Path. The *Dhammapada* is believed to date back to the first Buddhist Council in 477 BC.

Dharma

Dharma is Sanskrit, from the Aryan root *dhar*, to uphold, sustain or support. It is used in both **Hinduism** and **Buddhism**, its meaning varying according to context. Broadly speaking, it means 'law, truth or doctrine that defines the cosmos'. It also has connotations of duty, truth, righteousness and virtue.

Dianetics
See **Scientology**.

Dionysius the Areopagite

The only solid historical reference to Dionysius the Areopagite is a passing mention in the Acts of the Apostles. A body of early mystical writings, the real author of which is still unknown, was falsely attributed to him.

The writings themselves are in Greek and comprise the *Celestial Hierarchy, Mystical Theology, Ecclesiastical Hierarchy* and *Divine Names* along with several letters. They represent a synthesis between **Christianity** and **Neoplatonism** and underpin much of the Christian **mysticism** since the sixth century. They had a particular influence on the fourteenth-century mystical movements and many of their ideas are reflected in the famous *Cloud of Unknowing*.

Dissipative Structures

A term coined by the Nobel Prize-winning chemist, Ilya Prigogine. The idea that a new and higher form of order may manifest spontaneously in a highly perturbed state has obvious metaphorical attractions for those who believe we are moving towards a **New Age**.

Divination

Divination helps us to use our intuition so that we can harmonize our actions and face what may befall us, or indeed deal with what has already happened. At one level fortune-telling, at its highest level, divination is about what is best for psychological and spiritual growth. Divination tools, therefore, are rather like the weather forecast for the sailor.

Almost every method of divination is a philosophy about the world presented in a series of symbols. The *I Ching*, the **Tarot**, **oracle**s, **runes** and **astrology** are all systems of divination with a long history. There have also been many new systems developed in recent years using such tools as **crystals** (*The Crystal Oracle*), colour (*Know Yourself through Colour*), gypsy teachings (*Russian Gypsy Fortune-Telling Cards*), Greek mythology (*Olympus: Self-Discovery and the Greek Archetypes*) and Native American teachings (*The Sacred Path Cards*).

Dixon, Jeane

American society **psychic**, best known for her successful prediction of President Kennedy's assassination. Even more remarkable, given recent events in Eastern Europe, was a prediction she gave in 1953 when interviewed on NBC. Whilst talking about Russia, she said that in her crystal ball she had seen a dove strike its claws into the scalp of a completely bald man, but without drawing blood. The dove then looked eastwards. Jeane Dixon interpreted this as meaning that some day Russia would bring about peace by her own decision.

Djinn

In **Islam**ic mythology, **spirit**s, both good and evil, whose bodies are made of smokeless fire. The singular is *djinni*, hence 'genie'.

Dōgen

A thirteenth-century Japanese **Zen** master of the Sōtō-Zen school of Japanese **Buddhism**, Dōgen advocated a religion of practical simplicity, absolute faith and individual spiritual awakening. Although an aristocrat by birth, Dōgen avoided the imperial court, practising **meditation** deep in the remote countryside.

Dogon

The Dogon are a primitive farming people – many still living in caves – who inhabit the Hombori Mountains of southern Mali. They embody a most fascinating mystery, for preserved at the secret heart of their religion is accurate technical information about the star system Sirius impossible to gather without advanced astronomical equipment and only fully confirmed by professional astronomers in 1970.

Furthermore, the Dogon claim the information was originally given to them by extra-terrestrial visitors from the Sirius system itself.

The star called by the Dogon *Pō Tolo* is named *Sirius B* in modern astronomical charts. It is not visible to the naked eye and no postulation of its existence was made by Western astronomers until 1844 when irregularities were noted in the movements of the highly visible Dog Star, Sirius (A), in the Canis Major constellation. Calculations suggested these movements must be caused by the gravitational influence of a second, then undiscovered, stellar body.

In 1862, observers using high-powered telescopes finally detected the faint trace of the companion star. Today, Sirius B – as the companion was named – is known to be a white dwarf, the smallest and heaviest of all visible stars.

In the 1930s, visiting French anthropologists were, for the first time, initiated into the inner mysteries of the Dogon religion. There they discovered certain doctrines which, considering their source, were nothing short of astonishing.

The primitive Dogon knew, for example, that planets orbited our sun – they had working calendars for the sun, moon, Venus and the star Sirius. They knew that Saturn had rings and Jupiter was orbited by four major moons. But this astronomical knowledge paled beside the information they had about Sirius B. They were able to tell the anthropologists it was the smallest type of star, that it was white in colour and extremely heavy, since its natural constituents had been replaced by much denser metals (the precise process that takes place when a star collapses into a white dwarf). They were further able to say, quite correctly, that the orbit of Sirius B was an ellipse around Sirius A, that the star rotated on its own axis and that its orbital period was 50 years.

Where did all this fascinating information come from? It was brought from Sirius itself, say the Dogon, by amphibious aliens dispatched from their home to benefit humanity. They landed in a spinning vehicle which made a great noise. The Nommos, as they were called by the Dogon, appeared to be the result of a fish-like evolutionary line.

Perhaps it is no coincidence that there are ancient Babylonian accounts of the landing of amphibious aliens, called Oannes, in an egg-shaped vessel which dropped into the Red Sea. The beings, which 'had the shape of a fish blended with that of a man', taught humanity astronomy, writing, the rudiments of engineering and a legal system.

Don Juan
See **Castaneda, Carlos**.

Dowsing
A natural ability to find underground streams, minerals and even lost objects using no more than a forked stick, parallel rods or a **pendulum**. Dowsing is one of the most widely accepted of the esoteric arts (a number of local councils and water authorities employ their own dowsers to locate underground pipes or water sources) but one which, even today, lacks any satisfying theory, scientific or occult, as to how it actually works.

Doyle, Sir Arthur Conan

Although the creator of the world's most rational fictional detective, Sherlock Holmes, Sir Arthur Conan Doyle was himself fascinated by the irrational and mysterious. He was a keen student of the **psychic** and **paranormal** for almost half a century and in the last 12 years of his life was an active exponent of **Spiritualism**.

Doyle was born in Edinburgh in 1859 and brought up as a Roman Catholic, but became an agnostic while training to be a doctor. He practised medicine from 1882 to 1890, when the growing popularity of his Sherlock Holmes stories enabled him to abandon medicine for full-time writing and the pursuit of psychic interests. His attraction to Spiritualism strengthened when, in 1919, he attended a séance and heard the voice of his dead son Kingsley. He also saw his mother and nephew, revenants witnessed by two other observers.

The experience turned him into an active advocate of Spiritualism and he travelled world-wide lecturing on the subject with slides showing his own **spirit** photographs. Already a member of the **Society for Psychical Research**, he became president of the London Spiritualist Alliance, the British College of Psychic Science and the Spiritualist Community. He lobbied tirelessly for changes in the law regarding **medium**s right up to his own death in 1930.

Dreaming

Although greatly devalued with the growth of nineteenth-century rationalism, dreams have long held a fascination for humanity as carriers of messages from the gods. More recently, **Carl Gustav Jung** expressed a similar belief, except that his 'gods' had become psychic **archetype**s. **Freud** too stressed the value of dreams in investigating the content of the subconscious. More distant from the philosophical and scientific mainstream, several experts have suggested that dreams might be the key to such arts as **astral projection** and **etheric projection**.

Dreams of sexual love should always move through orgasm and the dreamer should then demand from the dream lover the poem, the song, the dance, the useful knowledge which will express the beauty of the spiritual lover to the group. If this is done, no dream man or woman can take the love which belongs to human beings.

The quotation is from the work of scientist Kilton Stewart, but it does not represent his own insights. Rather it forms part of a whole fascinating psychological system, based exclusively on dream analysis, developed by the Senoi people of the Malayan rain forest whom he visited in 1935.

Mornings with the Senoi are devoted to the analysis of dreams, first within the family unit where older members listen to and interpret the dreams of the young, then in a tribal council where adult dreams are recounted and analysed.

A typical analysis might be that of a falling dream, as common among the Senoi as it is in our own culture. The Senoi would first reassure the dreamer that such a dream was both wonderful and important, then ask where the fall led to. If it led nowhere (because the frightened sleeper had woken up, for example) they would explain this was a mistake. Everything done in a dream has a purpose, although this may be beyond one's understanding while asleep. Thus it was important to relax and enjoy the experience.

Falling, according to the Senoi, is the quickest way to make contact with the powers of the **spirit** world which are laid open to the individual in dreams. Meeting with the spirits may be a terrifying experience, but it is important to go on. Even when you believe you are dying in a dream, this only means you are receiving the powers of the dream world and these are actually your own spiritual power which has been turned against you and now wishes to be reintegrated.

Over a period of time, analyses of this sort gradually change the fear originally experienced in the dream into a joy for living.

Within their dream system, the Senoi believe a dreamer should always advance and attack in the face of dream danger, calling on friends for aid if necessary. Should the enemy appear to *be* a friend, the dreamer may be assured this is not actually the case: the hostile character is merely wearing the friend's face like a mask. If the dreamer successfully overcomes or kills the hostile element, the spirit of this dream character will henceforth become a servant or ally.

'Dream characters are bad only as long as one is afraid and retreating from them and will continue to seem bad and fearful as long as one refuses to come to grips with them,' wrote Stewart.

Since Stewart's visit to Malaya, scientists have discovered it is possible to know precisely when a sleeper is dreaming by monitoring rapid eye movements (REM). This has shown a) that everyone dreams (although not everyone remembers in the morning) and b) that the time spent dreaming varies considerably with age. Premature babies will typically spend as much as 80 per cent of their sleep time dreaming, but this drops to only 13 per cent among the senile.

There are clear indications that animals dream and substantial evidence that prey animals dream less than hunters, possibly because their sleep state is less secure. Lions, like most cats, have extraordinarily long dreams.

If, for any reason, an individual is deprived of his/her normal 'ration' of dreams, (s)he will typically indulge in an orgy of dreaming once (s)he is able to do so. Clearly, dreams are important, although there is considerable disagreement about exactly why.

Certainly dreams can be useful. Robert Louis Stevenson found the inspiration for his classic *Dr Jekyll and Mr Hyde* in a dream. So did Mary Shelley when she was writing *Frankenstein*. The poet Coleridge composed his masterpiece *Kubla Khan* in a dream and actually lost a substantial part of it through an interruption while he was writing it down the following morning.

Jim Fitzpatrick, the well-known Irish fantasy artist, had a series of dreams some years ago during which he watched spellbound as a whole epic saga of ancient Ireland passed before his sleeping eyes. Each night, the epic would carry on from the exact point where it left off the night before. The story continued, without a break, for months. Since that dream series, Fitzpatrick has devoted most of his working life to capturing the saga on canvas. Even now, years later, he remembers the dreams vividly enough to paint scenes from them.

Somehow the artistic use of dreams seems normal enough. But several hard-headed scientists have made important discoveries through dreams. The nineteenth-century chemist Friedrich von Kekulé, for example, spent many years trying to discover the molecular structure of the chemical benzene without success. Then, in 1865, he had a curious dream in which he could see the structures of various molecules, snake-like chains of atoms, one of which was swallowing its own tail. Kekulé awoke with the dream clear in his mind. He knew at once what it meant: the structure of benzene was a closed carbon ring.

Niels Bohr, the great physicist, created his famous model of the atom while dreaming as a student, leaving humanity with the uneasy realization that the whole of modern atomic physics and its various applications, including the atomic bomb, are all based on nothing more substantial than a dream.

But then several commonplace feats of engineering have the same source. Elias Howe, for example, was searching for that most elusive of all inventions, a sewing machine, when he had a dream. In it he was captured by cannibals who dragged him off to their king who told him he had 24 hours to invent a sewing machine, otherwise he was for the pot. But even with this incentive, Howe still could not figure out how to make one work.

The deadline came and went and Howe found himself (literally) in hot water. With nothing better to do, he watched the savages dancing round him waving their spears threateningly. Then he suddenly noticed each spear had an eye-shaped hole near its tip. He awoke at once and ran to his workshop where he built the first prototype sewing machine with the eye of its needle near the point.

As well as being practical, virtually every human culture has believed some dreams to be precognitive, a theory borne out by the work of **J.W. Dunne**. Biblical cultures accepted that God often sent messages in dreams, a belief shared by Jung, who remarked that the only reason these messages are not received in modern times is that humanity appears to have lost the capacity to listen. Jung's contemporary and mentor, Freud, theorized that dreams were the symbolic presentation of sexual impulses, a view still widely held.

But of all the various interpretations, the Senoi system remains by far the most intriguing, if only because the tribe has not experienced a single violent crime or intercommunal conflict for 300 years . . . and believes this happy state to rest on the psychological health created by their dream analyses.

Dream Journal

Everybody dreams and everybody dreams every night, but most people find it very difficult to remember what they have dreamed. The very few dreams that are remembered are nearly always those which occur early in the morning, just before waking up. This has produced speculation on how much more important material has been lost because so many dreams are simply forgotten. And that, in turn, has led many to record their dreams in a dream journal.

The technique of dream recording is at once simple and difficult. You leave a notepad and pencil within reach of your bed and promise yourself that you will write down every detail you remember of your dreams the *minute you wake up*. It is that promise that leads to the difficulty. Recording dreams is the last thing the average individual wants to do immediately on waking. But if dreams are not written down at once, they fade away like mist under a morning sun.

Dreamtime

As the mythic age of heroes by which the Australian aborigine explains the origins of his race, the Dreamtime is also that 'land' to which the **spirits** of the aborigine dead must travel and the dimension from which aborigine 'clever-men' (**shaman**s) draw their power.

Contemporary aborigine stories, traditional myths and art inspired by experience of the Dreamtime are all numbered among the most evocative cultural expressions of Australia today.

Druids

Victorian notions which linked Druids with the building of Stonehenge and other megalithic circles are today perpetuated by solstice ceremonies mounted by the modern Druid Orders. But the great stones far predated even the oldest of the historical Druids, who can only have used them – if they used them at all – as ceremonial sites.

Even this usage is questionable. The name 'Druid' probably derives from the Gaulish and Greek words for 'oak', and Pliny, one of many classical authors to mention the pre-Roman Celtic priesthood, describes a ceremony in an oak grove in which mistletoe was cut from an oak tree with a golden sickle on the sixth days of the moon.

The mistletoe, a parasite on the oak, is usually identified with Sir James Frazer's mysterious 'golden bough' which was believed to 'blaze out' into a supernatural golden glory. Since mistletoe itself is an evergreen with no hint of a golden tinge, this identification has led to speculation about an unknown species of mistletoe, possibly psychedelic, prized by the ancients on account of the visionary experience it would bring.

Certainly the ancient Druids themselves were widely known as visionaries and prophets, in communion with the gods. They were also believed to teach a doctrine of **reincarnation**, but this may be based on a misinterpretation of their actual doctrine. This insisted on the immortality of the soul which, after death, travelled to an otherworld where it entered a fresh body and proceeded to live again much as it had done on earth. The doctrine was novel in the classical world; which evoked the Pythagorean notion of the transmigration of souls to explain it. In fact, on closer examination, it bears more resemblance to the beliefs of **shaman**ism – further underlining the possibility that some form of mind-influencing drugs may have been used in Druid ceremonies.

Dunne, John William

John William Dunne was an aeronautics engineer who since childhood had harboured the conviction that he was destined to bring an important message to humanity. Throughout his life, certain incidents had conspired to confirm this. On one occasion, for example, a **medium** told him during a séance that he himself was to become the greatest medium the world had ever seen. It did not quite happen that way, but he certainly had a series of strange dreams and semi-mystical experiences.

It was, in fact, his dreams that were to make Dunne's name a household word among intellectuals in the 1920s and 30s and are today enjoying a resurgence of interest. In 1899, aged 24, Dunne had a dream in which his watch had stopped at half past four. He awoke, checked his watch and discovered it really had stopped . . . at half past four. Furthermore, he discovered he had awakened almost instantly when it happened.

This odd, but essentially unimportant, incident was the start of a series of precognitive dreams. Typical of these was one in which he dreamed of a disastrous volcanic eruption in the Far East and read about it in the newspaper a few days later. Details of the experience point to the fact that Dunne's dream forecast his reading of the newspaper account rather than the actual disaster.

He became intrigued by the fact that the human mind appeared capable of 'dreaming true' and began to collect similar dreams from friends and acquaintances. Gradually a pattern began to emerge. Dunne concluded, with **Freud**, that dreams were composed of distorted fragments of personal experience, often presented in a symbolic form. As an illustration of this, he quoted the dream of a man attacked by people throwing streams of lighted cigarettes towards his face. The corresponding reality was the cutting of a plank with a circular saw. The saw struck a nail in the plank and sent a stream of sparks towards the man's face.

But where Dunne differed from Freud was his theory that the incidents presented in symbolic form could just as easily be drawn from an individual's future as his past. For this reason, precognitive dreams tended to be trivial; they would typically relate to mundane matters like listening to the radio, meeting a friend in the street or chopping wood.

The important thing was not the content of precognitive dreams, but the fact that they occurred. Some quarter century after his own precognitive dreams began, Dunne published a book called *An Experiment with Time* in which he described them and urged his readers to keep their own **dream journal**. The book was an instant success and Dunne's ideas became an international talking-point.

Among his ideas was the notion of a serial universe, expounded in another work called *Nothing Dies* which was published in 1940. Broadly, Dunne argued that the fact of **precognition** in whatever small degree called for a 'time' which measured time as we normally experience it. This second 'time' was in turn measured by another 'time' and so on, in an infinite regress. But if time was an infinite regress and Einstein had shown the universe to be an indissoluble space/time continuum, then logically space must be an infinite regress as well, leaving us with an essentially serial universe.

Like his original insights into precognition, Dunne's theory of a serial universe attracted serious attention, but has not endured since it was based on the incorrect assumption that time flows like a river whereas, whatever our common sense experience, all we can validly say is that time represents a process, the exact nature of which is still unknown. His work with dreams remains extremely important, however.

E

Earth Magic
See **Feng Shui; Geomancy**.

Eckankar
A patented form of **astral projection** taught by the American **guru** Paul Twitchell. In a series of out of the body experiences, Twitchell found himself in touch with superior beings called the Eck Masters (*see* **Inner Plane Adepti**) who revealed a series of complex and comprehensive spiritual truths to him.

On the basis of these truths, Twitchell founded an international Eckankar organization, the followers of which attempt to practise projection according to the methods Twitchell has given.

Eckhart, Meister
A late thirteenth-century, early fourteenth-century German mystic (the exact dating of his life is uncertain) Eckhart von Hochheim became Prior of the Dominican Friary at Erfurt around 1298. He believed and taught renunciation of wealth and possessions in order to receive the divine light of God's wisdom which, he claimed, was open to creatures other than humanity, although in a lesser degree than to humanity itself.

Not all Meister Eckhart's doctrines proved acceptable to the ecclesiastical authorities. A papal bull of 1329 (around the time of Eckhart's death) condemned no fewer than 28 of his propositions as potentially heretical.

Egyptian Book of the Dead
Although commonly called *The Book of the Dead* by archaeologists and occultists alike, the actual title of this collection of funereal texts is *Chapters for Coming Forth by Day*, a clear description of what is promised for the soul of the deceased.

The texts contain spells, incantations and **ritual**s designed to help those who have died to navigate the dangers of the underworld and achieve a happy afterlife. Some rituals were meant to help the deceased join the sun god in the sky.

The practice of leaving such texts in the tomb seems to have dated to about the Eighteenth Dynasty (1580–1320 BC), but a number of the texts themselves are much older, deriving from the *Pyramid Texts* of 2350 BC.

Egyptian Mysteries

Orthodox scholarship has it that the Mystery Religions, with their secret doctrines, initiatory rites and ceremonial, were a phenomenon of ancient Greece and Rome, but the fact that Isis and Serapis were honoured in the Mysteries has led to widespread speculation that ancient Egypt had her Mystery Schools as well.

Much of the speculation has been romantic in the extreme. It has been suggested that the chambers of the major pyramids of Giza (*see* **Great Pyramid**) were initiation halls of the Egyptian Mysteries. Early authors wrote about a Mysteries temple beneath the statue of the Sphinx and one even claimed there was an entire underground city in the same area.

Elementals

Non-human Nature **spirit**s of which there are six main groups:

gnomes (spirits of the earth)
salamanders (spirits of fire)
sylphs (spirits of the air)
undines (spirits of water and rivers)
fauns or satyrs (spirits of animal life)
dryads (spirits of vegetation)

In an occult sense, elementals can be created by an individual through an emotional thought-form. Suffused with enough energy by the creator, they can become *tulpas* (*see* **Tulpa Creation**) or torment through possession or cause problems as **poltergeist**s.

Eliade, Mircea

A prolific author on a variety of subjects, including **yoga**, shamanism and comparative religion, Mircea Eliade was appointed Professor of the History of Religions at the University of Chicago in 1958.

Romanian-born Eliade is an accepted authority on **mysticism**, religious symbolism and initiatory patterns. His classic works include *Yoga: Immortality and Freedom*, *Shamanism: Archaic Techniques of Ecstasy*, *From Primitives to Zen* and his three-volume *History of Religious Ideas*.

Emerson, Ralph Waldo
See **Transcendentalist Movement**.

Emmanuel
Emmanuel first came through the channel Pat Rodegast during **meditation**. Pat Rodegast has compiled a widely-read collection, *Emmanuel's Book: A Manual for Living Comfortably in the Cosmos* (Bantam, 1987). Emmanuel says, 'The gifts I wish to give you are my deepest love, the safety of truth, the wisdom of the universe and the reality of God . . . The issue of whether there is a Greater Reality or not, for me at least, has been settled. I know that there is. So I will speak to you from the knowing that I possess.'

Encounter
A method for cultivating personal growth. The roots of the encounter group movement derive from the 1940s with training groups (T-groups), which explored ways of developing training methods in inter-personal relationships. Later on, personal growth became more important.

The aim of an encounter group is to make it possible, in the context of a mutually supportive environment, to communicate genuine feelings, expressing them both verbally and physically. There are various kinds of encounter group, but the main two are basic encounter, developed by **Carl Rogers** and his associates, and open encounter, developed by **Will Schutz** with others at **Esalen**.

Endorphins
The brain's own opiates, neurochemicals which deaden pain and produce euphoria.

Enneagram
A fragmentary science taught by **G.I. Gurdjieff**, who claimed it was the key symbolic device of the Sarmaun Brotherhood, a mystic order that existed in Central Asia for thousands of years.

The Enneagram is a remarkable system for clarifying and understanding human nature. The principle is simple – there are nine personality types divided into three groups (or triads): the Feeling Triad includes the Helper, the Status Seeker, the Artist; the Doing Triad includes the Thinker, the Loyalist, the Generalist; the Relating Triad includes the Leader, the Peacemaker, the Reformer.

Ennea is Greek for nine, so a rough translation of *Enneagram* is 'a nine diagram', which comprises nine equidistant points on the circumference of a circle, thus:

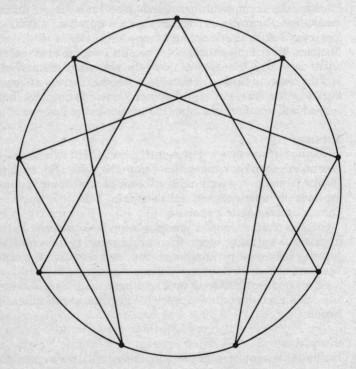

Enochian Language

When the Elizabethan magus, Dr **John Dee** and his seer **Edward Kelley** engaged in their most interesting series of magical experiments, they made contact with an entity which claimed to be an **angel**.

This being, visible only to Kelley, dictated a series of Calls or evocations to the Watchtowers of the Universe. The curious method of dictation – letter by letter and backwards – was explained by the fact that the Calls were so powerful even writing them down in the normal way might stir up potent and unwanted magical currents.

The process of transcribing the Calls was bizarre. Dee and Kelley had somehow obtained, or created, more than 100 large squares, or tablets, measuring 49×49 inches on average, each wholly or partly filled by a grid pattern of letters. During the course of the experiments, Dee would place one or more of these tablets before him on a writing table, while Kelley would sit across the room staring into a crystal shewstone.

When contact was made, Kelley would report sight of the angel in the shewstone, along with the angel's own copies of the tablets. Using a wand, the angel would then point to certain letters on the tablets and Kelley would call out the rank and file of the letter indicated. Dee would then locate the letter in the same position in his tablet and write it down. Thus the Calls were gradually built up.

The Calls themselves were not in English, but in a language Dee referred to as 'Angelic' or 'Enochian'. It was supposed to have been the tongue spoken on the lost continent of **Atlantis**. A fair example of the language is the following:

Micma Goho Mad Zir Comselha Zien Biah Os Londoh Norz Chis Othil Gigipah Vnd-L Chis ta Pu-Im Q Mospleh Teloch . . . Which translates as, 'Behold, saith your God, I am a circle on Whose Hands stand Twelve Kingdoms. Six are the Seats of Living Breath. The rest are as Sharp Sickles or the Horns of Death . . .'

Although considerable doubts have been cast on Kelley's *bona fides* as a seer, analysis has shown Enochian appears to be a genuine language fragment – as opposed to a code or cypher. Linguists claim it is not impossible to create a pseudo-language – it was, after all, done with Esperanto – but to do so requires highly specialist expertise and years of work. In the circumstances, it is difficult to imagine how Kelley might have faked Enochian at all, let alone managed the prodigious feat of memory involved in pretending to receive the Calls backwards.

The original diaries of Dr Dee, recording the experiments in which the Calls were produced, are now in the British Museum, but the story of Enochian does not end there. In Victorian times, initiates of the **Golden Dawn** used the material to create a vast, complex system of Enochian **magic**.

Esalen Institute

Founded in 1962 by Michael Murphy and Richard Price in Big Sur, California, the Esalen Institute has been the acknowledged centre of the **human potential movement**. Throughout the sixties and seventies it was a testing ground for new ideas and personal growth techniques. **Abraham Maslow, Fritz Perls, Will Schutz, Carl Rogers, Alan Watts** and **Aldous Huxley** were involved and many creative people visited and participated in seminars and workshops.

A community of about 100 is resident at Esalen today and it continues to have a flourishing programme of workshops, seminars and conferences.

ESP

ESP, the common abbreviation for Extra Sensory Perception, was originally coined as a respectable umbrella alternative to such terms as 'telepathy' and **'clairvoyance'** when serious laboratory efforts in psychical research began in the 1930s. Since then, however, it has become the subject of investigation in its own right as scientists discovered phenomena which did not fit into any of the older groupings.

Among these was the experiment set up by physicists at Stanford Research Institute in California in 1972. This involved the use of a special isolation chamber with thick steel double walls, capable of shielding any known electro-magnetic signal. One subject was placed in this chamber, while another was set before a photostimulator, an instrument which creates specific brain-wave patterns. This second subject was asked to attempt to 'contact' the man in the isolation chamber. Both subjects were then attached to electroencephalographs and the experiment began.

Under the influence of the photostimulator, the brain-waves of Subject 2 quickly adopted a novel pattern, exactly as the physicists would have expected. But then so did the brain-waves of Subject 1 locked away in the isolation booth: in moments they were an exact match of those of the man outside. Neither subject was aware of the changes which could only be detected by the electroencephalograph.

Essenes

A Jewish pacifist, pre-Christian mystical movement, the Essenes are today largely associated with the monastic settlement at Qumran and the famous Dead Sea Scrolls, but there were, in fact, lay Essenes as well as monastic.

The Essene community, lay and monastic, rejected the **rituals** of the Temple for a somewhat simpler and more inward observance and held firmly to a belief in the immortality of the soul.

As one of many Jewish messianic sects, their doctrines on the imminent appearance of a great Teacher of Righteousness so closely parallels the New Testament doctrines of Christ that a great many scholars have seriously considered the possibility that Jesus was an Essene before leaving the movement to establish his own following.

Dr Edmund Szekely, poet, scholar, linguist and Unitarian bishop, has translated and interpreted the Essene gospels and writings.

Etheric Body

A second body, mirror image of the physical and usually coincident with it, which can, in certain circumstances, be projected and become the primary vehicle of **consciousness**. In traditional **occultism**, the etheric body is believed to be composed of 'finer matter' but recent research suggests it may actually be a field phenomenon, electrical in nature.

Etheric Projection

In 1863 an American manufacturer named Wilmot was on board the *City of Limerick* as the ship hit a mid-Atlantic storm. During the night, he dreamed his wife visited him in her nightdress and kissed him. Although he had said nothing of the dream, his cabin-mate teased him the following morning about his midnight visit from a lady.

When he arrived home in Bridgeport, Connecticut, his wife at once asked him if he had received a visit from her in the night. She had, she said, been worried by reports of shipwrecks and decided to try to find out if he was safe. Consequently she visualized herself flying over the ocean, finding the ship and going to his cabin. A man in the upper berth looked straight at her, but she went ahead and kissed her husband anyway. When pressed, she was able accurately to describe the ship, the cabin and the man who had shared it with Mr Wilmot.

The case, which has been widely reported and examined, is an interesting example of etheric projection, the separation from the physical of a second, subtle body which can then travel substantial distances in a very short space of time.

Little was known about etheric projection until the publication, in 1929, of a book entitled *The Projection of the Astral Body*, jointly authored by the psychical researcher Hereward Carrington and an unknown American named Sylvan Muldoon.

In the book, Muldoon, who suffered from chronic illness, told how he had experienced dozens, even hundreds, of etheric projections over a period of years. During these projections, his **etheric body** was joined to the physical by a **silver cord**, but since the link was infinitely elastic, he was able to travel as freely as he wished.

Muldoon believed most people were capable of projecting the etheric body and gave a variety of techniques to facilitate the process. These included teaching yourself to wake up in a particular way from a dream and deliberately creating a condition of hunger or thirst while the physical body is incapacitated. Other experts have added sexual orgasm, **hypnosis** and sonic manipulation of brain-wave patterns to the list.

First indication of a full projection is often paralysis of the entire body – what Muldoon termed *catalepsy* or a 'glued-down' feeling.

'Shaking' or 'vibration' is often mentioned and is again almost universally experienced as unpleasant. When paralysis or vibration begin, it requires an enormous effort to break free of them – in some instances you are powerless to break free at all and can only wait for the condition to pass and the projection itself to begin.

Eurythmy

The art of movement, or spiritual dance, created by **Rudolf Steiner**. Meditative preparation ensures that the dancer, as microcosm, expresses the appropriate aspects of the macrocosm. Performers of Eurythmy employ sweeping and flowing movements to enact the essence of legends and stories.

Evans-Wentz, W.Y.

Formerly of Jesus College, Oxford, Dr W.Y. Evans-Wentz became, in the words of a colleague, a 'sort of scholar-gypsy' in the early years of the twentieth century. Following the publication of his *The Fairy-Faith in Celtic Countries*, a sympathetic book on Celtic folklore which influenced **W.B. Yeats**, Evans-Wentz spent several years in the Near and Middle East before, at the invitation of Maharaja Sidkyong Tulku, he went to live in India where he made an extensive study of the Eastern Esoteric Tradition. The outcome was a series of very fine books on the secret teachings of Tibet. These include his translations of *The Tibetan Book of the Dead* and *The Tibetan Book of the Great Liberation*, his fascinating biography of *Tibet's Great Yogi, Milarepa* and his extensive investigation of *Tibetan Yoga and Secret Doctrines*.

Exorcism

The process by which a person or place is freed of an evil **spirit**, ghost or **poltergeist**. Exorcism rites exist in many religions and their use is common in those societies where evil spirits are thought to cause illness, disaster and misfortune.

An exorcism is performed by someone with an appropriate training, either a religious official or a **shaman**. Rites can be very simple or elaborate ceremonies involving prayer, invective and the use of sacred herbs and water.

Explicate Order

See **Implicate Order**.

F

Fakir

From the Arabic word meaning 'poor person', the fakir was originally a Moslem ascetic who renounced the material world to follow Allah. Now a type of holy man in India who performs miraculous and magical feats, probably using **hypnosis**, such as lying on a bed of nails or the 'rope trick' in which the fakir appears to cause a rope to hang in mid-air and then shimmies up it.

Feild, Reshad

The author of a series of books described as 'classics of contemporary spiritual literature', Reshad Feild has developed a down-to-earth literary style which often manages to avoid the obscurity of so much modern metaphysical literature. One small example, quoted from the second volume of his *Travelling People's Feild Guide*, reads, 'The only purpose of being here is to be here yet a very small percentage of us ever get here.'

Feild had travelled extensively, visiting monasteries in Japan and the Himalayas. He studied Sufi mystical traditions in Turkey, where he was initiated into the order of Mevlevi Dervishes.

Feldenkreis Method

A school of **bodywork** devised by Moshe Feldenkreis, which attempts to correct faulty posture and promote co-ordination and flexibility through body movement and therapeutic touch. Whilst obviously of great value to dancers, actors and athletes, it is also for serious disability patients.

Feng Shui

Literally translated as 'Wind and Water' and sometimes translated as **geomancy**, *Feng Shui* is the peculiarly Chinese art of locating and/or creating fortunate places in which to live, work and even die. In his massive multi-volume study of *Science and Civilization in China*, Professor Joseph Needham defined Feng Shui as 'the art of adopting the residences of the living and the dead so as to cooperate and harmonise with the local currents of the cosmic breath'. The 'cosmic breath' is, of course, the universal *ch'i*, which also makes its appearance in Chinese **acupuncture**.

Feng Shui holds that Nature and the Earth are living entities and is convinced that humanity must integrate itself properly into Nature if happiness is to be achieved. In order to do so, Feng Shui recognizes that the surface of the Earth is a mirror – albeit a dim one – of astrological influences in the heavens. Because of this it is possible for experts to recognize or calculate those terrestrial features which carry benevolent or malevolent currents. Positive forces are, for example, associated with crooked, meandering lines (like a river) while straight lines tend to generate or reflect negative influences.

Because of this, there is in China, as Professor Needham points out, 'a strong preference for tortuous and winding roads, walls and structures, which seem to fit into the landscape rather than to dominate it'. Other experts have gone even further and suggest that the entire face of China has been heavily landscaped by thousands of years of Feng Shui practice in ancient times. The nineteenth-century traveller W.E. Geil was told that the position of the Great Mound of China was fixed by geomancers as being auspicious: 'The dragon pulse, meaning the magnetic currents with which the dragon is supposed to be connected, is good. The mountain south is a dragon at rest. The river north is a dragon in motion.' The author Ernst Borschmann wrote, 'Certain summits of the neighbouring mountains, often the main summit, are crowned with pagodas, small temples or pavilions to harmonise the magic forces of heaven and earth.' John Michell suggests artificial hills were formed on which to place cities.

Feng Shui was called upon to assist in the concentration of earth energy in the imperial capital Peking. Natural serpentine streams of energy were diverted into straight *lung mei* or 'dragon paths' which focused on the Emperor in his seat of government. No tomb or building other than those of the imperial family was allowed on a dragon path.

The art of Feng Shui has by no means died out. It is evident even in the highly practical and bustling business environment of present-day Hong Kong where corporations will typically commission a Feng Shui geomancer at the same time as an architect when a new building is planned. Where Western, or Westernized, executives do not themselves believe in the principles of Feng Shui, they realize an incorrectly-sited building will attract immediate trouble from a labour force which does.

Ficino, Marsilio

A Florentine philosopher and doctor employed by Cosimo de Medici to translate the *Hermetica* – the work supposedly of the Egyptian sage, **Hermes Trismegistus**. In 1489, Marsilio Ficino published a fascinating theory linking medicine, **astrology** and **creative imagination** in what was essentially a brand new therapeutic system. According to Ficino, the favourable astrological influences of a particular planet could be attracted by meditating on images characteristic of that planet's nature. When patients did so, he claimed, **healing** quickly followed.

Findhorn

The Findhorn Foundation was established in 1962 by Peter and **Eileen Caddy** and Dorothy MacLean, under **spirit** guidance. On a caravan park in the chill north-east of Scotland they discovered that, through collaboration with **devas** (i.e. Nature spirits), they could grow vegetables – often of monstrous size – in soil so poor that even weeds found it difficult to retain a foothold. As the community developed, astonished Press reporters carried back accounts of 40-pound cabbages actually growing in sand. The story of this remarkable experiment is told in Paul Hawken's book, *The Magic of Findhorn*.

Findhorn still flourishes and is one of the most successful of the **New Age** communities, continuing to experiment and evolve.

Firewalking

'I was in full possession of my senses,' wrote the Roman Catholic Bishop of Mysore in southern India in the course of a letter to the French author Olivier Leroy. He felt compelled to make the protestation, since his letter contained an account of one of the most unlikely ceremonies ever witnessed.

It happened in the spring of 1921 when Bishop Despatures was invited by the local maharaja to attend a demonstration of firewalking by a Muslim from northern India. When he arrived at the appointed spot, he found a 13×6 feet trench had been dug to a depth of about a foot. A fire was lit in it which burned so fiercely that the maharaja and his guests could only sit comfortably if they remained at least 25 yards away.

To the Bishop's surprise, the Muslim firewalker did not actually enter the pit himself, but stayed about a foot away from it. He called over one of the palace servants and after talking with him for a moment, pushed the man abruptly into the flames.

The panic-stricken servant struggled to get out, then the look of terror on his face gradually gave way to an astonished smile. He then casually walked the length of the pit, despite the fact his feet and legs were bare. When he emerged, other servants crowded round him to find out what it had been like, then themselves plunged into the pit. They were followed shortly after by the maharaja's bandsmen, marching three by three.

Dried palm leaves were thrown into the trench. They caught fire at once, sending flames higher than a man's head. The Muslim encouraged more servants to walk through and they did so without harm. Then the band marched through again, complete with instruments and sheet music which somehow did not catch fire. In all, the Bishop estimated, some 200 people must have walked on the fire without harm, including two Englishmen.

Two weeks later, the same Muslim gave another demonstration in Mysore, this one marked by the fact that three people forced their way into the pit after the Muslim had told them it was no longer safe to walk there. They were so badly burned they had to be hospitalized.

Firewalking is not confined to India. The traveller Rosita Forbes described a traditional fire dance in Dutch Guiana where men were able to walk through waist-high flames, embrace blazing boughs and chew glowing embers while a virgin priestess remained in trance. Once she emerged from trance to signal that the ceremony was over, they had to leap hurriedly from the fire to avoid being burned.

On the tiny Fijian island of Mbengga, there is an annual religious ceremony involving firewalking. The natives dig a pit 6 feet deep, 25 feet long and 10 feet wide, which they line with large stones. They then layer logs, brush, more stones and more logs until the pit is nearly full. A fire is then lit and allowed to burn all night while prayers are offered to Tui Namoliwai, the Water God.

The following morning, barefoot worshippers are led in a complete circle over the entire length of the burning pit. It is held that if they are properly prepared mentally and spiritually they will come to no harm. The fact that harm can come is borne out by an incident in 1940 when one man was so badly burned that he had to have both legs amputated.

In an attempt to discover how the firewalk is carried out, the scientist Harry B. Wright interviewed the man who led the worshippers. He proved perfectly willing to disclose the secret. The Water God, he said, sent hundreds of water babies to lie on the burning coals and the men simply walked across the cool backs of the babies.

The US physicist Jearl Walker had a different explanation. He believed the safety of firewalkers relied on nothing more mysterious than the Leidenfrost Effect – the same thing that keeps water droplets skeetering about on the top of a hot stove, levitating on a protective layer of vapour. It is an interesting observation, but one which fails to explain the cases in which firewalkers keep their socks (and sometimes shoes) on. Nor does it explain the safety of the sheet music used by the maharaja's bandsmen.

Nevertheless, it does seem likely that an explanation for firewalking will soon be found, if only because the occupation has been spreading. Since 1980, thousands of ordinary people in the US, Europe, Australia and South Africa, caught up in the **human potential movement**, have walked unharmed through 4-metre beds of red-hot coals after attending seminars which taught them how to utilize personal resources more efficiently.

Firth, Violet Mary
See **Fortune, Dion**.

Flotation Tank
The flotation tank was devised by the neurophysiologist **John Lilly**. Floating in heavily salted water at a temperature slightly less than body temperature in a darkened room induces altered states of **consciousness** and brings about physical and mental transformation. As well as reducing stress, flotation enables deep relaxation and creative **visualization**. It also effectively treats some physical ailments like high blood pressure, chronic pain and cardiovascular problems, and is also effective in reducing or eliminating smoking and alcohol and drug abuse.

Fludd, Robert

One of the most visual of the Elizabethan Qabalists, Robert Fludd published a number of esoteric works noted for their detailed diagrams of occult **cosmology** and symbolic **mandalas**.

Fludd, who lived between 1574 and 1637, was an accomplished musician as well as an astrologer and Rosicrucian, who expressed considerable interest in cosmic harmony and mystic hierarchies reflecting into the mundane world in accordance with the ancient esoteric maxim: *As above, so below.*

Flying Saucers

See **UFOs**.

Focusing

A technique developed in the 1960s by Eugene Gendlin and other psychological researchers at the University of Chicago. After analysing thousands of sessions between therapists and clients, they came to the conclusion that if able to be in direct contact with their felt experience, clients stood a far better chance of benefiting from therapy. Gendlin went on to discover the essential steps for helping individuals to contact their felt experience in a way which led to growth. The essence of Focusing is to be aware from the inside of our actual experience as it is occurring in the present moment, particularly when dealing with a problem or important life issue.

Formative Causation

See **Sheldrake, Rupert**.

Fortune, Dion

The pseudonym used by the **Freud**ian psychoanalyst Violet Firth (later Penry-Evans) who has had a more profound influence on **occultism** than almost any other figure in the twentieth century.

Born in 1891, Dion Fortune spent her formative years in a **Christian Science** household. She proved to be an independent child and showed early signs of the psychism which was to shape so much of her later life.

When she was aged about 20, she went to work in a private educational establishment and there fell foul of the principal, a domineering woman who had studied **yoga** and occultism in India. As a result of the clash, which seems to have involved the use of **hypnosis** by the principal, Dion Fortune plunged into a nervous breakdown from which she did not fully recover for a number of years.

The experience stimulated her interest in the human mind and led to her study of Freudian analysis, on which she eventually published several books. But she never believed Freud provided the total answer to her unpleasant experience or indeed to the continuing mystery of her own psychism. She turned to a study of the occult and was eventually drawn to join the Order of the **Golden Dawn**.

By this time, the Order was in decline. Dion Fortune found it composed of 'squabbling greybeards' but none the less sensed an **aura** of power associated with it. She stayed away from internal politics, kept her head down and studied **magic**. In the early 1920s, she founded her own Order, the Fraternity of the Inner Light, an organization which survives, quietly, to the present day and has profoundly influenced the development of the **Western Esoteric Tradition**.

Four Noble Truths
See **Buddhism**.

Fox, Matthew
See **Creation Spirituality**.

Freemasonry
When a candidate for First Degree **initiation** arrives at the Masonic Hall, his jacket and collar are removed and any money he may be carrying is set aside. He is then blindfolded and led by a guard (known as the 'Tyler') into the Lodge Room, a chamber furnished with an altar and twin pillars and featuring a black and white chequerboard floor.

The Master Mason in charge of the ceremony asks the Tyler, 'Whom have you there?' and the Tyler replies, 'A poor Candidate in a state of darkness.' The initiation then begins.

In the course of the **ritual**, the candidate swears an oath not to reveal the secrets of Freemasonry. When his blindfold is removed, he is shown certain grips and signs by which he may recognize a fellow of the Craft and told certain words referring to the building of King Solomon's Temple.

He is then presented with his working tools – a 24-inch gauge, a gavel and a chisel – the symbolic significance of which are each explained to him. Finally, he is shown the symbolism of the First Degree 'tracing board', a rectangular plank on which the Degree signs have been painted.

Following initiation, the candidate is known as an Entered Apprentice and may, in due course, proceed to the Degrees of Fellow Craft and Master Mason. This latter is the highest level of Craft Masonry, although the initiate is entitled to seek entry into the Royal Arch, an extension of Craft Masonry, with its own Degrees.

Despite its requirement of secrecy, there is a vast amount of information generally available on Freemasonry. As long ago as 1912, a Masonic bibliography issued in Germany listed 40,000 titles – and even this huge number represents no more than the tip of the iceberg today.

Freemasonry, which is banned in all Communist and most Roman Catholic countries (one surprising exception to the latter being Italy), is rooted in the medieval builders' guilds where signs and passwords were developed as proof by which itinerant stonemasons could establish they were masters of their craft. This 'Operative Masonry', as it is now called, evolved during the eighteenth century into 'Speculative Masonry', which took over many of the signs and rituals. All modern Masonry can ultimately be traced back to the Grand Lodge of England which was constituted in 1717 out of four existing London lodges.

At that time, the aspiration of a 'noble brother' to head the Grand Lodge was expressed, and this was actually achieved in 1721 when the Duke of Montague became Grand Master. Since then, the office has always been held by one of noble or royal birth. The present Grand Master is the Duke of Kent.

Freud, Sigmund

Physician and founder of psychoanalysis, Freud was a profound influence on the twentieth century. Born in 1856 in Moravia, he lived most of his life in Vienna, but fled to London in 1938 to escape the Nazi invasion and died there the following year.

His career began in Vienna General Hospital where he conducted brilliant work on the anatomy and physiology of the nervous system. He became interested in psychology whilst studying with the neurologist Charcot in Paris. When he returned to Vienna, he began to use **hypnosis** in treating neurotic patients. By investigating their minds he discovered 'free association' and developed psychoanalysis. Freud's emphasis on sexual repression and infantile sexual trauma as the cause of all neuroses caused misunderstanding and some of his key colleagues like Josef Breuer, and later Alfred Adler and **C.G. Jung**, broke with him.

In 1900 his seminal work *The Interpretation of Dreams* was published, followed by *The Psychopathology of Everyday Life* in 1904 and *Three Contributions to The Theory of Sex* in 1905.

Fuller, Buckminster

A brilliant, if eccentric, contemporary futurist philosopher concerned with humanity's place in the ecological scheme of things, whose architectural and engineering background enabled him to produce some remarkable inventions, of which the best known is the geodesic dome.

G

Gaia

The planet we live on flatly refuses to obey the laws of physics. The seas are not as salty as they should be. Computer calculations of the salt carried seaward by rivers clearly indicate a much higher concentration should by now have been achieved. The atmosphere, despite our heroic attempts to generate a greenhouse effect, does not contain nearly as much carbon-dioxide as it should for a planet the age of the Earth. Calculations show there should be nothing much else left in the air we breathe by now.

In fact, calculations based on the laws of thermodynamics clearly indicate that after five thousand million years, cold, lifeless inertia should have overcome our planet.

Although these anomalies had long been noted by scientists, it was not until 1979 that a theory was developed to explain them. It was postulated by Professor **James Lovelock** who suggested that the stability of our atmosphere could only be explained by the assumption that it was somehow linked to the biosphere, the collective name for every living plant and creature on the planet.

Lovelock then went further. He proposed that the lithosphere (the solid portion of the planet) combined with biosphere and atmosphere to form a single integrated system. Such a system would necessarily be the gigantic body of a living entity, the largest being in the solar system.

Lovelock did not retreat from the implications of his theory. He named the entity *Gaia*, after the ancient Greek Goddess of the Earth.

Gardner, Gerald

When he first began to attract widespread public attention towards the end of his life, Gerald Brosseau Gardner had developed a shock of white hair, a pointed grey-white goatee and bushy eyebrows which curled up at the ends like horns. In short, he looked what he was: a witch, and one of the first to engage in the now fashionable pursuit of declaring his interest openly.

Gardner was born in 1884 and spent most of his working life in Malaya where he was an officer of the Customs Service. He was an expert in folklore and spent a good deal of time investigating Far Eastern **occultism**. He retired from the service in 1936 and returned to Britain to begin an interesting occult career. Sometime in 1940, he joined a magical society in Christchurch, Hampshire, and discovered it was a front organization for a witch cult.

Never one to refuse an interesting experience, Gardner became an initiate of the Craft. But what he found there seems to have disappointed him, for about three years later he hired **Aleister Crowley** to compose **initiation** and other **ritual**s suitable for a reconstituted brand of **witchcraft**. The rituals, when complete, reflected both Crowley's and Gardner's sado-masochistic sexual interests.

Towards the end of the 1940s, Gardner published a novel about medieval witchcraft called *High Magic's Aid* in which he dropped several important hints about the real nature of the Craft. In 1954, having meantime joined the Council of the Folklore Society and picked up three rather questionable degrees, Gardner published his second book, *Witchcraft Today*. This was a factual work restating in very readable form Margaret Murray's thesis about the Stone Age origins of witchcraft as a fertility religion – Dr Murray herself wrote an introduction to the book – but Gardner added the startling information that this religion had survived and was being practised secretly to the present day. The book was a best seller, attracting a flood of disciples to its author. Whatever the truth of his allegation that witchcraft already flourished in secret, new covens began to spring up like mushrooms. Almost single-handedly, Gerald Gardner had created a witchcraft revival which continues to gather impetus to the present day. He was the acknowledged leader of the movement until his death in 1964.

Garrett, Eileen

One of the most remarkable **medium**s of the twentieth century, Eileen Garrett, who died in 1970, was unusual in that she was never prepared to take her psychical abilities at face value, but sought instead to give them a strictly scientific validation.

To this end she cooperated closely with several well-known parapsychologists, including **J.B. Rhine** of Duke University in North Carolina, Hereward Carrington and Nandor Fodor who tested her across a spectrum of **ESP** talents ranging from telepathy to **automatic writing**. Mrs Garrett herself inclined towards the belief that mediumistic communication and other phenomena were more likely to demonstrate unusual abilities of the unconscious mind than offer proof of post mortem survival.

Born in Ireland in 1893, Eileen Garrett received four years Spiritualistic training at the British College of Psychic Science under James H. McKenzie, the Scot who investigated so many trance mediums. In 1951 she was instrumental in establishing the Parapsychology Foundation, an institution devoted to encouraging scientific study of **psi** abilities.

Gauquelin, Michel

Contemporary French statistician whose lifelong interest in **astrology** persuaded him to attempt an analysis of the traditional astrological associations.

Although his work is sometimes hailed as proof that astrology works, it actually established quite the reverse. In an analysis of thousands of birth charts, Gauquelin could find no statistical correlation whatsoever between personality and/or career characteristics and traditional astrological doctrines.

What he did find, however, was clear statistical evidence of a relationship between the rise and culmination of the moon and certain planets (Mars, Jupiter and Saturn) on the one hand and successful career vocations on the other. Later work led him to believe the relationship was indirect. The planetary rise and culmination seems actually to be linked with the presence of certain personality characteristics, which in turn tend to lead towards specific career paths.

These relationships do not form part of traditional astrology and, despite their clear exposition in widely-read works like *The Cosmic Clocks* and *Cosmic Influences on Human Behaviour*, they have so far failed to stimulate the development of a new, statistically-valid astrological system.

Geller, Uri

On 23 November 1973, a young, charming 26-year-old Israeli appeared on a UK television chat show and started a controversy which continues to this day. The Israeli was Uri Geller. The controversy sprang from his claim that he could bend a variety of metal objects – keys, forks, spoons and the like – merely by applying the power of his mind.

The claim was not only substantiated in the studio, where forks bent and broken watches suddenly started up again, but also, incredibly, throughout the country. The studio switchboard was jammed with reports of cutlery-bending at home, particularly where children were watching the show.

The whole affair became an international sensation, with journalists seriously questioning whether Geller should be permitted to fly on commercial airlines (because of his possible influence on the delicate machinery of the plane). Scientists took an interest and sought permission to test Geller under laboratory conditions. Rather to the surprise of his more violent detractors, he agreed.

In fact, Geller was to undergo a wide variety of laboratory tests which indicated he could certainly produce phenomena under controlled conditions, but gave the scientists no idea how he did so. The prestigious Max Planck Institute announced that his powers were something which, in theoretical terms, could not be explained. Geller was also successfully tested for **clairvoyance** by the Stanford Research Institute in California.

His closest collaboration was with the parapsychologist Andrija Puharich, who witnessed such demonstrations as a thermometer rising, a compass needle spinning and a water-jet bending under the power of Geller's gaze, and came away convinced the wizard was genuine.

Following on a series of international appearances, Geller's fame increased, but so too did the insistence by his detractors that it was all done by conjuring. His supporters were not entirely heartened by claims that his powers derived from a meeting with aliens from space who had landed on Earth in a **UFO**. (In his autobiography, Geller claimed the flying saucer story had arisen out of a misunderstanding.) Geller responded by dropping out of sight and declining stage appearances for a number of years. He re-emerged in the limelight a millionaire, having successfully used his weird abilities to dowse for copper and gold.

Gematria

A branch of Qabalistic lore which derives hidden meanings from words or phrases by translating them into their numerical equivalents and analysing the result. Several ancient tongues – and notably Hebrew – have numbers assigned to the letters of their alphabets, so that discovering the number of a given word is little more than a matter of addition. When two or more things were found to have the same number, ancient Qabalists postulated a secret connection between them.

The most famous historical example of gematria is neither Jewish nor Hebraic, oddly enough, but arises in the New Testament Book of Revelation. Revelation 13:18 reads, 'Here is wisdom. Let him that hath understanding count the number of the beast: for it is the number of a man; and his number is Six hundred threescore and six.'

Here the reader 'with an understanding' is advised to 'count the number' of the Great Beast, a clear reference to gematria and an indication that the author of the book, John the Divine, may have been a Qabalist. This number, given as 666, is believed by scholars to have referred to the violently anti-Christian Roman Emperor Nero, since the Greek version of his name and title, *Nero Caesar*, totals 666. (*See also* **Crowley, Aleister**; **Qabalah**.)

Gendlin, Eugene
See **Focusing**.

Geomancy
The derivation of the term geomancy points clearly to its meaning as 'Earth magic', but like so many terms, this one had undergone a metamorphosis. In Napoleonic times, for example, geomancy was a system of **divination** by means of dots, tapped in random lines with a pencil on a piece of paper. If there was any connection with the earth, it lay in the graphite of the pencil, or possibly a suspicion that the dots may originally have been pebbles cast at random.

Today, however, the term is used very differently, although perhaps not quite so precisely. It is associated with Chinese **Feng Shui**, with **ley lines**, **dowsing**, *ch'i* and megalithic sites. Sometimes, though more rarely, those interested will even postulate a linkage with the mystery of **UFOs**.

Broadly speaking, modern theories of geomancy suggest the ancients knew a great deal more about earth currents (the sort that dowsers may be picking up) than we do today. The planet is seen as something analogous to the human body and is criss-crossed by the planetary equivalent of **acupuncture** meridians.

Prehistoric peoples in Britain, Ireland and Europe created megalithic monuments – like Stonehenge or the menhirs of Brittany – to manipulate these and certain cosmic currents for purposes we no longer understand, but which may have been associated with the fertility of the land.

Romantic though these notions may appear, there is a solid enough foundation for believing many – indeed most – **megaliths** have a special alignment. The dowser Guy Underwood visited hundreds of megalithic sites and discovered almost every one was aligned in relation to aspects of geodisic force perfectly discernible to his rod. Underwood speculated that:

> The philosophers and priests of the old religion seem to have believed that particularly when manifested in spiral forms [the geodisic force] was involved with the generative powers of Nature; that it was part of the mechanism by which what we call Life comes into being.

Even more telling was the work of Alexander Thom, a Professor of Engineering, who, as long ago as 1934, was taken by the possibility that the ancients were as much engineers as he was. The insight dawned the day he anchored his sailing boat in Loch Roag, in the Outer Hebrides, to take a look at a great stone circle on a nearby hillside. Staring along the avenue of menhirs, he noted they followed a north/south alignment and were pointing towards the Pole Star. But due to the precession of the equinoxes, the Pole Star was not in its present position in prehistoric times. So the megalith builders must have had some other means of determining true North.

The puzzle intrigued Thom all his working life and beyond. After his retirement, he began to take meticulous measurements at megalithic circles throughout the British Isles and Europe. What he discovered was astonishing. Every circle he examined was based on a single standard measurement he named a 'megalithic yard' of 2.72 feet. The circles themselves were astronomically aligned, the majority of them being huge machines for predicting eclipses of the moon.

Thom's findings ran completely contrary to the orthodox

archaeological theories of the day, but his published work contained his measurements and calculations, all of which could be – and soon were – checked for accuracy. It soon became evident he had made no mistakes.

But even now there is considerable controversy about what Thom's findings *mean*. Eclipses of the moon have no known effect on crops or the fertility cycles of human beings or domestic beasts. Nor do they mark any seasonal sub-division. Why then, did prehistoric humanity expend such time and energy predicting them? The geomantic mystery remains.

Gestalt Therapy

Gestalt therapy originated in the work of **Fritz Perls**, who was trained as a **Freud**ian psychoanalyst but was influenced by the work of **Wilhelm Reich**. Perls introduced Gestalt therapy at **Esalen** in the 1960s. The object of Gestalt therapy is to get the client to be aware and in contact with his/her world. It can be carried out in a group workshop or used on a one-to-one basis. One of the main techniques employed is talking to the 'empty chair'. This enables the client to say what they would really like to say or have said to an imaginary person sitting in the chair and then to play the part of the person sitting in the chair and responding. This dialogue, which can be very revealing, could also be taking place between different aspects of the personality. Always with Gestalt what matters is the here and now. For Perls, the object was, rather than to set out to change something, to become aware of something, and then that awareness may cause the thing to change of itself.

Ghost
See **Apparition**.

Gibran, Khalil

Author and poet from the Lebanon best known for his work *The Prophet*, first published in 1923 and reprinted countless times. It has been said of him, 'His power came from some great reservoir of spiritual life else it could not have been so universal and so potent, but the majesty and beauty of the language with which he clothed it were all his own.'

Gildas

The **spirit** entity who has communicated with Ruth White, a practising counsellor and healer, since the 1960s. The story of the development of this contact and Gildas's teachings are contained in her books *Gildas Communicates, The Healing Spectrum* and *A Question of Guidance*.

Glastonbury

Although a small market town in Somerset, Glastonbury has long been known as the magical capital of Britain. It is believed to rest at the intersection of powerful **ley lines**. Towering above Glastonbury is the Tor, a terraced volcanic rock 522 feet high with the remains of an old church tower at its peak. Legends of the **Holy Grail**, **Avalon** and King Arthur abound. The ever-flowing Chalice Well is reputed to have **healing** properties. St Patrick is said to have founded Glastonbury Abbey, and in the ruins the famous Glastonbury Thorn blooms every year.

Glastonbury is the site of Christian pilgrimages as well as seasonal **rituals** conducted by **pagan**s and other occult groups.

Glastonbury Zodiac

The sculptress Katherine Emma Maltwood (1878–1961) was researching traditional sites associated with **Arthurian legend** when, while tracing out the route of the Grail Quest on an Ordnance Survey map, she noticed that the River Cary between Somerton and Charlton Mackerell seemed to form the underside of a lion. She followed the figure and, to her considerable surprise, traced out the complete animal.

Excited and encouraged by this discovery, she began a map and field search for other figures. Soon the original lion had turned into a complete zodiac of animal and human forms. Mrs Maltwood did not, however, assume she had discovered an astrological connection. Steeped in Arthurian lore, she believed the Glastonbury Zodiac to be the enshrinement of certain archetypal myths, originally pre-Christian, from which the tales of King Arthur and his Round Table were subsequently derived.

There was some historical support for this theory. The Norman work, *La Queste de Sangraal*, clearly suggests the Round Table was not a table at all, but rather a massive earthwork laid out on the direction of **Merlin**. Essentially the same thought is echoed by Geoffrey of Monmouth, whose *High History of the Holy Grail* equates the Round Table with the 'Twelve Hides of Glaston', that area of land believed to have been granted by King Arvirgus to Joseph of Arimathea.

Several critics of Mrs Maltwood have suggested her zodiac exists largely in the eye of the beholder, pointing out that some at least of her figures are constructed with the aid of modern landscape features. But despite their best efforts, the mystery remains. Other, similar, terrestrial zodiacs definitely exist, in Britain and elsewhere, and even the Glastonbury Zodiac cannot be all that modern in its important elements, since it is mentioned in the writings of the Elizabethan magus, Dr **John Dee**, who was aware of its existence centuries before Mrs Maltwood.

Glossolalia

From the Greek *glossa*, 'tongue', and *lalia*, 'a talk', glossolalia is the act of speaking or writing in another unknown tongue. The ability first came to the apostles at Pentecost, but it has come to be regarded as a sign of demonic possession. It is important to Pentecostal Christians and to groups such as the **Shakers**, Quakers and Mormons.

Gnosticism

A loosely-defined movement rather than a religion or even a cult, Gnosticism is the term applied to a number of sects which emerged during the formative years of **Christianity**, all engaged in a search for hidden spiritual knowledge, by which they believed man was saved, rather than by faith or conduct.

The sects themselves varied considerably in their approach to esoteric truth, some emphasizing practical techniques like **astrology**, others concentrating on secret doctrines of Jesus. All seem to have been influenced by **Zoroastrianism** in that they tended towards a dualism of **spirit** and matter, the former equated with good and the latter evil.

Orthodox Christianity firmly rejected Gnostic doctrines as heretical. Indeed, the burning of the great library at Alexandria was the deliberate attempt to destroy the evidence for religions opposing the orthodox religion of the Western world. The movement, however, never lost its influence; it survived particularly in Qabalism (*see* **Qabalah**). The ill-fated **Cathars** drew much of their inspiration from the ancient Gnostics and Gnosticism surfaced again in the fifteenth century when the ancient Hermetic writings were rediscovered and translated. It also survived in secret societies such as the **Rosicrucians** and the Freemasons.

Goddess

When Archbishop Ussher calculated the date of the Creation at 4004 BC, he may have been closer to the truth than his scientific detractors have since claimed. Many feminist historians now believe that while the Creation must certainly have predated Ussher's calculation (substantially!) he may not have been too far wrong in pinpointing the creation of the world *as we know it*, a planetary culture dedicated to masculine values and ideals.

There is substantial evidence to suggest it was around 4000 BC that the religious concept of a supreme male God really began to take root in the human psyche. Prior to that time, while there had certainly been male gods aplenty, the dominant force in religious thought was the figure of the Great Goddess.

While most Western thinkers have little trouble with the realization that many ancient pantheons contained goddesses as well as gods, the idea of Goddess as the single, unitary, all-pervading divine principle remains as alien to many as the far side of the Moon. Centuries of habit have been invested in the unthinking assumption that the ultimate divinity must be male.

It was not always so. One of the most common archaeological finds throughout Europe is the so-called 'Venus Figurine', a stylized female figure with exaggerated belly and breasts almost certainly symbolic of the Great Goddess. So widespread have been these finds that they clearly suggest Goddess worship in prehistory must have been near universal.

The Goddess appears frequently in various guises in recorded history throughout the world. She is seen as the Sumerian Ishtar, the Phoenician Astarte, the Egyptian Isis, the Greek Demeter, the Roman Venus, the Indian Kali, the Chinese Kuan-yin, the African Oshun, the Japanese Amaterasu. Even the change in psychic dominance which led to the establishment of the more masculine Judaeo-Christian and **Islam**ic religions could not banish her altogether, as witness the Marian cults of **Christianity** (*see also* **Black Madonna**). In the late twentieth century there has been a resurgence of interest in the Goddess, in particular amongst neo-**pagan**s, feminists, psychologists and ecological activists (*see also* **Women's Spirituality**).

Golden Dawn

One day in 1886, Dr **William Wynn Westcott** was rummaging through the contents of a bookstall in Farringdon Street when he came across a number of manuscripts which excited him enormously. They were in code, but he surmised that they referred to something magical and bought them on the instant.

There are, in fact, several versions of the story. One states that Westcott found the manuscripts in the library of the Societas Rosicruciana and that they came originally from Freemason's Hall. Another version has him finding them in the library of the English clairvoyant Frederick Hockley. Francis King, the historian of **ritual magic**, accepts this latter version, but says the manuscripts reached Westcott from Hockley's library via a clergyman named Woodford.

Wherever they came from, Westcott needed someone to help him break the manuscript code. He selected for this task a colourful character named **S.L. MacGregor Mathers**, who was later to become curator of the Horniman Museum.

Together they discovered the manuscripts contained the skeleton of a fascinating system of technical magic, together with the address of an **adept**, Fräulein Anna Sprengler of Nuremberg in Germany. Westcott wrote to her in October 1887. In the course of their correspondence, she revealed many secrets of practical magic, and in 1888 granted him permission to establish his own magical lodge in England. This he did in conjunction with Mathers and a third Freemason, William R. Woodman. They called the new organization the Hermetic Order of the Golden Dawn.

The Golden Dawn turned out to be something better than just another pseudo-Masonic secret society. Although its impressive sounding 'Isis-Urania Temple' was a smallish set of rooms in a dingy back street, it soon attracted some of the best minds of its day. The Astronomer Royal of Scotland became a member. So did Florence Farr, the actress, **W.B. Yeats**, the Irish poet, and the writers Sax Rohmer, Arthur Machen, Bram Stoker and Algernon Blackwood.

The attraction of the Golden Dawn for individuals of this calibre almost certainly lay in the fact that the magical methods it used were a far cry from, for example, the lunatic collection of naïve spells which go to make up the average medieval *grimoire*. Rather what Westcott and his colleagues put together was a system of Occidental **yoga** aimed at developing human **consciousness** and, ultimately, provoking mystical experience.

The system was based on the Jewish **Qabalah**, but with considerable Christian and some Oriental overlay. It was to set a standard for ritual magical organizations which is followed to the present day.

Internally, the Golden Dawn was organized as a hierarchy. Mathers led it under the guidance of mysterious and largely invisible Secret Chiefs. (*See* **Hidden Masters**.) Structurally, it was divided into outer and inner Orders, which were in turn subdivided into ten grades, each related to a sphere of the Qabalistic **Tree of Life**. Entry into each grade involved a course of study, a successful examination and a ritual **initiation**.

The Golden Dawn flourished for a time and even expanded modestly. (At one period it had a Temple in Edinburgh.) But while there are branches of the organization still operational today in New Zealand and America claiming direct descent from the parent, there seems little argument that the original Order crumbled under the impact of the political machinations of its most notorious member, **Aleister Crowley.**

Crowley, who even as a young man showed an enormous natural aptitude for magic, swarmed up the early grades in the shortest time possible, then created a split from which the Order never really recovered. It arose when Crowley presented himself for a new initiation and was refused by the then head of the organization, W.B. Yeats. Yeats loathed Crowley and it may well have been he was unfair in his attitude. But Crowley was not one to let small difficulties stop his progress and promptly travelled to France where he received the initiation he wanted from MacGregor Mathers, then living in Paris. He returned to London demanding the papers and rituals of his new grade, but was still refused by Yeats. The disagreement ended in legal action and the Order, which required its members to take the most fearsome oath of secrecy, washed its dirty linen in public. Somehow things were never quite the same again. By the time **Dion Fortune** came to join, she found the once powerful Golden Dawn composed of 'squabbling greybeards'.

Goodheart, Dr George
See **Kinesiology**.

Grail, The Holy
See **Holy Grail**.

Grant, Joan
The British author of *Winged Pharaoh* and several other historical novels, Joan Grant claimed she incorporated into her fictional works recollections of her own past incarnations (*see* **Regression**; **Reincarnation**) not only in Egypt, but in Palestine and pre-Columbian America.

Joan Grant, who was born in 1907, also produced two autobiographical works, *Time Out of Mind* and *A Lot to Remember*, in which she dealt with the reincarnation theme. A great many readers have been prepared to accept her claims of past-life recall because of the unusual wealth of incidental details about ancient cultures which is typical of her novels. She died in 1989.

Great Pyramid
The Great Pyramid of Cheops (in Egyptian *Khufu*) covers a base area of 13 acres on the Giza Plateau some 10 miles from Cairo. It contains an estimated 2,300,000 stone blocks, each weighing on average 2.5 tons and some reaching an actual weight of 70 tons. The original limestone casing has all but disappeared, as has a (possibly metallic) cap. Nevertheless, the structure still contains enough masonry to duplicate every church ever built in England from the dawn of history to the present day.

There are two major mysteries surrounding the Great Pyramid: how was it built and what was it used for?

The mystery of construction is not entirely related to size, even though the Pyramid remains the largest building, ancient or modern, in the world. The real puzzle is how the Egyptians achieved the precision they did. Engineers long ago discovered the base on which the structure rests was levelled to within a fraction of an inch, an amazing feat over 13 acres. The casing stones are finished and laid to a tolerance of one hundredth of an inch.

Orthodox archaeology has it that the Pyramid was built as a sort of winter relief work by peasants without construction experience, who quarried the blocks, floated them by raft down the Nile, then hauled them into position without benefit of wheels or pulleys, both of which were unknown in the culture.

A very old Middle Eastern tradition solves the problem by

asserting the Pyramid was built by **magic**. The stones were laid on pieces of papyrus inscribed with curious symbols, then struck by a rod. This allowed them to move 'the length of a bowshot' before the process had to be repeated. Some authors insist this was not magic at all, but a distorted recollection of a largely-forgotten science based on sonics: the rod used was a precision instrument analogous to a tuning-fork, manufactured to the exact vibration of the stone block it was supposed to move. They point to travellers' tales of a similar operation in pre-Communist Tibet, where sonorously chanting monks were reputed to levitate massive boulders.

But the mystery of how the Great Pyramid was built is superseded by the mystery of why. Orthodox archaeology still insists the massive structure was a tomb, but there have always been serious doubts about this theory. Most of them date back to AD 820 when Caliph Abdullah al-Mamun's men broke through several seals and plugs (obviously untouched since the Pyramid was built) only to discover an empty sarcophagus in the King's Chamber. If a mummy had ever lain there, it is difficult to imagine where it went.

The Caliph had heard rumours that the Pyramid might contain accurate planetary and celestial measurements. But those who followed him looked more successfully at the structure itself than in secret chambers. The Victorian mathematician John Taylor, for example, concluded that the Pyramid embodied the value *pi*. From this he speculated that the Egyptians had known the Earth was round, had somehow managed to measure its circumference and had built the Pyramid as a permanent record of the result.

Taylor also derived a value of 25 'pyramid inches' for the Egyptian cubit, each inch almost indistinguishable from the standard British inch, which is itself a minute fraction short of being one fifty millionth of the polar axis. His figures were confirmed by satellite to four decimal places during the 1957–8 International Geophysical Year. Like at least one other scholar before him, Taylor suggested that the sarcophagus in the King's Chamber was never meant to be a coffin at all, but was actually a standard unit measurement of volume – in this instance the British grain measure of a 'quarter' multiplied by four.

The great archaeologist, William Flinders Petrie, who began his investigation of the Pyramid in 1880 (and is still considered by many to be the definitive authority on its measurements) discovered the Pyramid was aligned to the cardinal points more finely than any other known construction, ancient or modern. Upright surfaces were perpendicular to a tolerance of a quarter of an inch in 350 feet. The value *pi* was not only incorporated in the overall building, but in the King's Chamber as well. This room also showed the ancient Egyptians had been aware of the Golden Section and the Theorem of **Pythagoras**.

Petrie pointed out that given the hardness of the granite from which the chocolate-coloured sarcophagus was made, drills reaching a pressure of two tons would have been required to hollow it out – an incredible figure in the context of a supposedly primitive society. Casing stones were square and straight to optical precision.

Although Petrie denied that the Pyramid incorporated calendar measurements, he only did so by overlooking the implications of his own discovery that each face of the structure was slightly hollowed, an effect not observable with the naked eye. By taking this into consideration, the Leeds engineer David Davidson concluded accurate values for solar, sidereal and orbital years had been included in the building. Later computations showed the sum of the base diagonals give a good approximation of the number of years in a total precession of the equinoxes – a figure impossible to calculate accurately due to unpredictable astronomical valuations.

The discovery of these values has led to widespread speculation that the Pyramid was built to perpetuate them, that it was, in essence, a sort of complex, gigantic version of the Standard Metre in France. But those values contained in the internal chambers are yardsticks which could never be used, so this theory remains unsatisfactory. Other theories abound and several areas of speculation are frankly bizarre, ranging from the idea that the Pyramid functions as an aid to mummification to it being an observatory.

A number of occult writers, including **Madame Blavatsky**, have suggested that the structure was used as an **initiation** chamber in the **Egyptian Mysteries**, and that candidates placed in the sarcophagus of the King's Chamber, far from being mummified, experienced **astral projection** which allowed them to visit other planes and convinced them of their survival after death. Romantic though the idea might appear, the ability of the Pyramid to trigger astral projection seems to have been confirmed in the present century by Dr **Paul Brunton**.

Grof, Stanislav

Dr Stanislav Grof, a Czechoslovakian by birth, is an acknowledged authority on LSD who believes that psychedelics, carefully and intelligently used, can give access to mythic levels of **consciousness**. In recent years he has shifted away from LSD psychotherapy to work with what he calls 'Holotropic Breath Therapy', which has some similarities with **rebirthing**. In 1980, together with his wife Christina, Grof founded the Spiritual Emergence Network after Christina had suffered a psychospiritual crisis.

Guardian Angel

The medieval Christian notion that each individual is born with an accompanying guardian **angel** who stands by his/her right shoulder and provides the voice of conscience, has been dramatically extended by occultists, many of whom believe it is actually possible to communicate with this entity and derive from it substantial magical powers.

The belief stems almost exclusively from a very curious fifteenth-century manuscript entitled *The Book of the Sacred Magic of Abra-Melin the Mage* which was discovered in the Bibliothèque de l'Arsenal in Paris and translated by the Victorian scholar and magician, **S.L. MacGregor Mathers**.

The book describes a ceremony which promises 'knowledge and conversation of the Holy Guardian Angel' leading to power over **elementals** and demons which are then obliged to do the operator's will. The ceremony itself must be started at Easter and takes six months to complete. It was attempted, but abandoned unfinished, by **Aleister Crowley**, who none the less claimed contact with his Guardian Angel at a later date. More recently, a contemporary magus, writing under the pen-name 'Chevalier' claimed to have carried the operation through to completion, but coyly declined to give precise details of the final result.

Guénon, René

Born in 1886, René Guénon was a brilliant metaphysician. After being involved with various esoteric groups he became a convert to **Islam** and spent the latter part of his life in Egypt, dying in 1951. He wrote extensively and his published work includes

occultism, theology, **mysticism**, **Sufism** and the **Perennial Philosophy**.

Guide

Possibly separate **spirit** entities, human spirits who have lived before and whose task it now is to help us to follow our own spiritual path, or else inner guides, perhaps archetypal figures in the **collective unconscious**, who can help us attain our own inner wisdom.

Guided Imagery

See **Pathworking**.

Gurdjieff, G.I.

In the later years of his life, George Ivanovitch Gurdjieff took to driving at a furious rate in an extremely powerful sports car. The inevitable happened and he crashed, injuring himself so badly that his followers feared he could not possibly recover. When he regained **consciousness**, however, he insisted on discharging himself from the intensive care unit of the hospital so that he might have the opportunity of 'curing himself.' Within two weeks he was fit, well and as full of energy as ever.

The story is one of many which surround this enigmatic occultist. (Another tells how he brought an American woman to orgasm in a café just by glancing at her.) Like details of his early life, these reports are sometimes difficult to substantiate, but all contribute to the mythos of what was certainly a most remarkable individual.

Gurdjieff was born around 1877 in Caucasian Russia near the Persian border. Where he received his mystical training is something of a mystery. **J.G. Bennett** claims he studied pre-Christian esoteric traditions like those of the Mithraic cult and there certainly seem to be clear indications of Sufi influence in his methods. Rom Landau suggests that, like **Madame Blavatsky**, he visited Tibet and studied with the lamas there. He has even been identified with the notorious Russian spy, Dorjieff and there have been writers who speculate that he was the 'Hidden Master' who influenced Hitler and the Nazis.

He arrived in Moscow in 1912, creating sufficient impact to gain entrance to important Court, aristocratic and creative circles. He began, almost at once, to attract pupils, among them the mathematician **P.D. Ouspensky**. After the Russian Revolution he travelled widely throughout Europe, but by 1923 had established an Institute for the Harmonious Development of Man (his third to date) in Paris. He promoted himself by staging public shows of his esoteric dance techniques and attracted a steady stream of pupils, including the French author Louis Pauwels, who claims Gurdjieff's system almost killed him and actually did kill several other pupils, among them Katherine Mansfield.

Gurdjieff is well-known both through Ouspensky's writings and his own books, the most accessible of which is *Meetings with Remarkable Men*, made into a successful film by Peter Brooke.

Gurdjieff died in 1949.

Gurdjieff Work

The **cosmology** propounded by **G.I. Gurdjieff**, which talks of rings within rings and souls sucked up to feed the moon, is so symbolic that a great many of his followers have given up on it altogether and rely on the work of his early disciples, like **Ouspensky**, Orage or **Bennett** for clarification. But Gurdjieff's psychology is something else again.

At the root of all his teachings is the notion that human beings, with only rare exceptions, live their lives in a state analogous to sleep. Although we feel ourselves to be awake and in control of our actions, the reverse is actually the case. Things happen to us so that we go through our lives like robots, the effect of a multitude of causes.

Words like 'evolution' and 'progress' are, according to Gurdjieff's viewpoint, meaningless when applied to the life of the average individual. No real progress is possible until we somehow manage to pass out of our curious sleep state. To help his followers do so, Gurdjieff devised a series of physical and psycho-spiritual exercises, referred to as 'The Work'.

Although drawn from diverse sources, the system drew on a fundamental insight: human beings remain asleep because for most of the time they forget themselves – that is to say they are not consciously aware of themselves as active participants in the drama of life. Their attention is continually focused outwards so that their reactions are merely trigger responses to external stimuli. In order to awake, Gurdjieff taught that self-remembering was necessary. The individual had to build up a habit of self-awareness.

Several exercises designed towards this end were bizarre. At one group, for example, it was a firm rule that, at a given signal, each and every member should freeze into immobility in whatever position he happened to find himself. He was then obliged to maintain this position, however uncomfortable it might be, until a second signal released him.

Guru

Literally, one who dispels darkness, from the Sanskrit *gu*, meaning 'darkness' and *ru*, meaning 'light'. A guru is a spiritual teacher, who by example helps the devotee to attain enlightenment.

H

Hall, Manly P.

Born in 1901 in Ontario, Manly P. Hall is the author of over 100 books. His most famous work is *The Secret Teachings of All Ages*, an encyclopaedic volume on the **Western Esoteric Tradition**, published in 1928. In 1934 Manly P. Hall founded the Philosophical Research Society in Los Angeles.

Harmonic Convergence

On 16 and 17 August 1987 the world's largest **New Age** participatory event to date took place. Many thousands of people all over the world gathered at such sacred places as **Glastonbury** in England, the Pyramid of the Sun in Mexico and Mount Shasta in California.

According to Dr José Argüelles, who is credited with originating the idea for the celebration, the date was set long ago by the ancient Mayans. According to Argüelles' calculations, the Earth is entering a new period and the uniting of minds in harmony creates a special energy field which helps promote world peace and make possible contact with beings from other planets.

Harner, Michael

In 1959, Michael Harner, then Associate Professor of Anthropology at the New School for Social Research in New York, was invited by the American Museum of Natural History to study the Conibo Indians of the Peruvian Amazon. He accepted, set off the following year and quickly established a close rapport with the Indians. His interest went beyond academic anthropology, however, since he wished to experience at first hand what it was like to be a **shaman**. In order to achieve this, he drank a potion concocted from the 'soul vine' *ayahuasca* and was plunged into a visionary experience which included a giant crocodile and a dragon-headed ship. (*See* **Astral Plane**.)

Since then, Harner has become one of the world's leading authorities on shamanism and has studied among the Coast Salish, Jivaro, Lakota Sioux, Pomo, and Wintun peoples. On the academic front he has been a visiting professor at Columbia, Yale and the University of California.

Professor Harner, who has published a number of books including *The Jivaro, Hallucinogens and Shamanism* and *The Way of the Shaman*, travels extensively to give workshops on shamanic development and **healing**.

Hasidism

A Jewish mystical movement drawing its name from the Hebrew *hasid*, meaning 'pious'. The movement was founded in eighteenth-century Poland by Eliezer Ba'al Shem Tov, who, as a firm believer in joyful service of God, conducted services noted for wild singing, dancing and drinking.

Ba'al Shem was himself an ecstatic who seemed to enter trance states during prayer, his body shaking like that of a primitive **shaman**. The movement he founded drew heavily on the doctrines of the **Qabalah** and survives today as a movement within mainstream **Judaism**.

Healing

There are many forms of healing which have been used throughout history – prayer, invocation, magical medicines, special foods, the projection of will and the laying on of hands. True healers act as a conduit for healing energy from a higher source of power. (*See also* **Psychic Healing**; **Psychic Surgery**.)

Hellerwork

Along with **Rolfing** and certain other forms of **bodywork**, Hellerwork shares the premise that physical and emotional traumas accumulate in the body over a person's lifetime, resulting in muscular rigidity and tension.

Such tensions can be broken down and the body restored to a more supple state via massage and physical manipulations, but Hellerwork goes further in that its clients are taught to link the problems arising in their bodies with problems arising in their lives, so that a therapeutic approach to one automatically influences the other.

Herbalism

Arguably the oldest form of medical practice, herbalism is enjoying an unprecedented revival of interest and practice. Part of this development has been occasioned by an increasing realization of the side-effects frequently caused by the use of drugs in conventional medical practice. Although not without its own dangers, herbalism – which makes use of natural plant extracts rather than chemicals – is much less prone to negative interactions and side-effects. It is also quite capable of achieving results where orthodox medicine has failed.

Hermetica

A body of magical doctrine, mainly Greek in origin, which includes elements of Christian **mysticism** alongside references to **healing** techniques related to pre-Christian deities like the Egyptian Thoth and Isis. The cornerstone of the Hermetica is the principle 'As above, so below'.

Central to the literature of the Hermetica is the figure of **Hermes Trismegistus** (Hermes the Thrice-Greatest), the Greek name for the Egyptian god, Thoth, the scribe of the gods and the inventor of writing and all the arts.

Not all of the Hermetica texts have survived, but those remaining have been the subject of several English-language translations, among the best of which is that published in 1906 by G.R.S. Mead. **C.G. Jung** found much of value in the Hermetic writings and drew on them in his work.

Hesse, Hermann

A major work written in the 1960s, *The Glass Bead Game*, earned author Herman Hesse the Nobel Prize, but it is the less well-known *Journey to the East* which probably gives greater insights into the man, since it is intrinsically a semi-autobiographical novel which details his own spiritual quest.

Hesse was essentially concerned with the conflict between caution and impulse, reason and instinct, intellect and emotion, social values and individual desires. Possibilities for resolving such conflicts are outlined in various of his works including his famous *Steppenwolf* and his *Siddhartha*, which describes the spiritual life of its hero in India at the time of the **Buddha**.

Hexagrams

Special figures comprising broken (**yin**) and unbroken (**yang**) lines used in *I Ching* **divination**.

Hidden Masters

In 1887, **Madame H.P. Blavatsky** published a peculiar two-volume book which was destined to become an unlikely best-seller. The book was called *Isis Unveiled* and claimed to be the 'master-key to the mysteries of ancient and modern science and theology'. It also claimed, as did Blavatsky's later work *The Secret Doctrine*, that the welfare of humanity was watched over and guided by an esoteric Brotherhood of Hidden Masters.

These Masters were described as superhuman beings with mystic powers hidden in the Himalayan fastness of Tibet. Blavatsky herself was supposed to have met them face to face, learned much of their ancient wisdom and, indeed, to have been chosen to break the news of their existence to the Western world.

In the latter task, Blavatsky was soon to be assisted by a newspaper editor in British India, Mr A.P. Sinnett, who began to publish letters written by two members of the mystic Brotherhood, outlining a world view that was at once mysterious and romantic.

Public interest in the Hidden Masters, which peaked with the growth of Blavatsky's Theosophical Society, was to prove remarkably enduring. A compilation of the letters to Sinnett appeared in book form as late as 1923 and has proven commercially viable over multiple editions ever since.

The Blavatsky/Sinnett Hidden Masters were very definitely a part of the Eastern Esoteric Tradition, accepted more or less as Blavatsky portrayed them by those interested in such matters throughout the Orient. There is, however, a **Western Esoteric Tradition**, rooted in the **Qabalah**, which propounds a remarkably similar doctrine.

This teaching first became public knowledge in Renaissance times with the distribution of a pamphlet entitled the *Fama Fraternitatis* describing the existence of a secret 'Rosicrucian Brotherhood' comprising occult adepts who were subtly guiding the destinies of Europe.

The concept of Hidden Masters was further extended in the mid-nineteenth century with the formation of the Hermetic Order of the **Golden Dawn**. One of its most colourful leaders was the eccentric Victorian author and scholar, **S.L. MacGregor Mathers**, who first announced that behind the mundane structures of the Order stood certain Secret Chiefs from whom he received his instructions. These instructions concerned the running of the Order and what doctrines it propounded.

Apart from the fact that they were not (necessarily) Tibetan, the Secret Chiefs, as described by Mathers, seem more or less identical to Blavatsky's Hidden Masters. They were adept in the occult arts, interested in the welfare of humanity and intervened subtly to guide the evolution of the human race. Like Blavatsky, Mathers insisted on the physical reality of his Secret Chiefs. On one occasion he claimed to have met two of them on a train.

But he also held that many, perhaps most, of these super-beings spent much of their lives in **spirit** form and only occasionally incarnated for special missions.

Although there are lodges of the Golden Dawn in America and New Zealand to the present day, the British aspect of the organization went into a serious decline about the turn of the present century and was more or less defunct by the end of the First World War. The Western Esoteric Tradition was, however, carried forward by a new organization in Britain called the Society of the Inner Light, founded by a former Golden Dawn initiate called Violet Penry-Evans, more often known by her pen-name, **Dion Fortune**. Like Blavatsky and Mathers, Dion Fortune insisted on the existence of Hidden Masters (whom she called **Inner Plane Adepti**) and claimed her own society was ultimately run by them.

Dion Fortune stated openly that her Inner Plane Adepti included both Blavatsky's Hidden Masters and Mathers' Secret Chiefs (that is to say she claimed the same entities who had communicated with Blavatsky and Mathers were among those who were now communicating with her). She felt, however, that the natural habitat of the Masters was the **astral plane** and several other even more spiritual environments and that they seldom took on physical bodies any more.

At first, Dion Fortune's society used trance **medium**s, similar to Spiritualist mediums, in order to talk to the Masters, but later a special breed of **psychic**, called a 'mediator', was developed. Mediators were individuals, usually women, with the special ability of seeing into the astral plane. Since they did not go into trance, the messages they brought back from the Hidden Masters were supposed to be less subject to distortion.

Several other organizations claim to be 'contacted' i.e. to function under the guidance of one or more Hidden Masters.

Higher Self

The interlaced triangles of the *megan David* on the flag of Israel have an esoteric symbolism unsuspected by many residents of that country. In its occult form, the symbol (referred to in medieval times as the Seal of Solomon) displays each triangle in a different colour and is interpreted as representing the Higher Self intermingled with the mundane nature in the perfectly balanced and evolved individual.

The concept of a Higher Self is commonplace in esoteric thought (where it is frequently linked with the theory of **reincarnation**) and not all that rare in religion either, where it is often thought of as conscience or the god within.

Manly P. Hall once stated, 'Suicide thwarts the plan of the entity which sends out the personality.' When asked about reincarnation, the **spirit guide** Silver Birch remarked, 'There is reincarnation, but not in the same sense in which it is generally expounded. There is in our (spirit) world a spiritual diamond which has many, many facets. These come into your world to gain experience and to add their quota to the diamond's lustre and brilliance. Thus the personalities that are incarnated are facets of the one individuality.' In the opening of his book *Past Lives*, John van Auken writes, 'The idea that you and I have reincarnated is somewhat of a misconception. The "you" and "I" that we consider to be our normal, everyday selves has actually not reincarnated. However, there is an inner part of us that has been alive before. This part has incarnated in the Earth's dimension many times.'

Hall's 'entity which sends out the personality', Silver Birch's spiritual diamond and Aukin's 'inner part' are all examples of the Higher Self. **Ralph Waldo Emerson** referred to it as the Oversoul and claimed it existed 'before Time'.

Interestingly, there is a growing body of evidence within orthodox psychology for the existence of a Higher Self. In examining a cousin who exhibited symptoms of multiple personality while in trance, **Carl Jung** noted that one was far more mature, intelligent and developed than the woman's waking personality. Such a phenomenon is commonplace in cases of multiple personality and some psychologists are beginning to suspect it is present, in a non-pathological sense, in us all. Dr Eric Berne's **Transactional Analysis**, for example, structures the psyche into three differing types of 'self' which emerge in relation to current circumstance. The author **Colin Wilson**, driven to the edge of a breakdown through overwork, became aware of an extensive hierarchy of selves presided over by a mature and powerful entity which could be persuaded to 'take charge' by an act of will.

Hildegard of Bingen

A twelfth-century German abbess who was known as 'the Sibyl of the Rhine' because of her visions and prophecies which occurred throughout her life. In spite of poor physical health, she was a remarkable woman, founding two convents, getting involved in ecclesiastical politics, travelling long distances in the pursuit of her duties and writing hymns and a herbal. She died in 1179.

Hinduism

One of the world's greatest and in many ways most subtle religions, Hinduism is the product of an ancient wisdom almost certainly rooted in the mystical experiences of its founders, the semi-legendary Vedic Sages.

Although, like most religions, degenerate in its everyday practice, the stamp of **mysticism** is clearly evident in the fundamental precepts of Hinduism. It teaches an ultimate Unity behind the multiplicity of manifest appearance, personified in the deity figure of Brahma, about which all speculation is futile. It encourages the practice of **yoga**, the various Indian systems of which were almost exclusively Hindu developments. And the ultimate aim of the individual practitioner is openly defined as mystical transcendence.

Against this mystical background, there are several interesting and important overlays. Despite the ultimate Unity of Brahma, Hinduism has developed for practical purposes a vast pantheon of gods and populated the universe with an even larger multitude of **spirit**s and devils.

Of the various deities, the two which stand supreme under Brahma are Vishnu the Preserver and Shiva the Destroyer. The Brahma-Vishnu-Shiva triad has, in its abstract essence, much in common with the ancient Chinese concept of **Tao** manifesting in the complementary forces of **yin** and **yang**.

Fundamental to the practice of Hinduism are the interlocked beliefs of **karma** and **reincarnation**. The latter is held to be such an absolute that even gods reincarnate. (The great hero Krishna was believed to be an incarnation of Vishnu.)

A great many Hindu concepts are familiar to, and accepted by, followers of **Buddhism**, which stands in almost exactly the same relationship to Hinduism as **Christianity** does to **Judaism**.

Holographic Theory

Deriving from holography (three-dimensional photography by laser, whereby any part of the holographic plate can be used to reproduce the whole image), holographic theory postulates that as well as a whole containing parts, the parts also contain the whole. **David Bohm** has developed a theoretical model of the universe as holographic while **Karl Pribram** has applied holographic theory to his study of the brain. The holographic **paradigm** is an attractive one to those who subscribe to alternate realities and makes sense of the paradoxical sayings of mystics.

Holy Grail

Although the Holy Grail is usually referred to as the cup used by Jesus Christ at the Last Supper, there are clear indications that the myths and legends which encrust this mystical vessel are substantially older than the advent of Christ himself.

The fundamental Grail legend tells of a knight who journeys through a wasteland until he reaches a magnificent but eerie castle. Entering the building, he meets its master, the mysterious *Rex Piscator* or 'Fisher King', a crippled, wounded monarch who invites him to a sumptuous feast. The knight accepts and during the feast sees a magic sword, a bloodstained lance and, finally, the Grail itself, carried in procession.

The knight is then challenged to ask a question. If he finds the correct question, the Fisher King is healed and the wasteland restored to fertility. If not, calamities follow.

Various forms of this story are incorporated in the myth cycles of **Arthurian legend** and related by early (and even some modern) historians to the belief that the Holy Grail was carried from Palestine to Britain by Joseph of Arimathea and hidden at or near **Glastonbury**. But there is a difficulty with this in that the Grail of the Fisher King is not always described as a cup. It sometimes appears as a dish, a ciborium, a stone or even a cauldron.

Modern analysis of the story suggest links not with the Last Supper, but with pre-Christian Celtic mythology which tells of many similar feasts and many similar vessels, some of which conferred immortality or raised the dead. The Fisher King is equated not with Christ (who told his disciples he would make them 'fishers of men') but with Bran the Blessed, who appears in the *Mabinogion*.

Scholars believe the myth reflects the very ancient belief that the fertility of a land depends on the strength, behaviour and, in particular, the sexual potency of its ruler. Various versions of the legend indicate the Fisher King's wound was genital.

Whatever the source of the legend, there is little doubt that the real importance of the Holy Grail is its mythic power – that is to say, its ability to fascinate the human mind. Because of this, several modern esoteric schools and many more solitary occultists have used the myth as a **pathworking** designed to lead closer to enlightenment.

Home, Daniel Dunglas

Something bizarre happened in the home of Connecticut silk manufacturer Ward Cheney in August 1852. Cheney, who was interested in the Spiritualist movement sweeping the country at the time, had organized a séance for a few of his close friends and called on the services of a 19-year-old **medium** who, despite his youth, was supposed to be able to produce the **spirit** rappings which characterized such meetings.

But as the séance got underway, one of the participants, *Hartford Times* editor F.L. Burr, reported that suddenly, without any expectation on the part of the company, the medium was taken up in the air.

'I had hold of his hand at the time,' Burr stated afterwards, 'and I felt his feet – they were lifted a foot from the floor. He palpitated from head to foot with the contending emotions of joy and fear which choked his utterances. Again and again he was taken from the floor, and the third time he was carried to the ceiling of the apartment, with which his hands and feet came into gentle contact.'

The medium in question was Daniel Dunglas Home. The séance described was the first at which he levitated, but not the last.

Home was born in Scotland in 1833, but emigrated with his aunt to Connecticut in 1842. His curious abilities seem to have manifested early, for the family had him exorcised as a boy following an outbreak of **poltergeist** activity. Fortunately the **exorcism** failed and Home grew up to become one of the most famous mediums of all time.

Unlike many of his contemporaries, he held his séances in full light and refused, throughout his entire life, to charge a fee. The range of his associated phenomena was enormous. Along with the usual raps and noises, he could make tables and chairs move of their own accord, materialize spirit hands, play musical instruments without touching them and handle red-hot coals without injury.

Not everyone approved of his activities. The Roman Catholic Church expelled him for 'sorcery' in 1864 and Robert Browning lampooned him in his poem, *Mr Sludge the Medium*. For all this, Home was never caught cheating and, more positively, was pronounced genuine after tests by the noted psychical researcher Sir William Crookes. His most spectacular feat was another **levitation** in 1868, when he had mastered the trick of defying gravity at will. Three witnesses at the London home of Lord Adare watched him float out of one third-storey window and in another.

Home produced two books on his abilities and the phenomena of **Spiritualism** before his death in 1886.

Homoeopathy

An alternative therapy now so widely accepted as valid that it has almost become part of Establishment medical practice, homoeopathy stands traditional theory on its head with its insistence that like should be used to cure like.

The system was developed by the German doctor Samuel Hahnemann (1755–1843) who came to believe that drugs and even poisons which caused certain symptoms when ingested could be used to cure diseases showing those same symptoms if administered in tiny doses. The belief was based on the idea, now widely accepted, that disease resulted primarily from an imbalance in the body.

Hahnemann experimented with such deadly toxins as aconite and strychnine, but used a technique known as 'potentizing' to create dosages so minute that not a single molecule of the original substance could be chemically detected in the actual medicine. When his system worked, he concluded he was actually stimulating the body to call upon its own substantial reserves of **healing**.

Because of its effectiveness, homoeopathy is now practised world-wide and continues to gain popularity since it avoids many of the side-effects associated with more orthodox drug usage.

Horned God

Consort of the **Goddess** in **witchcraft**, the Horned God is often associated with the Celtic Cernunnos and represents the balancing male principle in what is essentially a feminine religion. There are fairly obvious links with the classical Pan, who signified the totality of Nature, but historically the orthodox Christian Churches have required little more than the horns and their traditional antipathy to witchcraft in order to equate the Horned God directly with Satan.

Houston, Jean

Jean Houston is one of the best-known names in the field of **transpersonal psychology**. As Director of the Foundation for Mind Research in Pomona, New York, she has spent many years researching the development of human potential. Her training programmes in spiritual studies are modelled on the ancient **Mystery cults**. She is particularly interested in the role of myth in shaping **consciousness**. Her most recent books are *The Possible Human*, *The Search for the Beloved* and *The Hero and the Goddess*.

HPB

See **Madame Blavatsky**.

Human Potential Movement

Increasing dissatisfaction with **Freud**ian theory and a variety of existing psychological models led to the development in America of a vital new movement known as **humanistic psychology**, which sought to expand the perceptions of the human psyche held by the more orthodox systems.

Under the dynamic leadership of **Abraham Maslow**, humanistic psychologists preferred the study of healthy individuals to the pathological studies on which many earlier psychologies were founded. A holistic approach was taken with emphasis on personal growth, self-actualization, the recognition of human potential and a focus on experience as distinct from intellectual analysis. Other key figures were **Carl Rogers**, **Fritz Perls**, **Roberto Assagioli**, Virginia Satir, Ira Progoff and **Jean Houston**. The term 'human potential' was first used at **Esalen** (the first major growth centre in the USA) in 1962.

Numerous new psychotherapies and **bodywork** schools have been developed, now collectively referred to as the human potential movement.

Humanistic Psychology
The third force in psychology (psychoanalysis being the first, behaviourism the second, and **transpersonal psychology** the fourth). The pioneer figure in its emergence was **Abraham Maslow**. In 1949 Anthony Sutich and Maslow agreed to work together on developing a psychology which would deal with the healthy human being. Humanistic psychology deals with personal growth, existential choice and the fulfilment of human potential.

Humphreys, Christmas
Lawyer and judge known in his lifetime as the 'Dean of English **Buddhism**'. He founded the Buddhist Society, the West's oldest, most respected organization of its kind, in 1929.

Huna
The native religion of the Hawaiian islands, outlawed, suppressed, but not entirely obliterated following the arrival of Christian missionaries in 1820.

Max Freedom Long, the leading twentieth-century investigator of Huna, believed it to contain a very potent system of ancient **magic** based on a highly sophisticated model of the human psyche. Practitioner Kahunas, the 'Keepers of the Secret', were able to cure or curse, develop immunity to fire, see and change the future and even raise the dead by application of the ancient methods.

Extravagant though the claims for Huna might seem, Kahuna doctrines of twin souls and a **spirit** as the essential inner structure of humanity continue to be studied and there seems substantial evidence to suggest that the few Kahuna initiates remaining on the islands still exhibit unusual psychic powers.

Hundredth Monkey

An old folk-tale tells how a monkey, captured and placed in a cage, was unable to get out. As were a second, third and fourth monkey incarcerated with him. But the number of captured monkeys increased until, with the arrival of the hundredth monkey, the cage burst asunder and all escaped.

The original moral of the tale may have been that while the individual alone is almost powerless, a group acting together can break through the strongest bonds. But it has increasingly been applied to the weird phenomenon of critical mass information transfer through animal and perhaps even human species.

The phenomenon was first noticed in Britain when, in 1952, dairies began to deliver milk in bottles with foil caps. (Until then milk bottles had been sealed with cardboard.) *Parus caeruleus*, the blue tit, soon discovered it was possible to peck through the foil and drink the cream. The discovery by these little birds was made in London and spread steadily through the south of England.

At first the spread was at a pace which could be explained in perfectly mundane terms. The habit was growing in relation to observation: one tit would see another pecking at a milk bottle top and copy the technique. But then, in 1955, a quantum leap occurred. Suddenly all of the blue tits and most of the great tits throughout Europe could do the trick. The number of birds with the knowledge had reached critical mass, producing an explosion of the relevant information throughout the species. The scientist **Rupert Sheldrake** coined a name to describe the phenomenon. He called it **morphic resonance**.

Huxley, Aldous

Aldous Huxley was almost blind when he ingested mescaline in the early 1950s and the intense visionary experiences it produced had a profound impact on the direction of his personal philosophy.

Huxley, who was born in 1894, was already an internationally respected novelist and essayist, noted for his social and political insights, when he became interested in Eastern philosophy, **mysticism**, alternative medicine, psychical research and altered states of **consciousness**. In 1952, he wrote the definitive study of the diabolic possession of seventeenth-century nuns in the Ursuline Convent at Loudun, in France, and his book *The Devils of Loudun* subsequently formed the basis of the Ken Russell film *The Devils*.

His ideas on the nature of psychedelic experience and mysticism are contained in two essays, *The Doors of Perception* and *Heaven and Hell*. He described and analysed his mescaline visions, relating them to the development of the religious impulse in humanity. Huxley believed that the brain was a reducing valve for something he called 'mind at large' ensuring that in normal consciousness we are only able to sense such information as is useful for physical survival. Certain drugs like mescaline and certain practices like fasting, **yoga** and even self-mortification, reduced the efficiency of the brain as a filter, allowing a much wider perception of reality to flood through.

Aldous Huxley died in 1963.

Hypnosis

It is still possible – indeed fairly easy – to find reference works which refer to the eighteenth century's **Franz Anton Mesmer** as an early exponent of hypnosis. In fact, he was nothing of the sort. Mesmer, who believed he was using a mysterious force he called 'animal magnetism', induced violent convulsions in his patients far distant from the passive trance known as hypnosis today.

But if Mesmer never practised hypnosis, the phenomenon seems to have been discovered or, more properly, rediscovered by one of his followers, the Marquis de Puységeur. The Marquis was attempting to 'magnetize' a peasant using Mesmer's technique when the man fell into what appeared to be a profound sleep. The state bore no resemblance to the familiar Mesmeric crisis, but de Puységeur soon discovered it had its own benefits: notably the fact that the subject was hyper-susceptible to suggestion.

James Braid, a nineteenth-century medical practitioner of the art also noticed the similarity of the trance state to sleep and coined the word *hypnotism* (from the Greek *hypnos* meaning 'sleep') to describe it. The name stuck, despite the fact that later research showed the hypnotic trance has nothing in common with sleep. Subjects do not even lose **consciousness**, although they often suffer from post-hypnotic amnesia which leads them to believe that they had lost consciousness.

While the techniques of hypnosis have been known and used for millennia – it seems to have been practised in Ancient Greece and Egypt and, even earlier, in Ancient India – any genuine understanding of the phenomenon remains elusive.

An older, more descriptive, term for hypnosis is *mekhenesis*, meaning 'the taking away of responsibility', which pin-points one of the most important characteristics of the trance state. When someone is placed under hypnosis, their responsibility for their actions is removed and placed in the hands of the hypnotist.

This is a disturbing situation which has created its own mythology. It is often alleged that hypnotized subjects can never be made to do anything that runs contrary to their moral principles. The allegation is based on a frequently-quoted story about Charcot, one of the founding fathers of modern psychology.

According to this story, Charcot was demonstrating hypnosis to a group of male students with an extremely attractive young woman as his subject. Charcot had placed her in trance when a message arrived calling him away to attend to some urgent business. He passed control of the subject to an assistant and left the lecture hall. The assistant promptly commanded the young woman to remove all her clothes. Her eyes flicked open, she emerged at once from trance and slapped his face.

In his *Sense and Nonsense in Psychology*, Professor H.J. Eysenck remarks that, 'There are many observations of this kind to be found in the experimental literature and it may be said with a reasonable degree of confidence that in many cases an *explicit suggestion to do something unethical or immoral will not be carried out by the subject.*'

But research has shown that with a little imagination, a deeply hypnotized subject can be made to do just about anything, so long as the suggestion given is *not* explicit. A straightforward command while the subject is in trance will be obeyed, provided it is properly framed.

This has been clearly shown in an experiment involving a 20-year-old army private with an excellent service record. He was hypnotized while several senior personnel looked on. One of them, a lieutenant-colonel, was placed directly in front of him, about ten feet away. It was then suggested that when he opened his eyes he would see 'a dirty Jap soldier'. This soldier, he was told, had a bayonet in his hand. The subject was urged to 'strangle him with your bare hands'.

In a moment the subject opened his eyes and began very slowly to move forward. Then he launched himself in a flying tackle and brought the lieutenant-colonel crashing to the floor. He then knocked the officer against a wall and tried to strangle him. Three people were required to pull him off.

An even more disturbing experiment was carried out in the early 1950s. Here subjects were shown the destructive power of nitric acid when a penny was thrown into a bowl of the liquid and disintegrated. They were then placed in trance and instructed to throw the acid into the face of an assistant.

For obvious reasons, a substitute was made for the actual acid. While the subject was distracted, the experimenters put in its place a similar bowl of water to which methylene blue and barium peroxide had been added. The mixture resulted in an impressively boiling liquid indistinguishable from the real thing.

Direct orders to throw the acid resulted in the same sort of rejection suffered by Charcot's assistant. But the experimenters quickly discovered they could persuade subjects to take violent action. One entranced woman was, for example, told that the assistant was a murderer who was coming to kill her child. She threw the 'acid'.

Individual reactions to hypnosis vary enormously. One measure of this variation is something called the Eysenck-Furneaux Scale, based on how often a particular suggestion was accepted within a large group of hypnotic subjects.

The scale runs from simple fundamental suggestions like those of tired eyes or complete relaxation, which are accepted in 76 per cent of cases, all the way through to suggestions which create the illusion of an electric bulb lighting up, something successfully achieved in only 12 per cent of cases. Scientists often refer to a fivefold categorization of hypnotic reactions as follows:

Insusceptible
Here subjects show a total lack of response to suggestion. They may be perfectly willing to be hypnotized, but the technique simply does not work.

Hypnoidal
This category is characterized by relaxation, some fluttering of the eyelids usually followed by actual closing of the eyes. Subjectively the body feels heavy.

Light Trance
It is now virtually impossible for subjects to open their eyes or

move their limbs without specific instructions to do so. Suggestions of rigidity are readily accepted and it is possible to induce 'glove anaesthesia' in which no pain can be felt in the hands.

Medium Trance

At this level spontaneous amnesia arises – a partial or total inability to remember what happened during trance. Subjects may be persuaded to undergo temporary personality changes and will react to simple post-hypnotic suggestions, including post-hypnotic anaesthesia.

Deep Trance

Deep trance is characterized by subjects' ability to open their eyes without affecting the trance, the acceptance of bizarre and complex post-hypnotic suggestions, including post-hypnotic hallucination, auditory hallucinations and selective directed post-hypnotic amnesia.

Statistical analysis caused Professor Eysenck to suggest that about 15 per cent of the population are insusceptible, 40 per cent can achieve either light trance or the hypnoidal state, 25 per cent reach medium trance and 20 per cent are capable of going all the way to deep trance.

Hypnotherapy

The use of hypnosis as a curative agent has a long, but somewhat chequered history. The ability of hypnosis to control pain is so dramatic that the technique was originally used as an anaesthetic in surgical operations, but largely abandoned following the discovery of ether. In recent years, however, hypnosis has been making a comeback in this area since its use with suitable patients substantially reduces incidences of post-operative shock and bleeding.

Freud used hypnosis extensively in his early psychiatric practice, although he largely abandoned it in later years in favour of psychoanalysis. It is still used fairly extensively in psychiatry, however, as an aid to relaxation and a door to the unconscious. Many forms of hysterical illness react directly to suggestion.

But one of the most promising areas of investigation is undoubtedly the use of hypnosis as a therapy in purely physical illnesses. It has long been recognized that hypnosis can get rid of warts, a virus ailment, and help in various other types of skin condition. This has led to cautious experimentation in other forms of illness, with at least some evidence to suggest hypnosis may be useful even in severe maladies like cancer.

I

I Ching

The Chinese *I Ching*, sometimes claimed to be the oldest book in the world, is a process of **divination** which has somehow avoided the stigma of fortune-telling and become, even to a great many Western scholars, a system of profound philosophy. Once the province of an élite intellectual few outside China, the *I Ching* has become one of the most widely studied branches of Chinese esoteric practice.

The basic principle of the *I Ching*, the subdivision of phenomena into negative and positive forces called **yin** and **yang**, is an aspect of Chinese thought dating from the furthest reaches of prehistory. Technically, the **oracle** professes to read the current state of yin and yang through the development of six-lined figures known as **hexagrams**.

I Ching Hexagrams

The hexagrams themselves have a long, if somewhat disreputable, history in that they sprang from a very ancient form of fortune-telling: the tortoise-shell **oracle**. In China, from a time dating back literally into prehistory, tortoise-shells were heated until they cracked and the patterns interpreted as indicators of the future or answers to specific questions.

In time the cracks became stylized into three-lined figures, known as *trigrams*, which were composed of broken (*yin*) and unbroken (*yang*) lines. Diviners eventually began to study trigram patterns in their own right, divorced from the original tortoise-shell **rituals**.

Some time prior to 1150 BC (actual dates in ancient Chinese history are notoriously uncertain) a provincial noble named Wen fell foul of the Emperor, who had him thrown into prison. The essential problem seems to have been Wen's personal popularity. Rulers then, as now, had a sharp eye for prospective rivals.

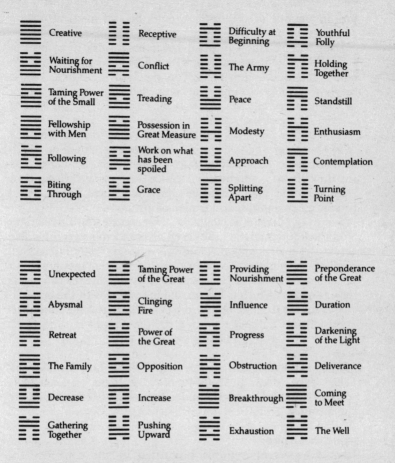

Wen turned to intellectual pursuits in prison and began to assign definitive meanings to the trigrams already in wide use for **divination**. But he broke with tradition in a highly creative development by combining them into six-lined figures (*hexagrams*) and adding his own brief commentary, called a *Judgement*, to each.

On his release from jail, Wen led a rebellion which overthrew the Emperor. He himself died before he could seize the throne, but his son, the Duke of Chou, consolidated the victory to found a new dynasty. Scholars have tended to award Wen the postumous title of king, even though he was never actually a sovereign in his own lifetime.

The Duke of Chou finished his father's work in respect of something even more important than his military adventure. He added his own commentaries on the individual lines of the newly-created hexagrams. The completed work became known as *The Changes of Chou* (*Chou I*) or, more simply, *The Book of Changes* (a literal translation of *I Ching*).

Even at this stage, the work had really ceased to be simply a method of fortune-telling and become a profoundly philosophical tome masquerading as a system of divination. The metamorphosis continued centuries later when **Confucius**, already an old man when he came upon the *I Ching*, added further commentaries and explanations.

The work contains a total of 64 hexagrams, each of which has a different interpretation. But each *line* of each hexagram is also capable of interpretation. Lines are, however, only interpreted when it is thought they contain such 'tension' that they are about to change into their opposites. Once they do so, they produce a new hexagram which is interpreted in context with the original.

This means that the oracle is capable of delivering more than 4,000 answers without repeating itself.

Ichazo, Oscar

Modern Chilean **guru** championed by **John Lilly** in his book *Centre of the Cyclone* and founder of **Arica**. Ichazo's teaching has similarities with **Gurdjieff**'s and is supposedly derived from the same source.

Implicate Order

Central aspect of a thesis postulated by the contemporary physicist **David Bohm** who argues that quantum theory, while offering little enough direct explanation for the behaviour of matter at a macroscopic level, has provided one vital insight: that fragmentation is purely illusory and reality can best be understood as a whole, which changes all the time.

Bohm uses the analogy of the hologram to describe his insight, based on the fact that each part of a hologram contains the whole. (If light shines on any part of a hologram, the whole of the image is reconstructed.) Bohm believes the universe is similarly structured, with the whole enfolded in each of its parts.

At subatomic levels, however, he accepts that the holographic analogy is limited by its static nature and has coined the term 'holomovement' to describe his postulate of a dynamic phenomenon out of which all forms of the material universe flow. The excitement the suggestion has engendered is occasioned by the fact that this approach aims to study the structure of movement rather than matter, thus allowing for the possibility of progress in a new direction at a time when traditional subnuclear physics seemed to have reached the end of a cul-de-sac.

Initiation

Although frequently corrupted into little more than an outward ceremonial show, initiation is essentially an individual transformation which involves a transition from one level of awareness and development to another.

Initiatory **ritual**s, designed to stimulate such transformations, have been a feature of human culture from earliest times, ranging from the initiations at puberty in primitive societies all the way to the elaborate ceremonial initiations of **Freemasonry** or the **Golden Dawn**.

Most occultists believe, however, that the only really worthwhile initiations are inward, often occurring in mystical or visionary experiences which induce changes in the character, outlook or abilities of the individual.

Inner Plane Adepti

These are superhuman entities, manifesting on the **astral plane** (although usually held to have their real existence in even more remote dimensions) in order to guide the evolution of humanity through occult contacts. (*See* **Hidden Masters**.)

Intuition

Intuition is generally defined as knowledge arrived at spontaneously, without conscious steps of reasoning or inquiry. The keyword here is *conscious*, for it may be that the talent derives from a logical process of which we are consciously unaware. But many experts remain wary of this explanation since it runs contrary to what we know of the general workings of the unconscious mind.

Some psychologists, however, attribute intuition to thought processes too fast to be recognized. According to this theory, numerous minimal cues may be rapidly integrated, making possible conclusions without any apparent intermediate steps.

An alternative explanation put forward is that intuition is the result of a special ability, or sympathy with the object under consideration – something almost akin to a **psychic** talent. Some philosophers claim that certain phenomena can be understood only by intuition, that is to say, grasped directly without intervention of rational thought processes.

Iridology

A diagnostic system which relies on close examination of the iris of the eye, portions of which are believed to correspond with various internal organs. Iridologists claim that the whole body is reflected in the eye because this is where the entire nervous system comes to the surface. With the spread of iridology practice, there has been increasing scientific interest, but early tests to establish the validity of the system have not proved encouraging.

Isis Unveiled

A two-volume work in which **Madame Blavatsky** introduced the concept of a secret tradition of Oriental wisdom to an enthusiastic Western audience.

Islam

The name of the religion means 'submission [to God]', so that a Moslem surrenders himself unconditionally to the divine will. Tradition regards Islam as a more perfect revelation to mankind than that given to the Jews or Christians. The all-embracing law of Islam covers all facets of human activity, and inner faith is seen as leading to the performance of the external duties of Islam.

J

Jainism

A religion of India, its adherents tracing their history back to the life and work of Mahavira. The Jains have maintained strict vegetarianism, stemming from their cardinal doctrine of *ahimsa*, non-violence. Mahatma Gandhi was influenced by their doctrine and practice.

James, William

An American psychologist whose *Varieties of Religious Experience*, published in 1902, still remains a classic in its field, William James stands out as a man clearly ahead of his time. Born in 1842, his activities throughout a 68-year lifespan would seem more typical of the psychedelic sixties than the Victorian era.

James experimented with nitrous oxide, which he believed to be a chemical key to mystical **consciousness**. He was a founder member of the American Society for Psychical Research in 1884. He tested Spiritualist **medium**s, notably the famous Leonore Piper, whom he considered genuine. He accepted ghosts and hauntings, but considered them natural phenomena for which science had not yet found an explanation.

But it was his fascination with trance states and mystical experience for which he is best remembered. He stressed individual evolution and many of his views on personal growth have exercised a profound influence on the **human potential movement**.

William James died in 1910.

St John of the Cross

Born in 1542, not far from Avila in Spain, St John of the Cross entered the Carmelite Order and became the devoted companion of **St Teresa of Avila**.

Controversy over reform within the Carmelite Order resulted

in his being flogged and imprisoned. This was a decisive factor in his development as a mystic, for it was in prison at Toledo that he began to write his famous mystical poems. He escaped from Toledo and went on to write four great prose works: *The Ascent of Mount Carmel*, *The Dark Night of the Soul*, *The Spiritual Canticle* and *The Living Flame of Love*.

With scientific precision, St John of the Cross teaches absolute detachment and absolute love. He has been called 'the mystic's mystic'.

Judaism

The religion of the Jewish people in the period following the destruction of the second Temple in Jerusalem by the Romans in 70 AD. There was a shift in emphasis from Temple cult to a religion of the home and synagogue. The role of the priest virtually disappeared. The Torah is considered a teaching of divine origin and the commandments of God contained therein determine Jewish norms and extend into every aspect of the life of the individual and the community. The belief in one god who will send a messiah to usher in the redemption, who judges man's actions and who rewards and punishes is essential to Jewish faith.

Julian of Norwich

Born in 1342, Dame Julian is the most approachable of the medieval English mystics, because of her simplicity and joyousness. In her book the *Revelations of Divine Love* she describes her visions of both the suffering and glorifying of Christ. Her most famous lines are 'all shall be well, and all shall be well, and all manner of things shall be well'.

Jung, C.G.

It is a curious fact that the fundamental infrastructure of Jungian psychology which, with the work of **Freud** and Adler, represents the underpinning of almost all our ideas about the human mind was revealed to Jung in a dream.

In this dream, he was in a two-storey house which he somehow knew to be his own. The upper storey was a kind of salon furnished in rococo style with some fine paintings on the walls. It seemed a pleasant place to live, but Jung realized suddenly he did not know what the other storey was like.

He descended the stairs and reached the ground floor. There he discovered everything was much older, in a style dating to the fifteenth or sixteenth century. The floors were red brick, the furnishings medieval, and everywhere was rather dark.

As he continued to explore, he happened on a heavy door. He opened it and found a descending stairway. This took him into a beautifully-vaulted chamber with walls of stone block and brick. The architectural style convinced him this portion of the house must be Roman. He examined the stone slab floor and in one of the slabs discovered a ring.

'When I pulled it, the stone slab lifted,' Jung wrote in his autobiography *Memories, Dreams, Reflections,* 'and again I saw a stairway of narrow stone steps leading down into the depths. These too I descended and entered a low cave cut into the rock. Thick dust lay on the floor and in the dust were scattered bones and broken pottery, like remains of a primitive culture. I discovered two human skulls, obviously very old and half disintegrated. Then I awoke.'

On this dream Jung founded what was to become the second most influential model of the human mind (after Freud's classical Ego, Id, Superego, conscious and subconscious subdivisions) and a model still extremely popular with intellectuals and mystics.

'It was plain to me that the house represented a kind of image of the psyche – that is to say of my then state of consciousness, with hitherto unconscious additions,' Jung wrote. 'Consciousness was represented by the salon. It had an inhabited atmosphere, in spite of its antiquated style. The ground floor stood for the first level of the unconscious. The deeper I went in, the more alien and darker the scene became. In the cave, I discovered remains of a primitive culture, that is, the world of the primitive man within myself – a world which can scarcely be reached or illuminated by consciousness. The primitive psyche of man borders on the life of the animal soul, just as the caves of prehistoric times were usually inhabited by animals before men laid claim to them.'

In that primitive bottom layer Jung found his most famous postulate – the **Collective Unconscious**, a stratum of mental patterns common to us all. Out of the Collective Unconscious came his theories of archetypes, his insights into **alchemy**, his fascination with symbols and much more.

Carl Jung was born in Kesswil, Switzerland in 1875. His father was a minister of religion, a fact which had substantial influence on Jung's own intellectual development. He studied medicine at Basle and Paris and worked for several years with the founder of modern psychology, Sigmund Freud, who, for a time, considered him his most likely intellectual successor.

But Jung's psychological make-up was that of a visionary. He experienced visitations from a discarnate entity he called Philemon which was capable of walking and talking with him in his garden. He had a waking dream of floods of blood shortly before Europe plunged into war. Towards the end of his life, when very ill, he had an **out-of-body experience** in which his consciousness left the planet. From childhood he had vivid, symbolic dreams.

For anyone with such a rich subjective life, Freud's insights must have seemed sterile. Jung's most famous disagreement with his mentor arose out of the importance Freud placed on sex. But it was not just the sexual doctrine which Jung cast aside. He threw away much of Freud's whole basic model of the mind and set out on a personal odyssey which took him into the realms of alchemy, mythology, folklore, **Gnosticism**, Oriental esotericism and even as far afield as **astrology** and the *I Ching*. An intellectual collaboration with the physicist Wolfgang Pauli produced one of his most curious theories, that of **synchronicity**, an acausal connecting principle postulated to exist in nature as the foundation of meaningful coincidences.

Jung was a prolific writer up to the time of his death in 1961. His impact on twentieth-century thought has been enormous.

K

Kabbalah/Kabbalist
See **Qabalah**.

Kabir
An Indian mystic, born in 1440, who developed a philosophy combining **Hinduism** and **Sufism**. During his lifetime he was strongly influenced by Guru Nanak, founder of the Sikhs.

Kabir, who is credited with the performance of several miracles, rejected the caste system completely, holding that mystical truth should be open to all. He died in 1518.

Kahuna
Literally, Keeper of the Secrets. A traditional Hawaiian doctor-priest-teacher, a practitioner of the **Huna** magico-religious system, who has mastered the various arts of **healing** and **prophecy**.

Kali Yuga
In Hindu and Buddhist mythology, the Dark Age which marks the ultimate degeneration of the human species. By the end of the *Kali Yuga*, it is believed that fire, drought and famine will ravage the Earth, piety will be dead and even the holy Brahmins will have come to neglect their devotions.

At this point, the final disaster will strike. A century of dearth will be the prelude to a drying up of all moisture, followed by a conflagration that will not only destroy the remnants of humanity, but the entire known universe.

What is left, according to Oriental theory, is Brahman, the uncreated unmanifest background from which all else springs. Following the universal destruction, the timeless cycle begins again with the emergence of a new golden age, the *Krita Yuga*. (*See also* **Yuga**.)

Karezza

Sexual intercourse in which orgasm is deliberately suppressed, sometimes as a form of birth control, but more often for mystical or magical purposes.

Karma

An Oriental doctrine related to **reincarnation** which teaches essentially that every thought and deed must eventually create its own effects, which must then be endured or enjoyed by the individual concerned.

In its more elaborate form, the doctrine refers to the 'Lords of Karma', divine beings responsible for maintaining the balance of cosmic debt, but Western notions of judgement are actually quite foreign to the thought processes which produced karmic theory.

On the personal level, an individual typically generates a 'burden of karma' (which may be good or bad) carried from one life to the next and worked out (repaid) over aeons of time until – particularly in **Buddhist** thought – enlightenment permits a situation in which no further karma, of any sort, is generated and the reserve is dissipated.

Kelley, Edward

Partner of Dr **John Dee** in numerous magical and alchemical experiments. Kelley, who had his ears cropped for coining, seems to have been a mixture of **psychic** and charlatan. He died a pauper and later reincarnated as **Aleister Crowley** . . . or so Crowley believed.

Thomas à Kempis

Born in 1380, Thomas à Kempis spent the greater part of his life at the monastery of Mount St Agnes in the Lowlands. Much of his time there was spent copying scriptural and devotional texts, but he was also a prolific author. His most famous work, the *Imitation of Christ*, is one of the greatest and most enduring classics of Christian devotional literature and has had a profound influence on many.

He died in 1471.

Keyes, Ken

In spite of having polio, Ken Keyes became a successful businessman, but he decided he wanted to discover the laws of happiness. He developed the Living Love method of personal growth to help people achieve fulfilment and happiness. His *Handbook to Higher Consciousness* has become a classic.

Kinesiology
From the Greek *kinesis*, 'motion'. Developed by the American chiropractor Dr George Goodheart, Kinesiology is a system of natural health care which combines muscle-testing with the principles of Chinese medicine to assess energy and body function. It uses a range of gentle yet powerful **healing** techniques to improve health and increase vitality. Whatever the symptoms, Kinesiology balances the body and puts it in the optimum state to heal itself. It is useful for everyday complaints.

Touch for Health is the system developed for non-professionals.

King, George
The founder of the **Aetherius Society**, George King is a British occultist guided, on his own claim, by the **spirit**s of several notable historical figures, including the psychical researcher, Sir Oliver Lodge. In 1954, at the age of 35, he was visited by a **yoga** adept, who told him he had been selected by the **Hidden Masters** to represent spirit in its coming battle with materialism. A basic tenet of the Aetherius Society, which he founded shortly afterwards, is that the Masters, including Jesus Christ, periodically visit humanity in flying saucers.

Kirlian Photography
When the Russian Professor of Engineering, Semyon Kirlian, visited Krasnodar hospital in 1939, he chanced to see a patient receiving treatment from a new high-frequency generator. As the electrodes were brought close to the patient's skin, there was a small flash. Kirlian recognized this as the type of flash which occurs as a gas is being charged by an electric spark and wondered what was being charged here, since no gas was present.

The problem intrigued him sufficiently to prompt an experiment. He and his wife Valentina set up two metal plates to act as electrodes and placed a photographic film on one of them. Then he put his hand between the plates and switched on a high-frequency current. When the film was developed, it showed Kirlian's hand surrounded by an **aura**.

It was the start of something very interesting indeed. The Kirlians used their new method of high-frequency electronic photography to make a great many pictures. Those which involved living tissue – even plant tissue like a leaf – showed sparks and flares of energy in patterns as dramatic as they were beautiful. A dead leaf showed nothing of these patterns.

Eerily, when a portion of a leaf was torn or cut away, Kirlian photography clearly showed a ghostly image of the missing piece.

What all this meant was anybody's guess and those doing the guessing were, for almost 40 years, all Soviets. Then two American travel writers, Sheila Ostrander and Lynn Schroeder, published a best-selling book entitled *Psychic Discoveries behind the Iron Curtain* which described the discovery and suddenly everybody in the West wanted to know more about Kirlian photography.

Everybody, that is, except the scientific establishment, which pointed out that similar effects had been recognized since the early years of the twentieth century. If a roll of film is connected to electricity lines, it will show distinctive tree-like patterns if there is a sudden surge in voltage: the patterns are known as Lichtenburg figures after their discoverer, Jiri Lichtenburg. Closer to the actual Kirlian technique, it was argued that since the voltage in any high-frequency condenser is far from constant, the ionization it causes is bound to show up as strange spots and flares on any photograph.

This was all very well except that more adventurous and open-minded research projects using Kirlian photographs of human volunteers soon showed that the aura effect varied in relation to a subject's mood and were influenced by personality interactions: the Kirlian auras of young men brightened when a pretty woman entered the room. One of the most dramatic results of the experiments was the discovery that subjects lit up like a Christmas tree moments after drinking a shot of vodka. (The experiments themselves were carried out in the United States. The choice of vodka, as opposed to, say, bourbon, seems to have been made in deference to the Russian origins of the Kirlian camera.)

Worse was to follow. Careful analysis of Kirlian photographs of the human body showed flares at precisely those points used for thousands of years in the practice of Chinese **acupuncture**. From there it was a short step to the discovery of a relationship between the strength of the Kirlian 'field' and health: illness showed up as a weakening in the aura, sometimes before physical symptoms manifested. In the Neuropsychiatric Institute at UCLA, California, the scientific team of Thelma Moss and Ken Johnson constructed Kirlian apparatus which showed energy flares emitted by the fingertips of faith healers as they exercised their art.

Work with Kirlian photography continues, with indications that it may yet add substantially to our knowledge of such subjects as the **etheric body**, life after death and **healing**.

Knight, Gareth

Pen-name of Basil Wilby, one of the better-known contemporary British Qabalists. Knight was, with **W.E. Butler**, instrumental in creating the Helios Course in Practical **Qabalah**, which was the foundation of the flourishing esoteric school, the **Servants of the Light**, and wrote several of the early lessons of the course.

As his personal development diverged from the path taken by SOL, he broke from the organization to establish his own esoteric school with emphasis on a more Christianized version of the Qabalah. He is the author of several books and numerous articles, but his masterwork undoubtedly remains his two-volume *Practical Guide to Qabalistic Symbolism*.

Knight, J.Z.

See **Ramtha**.

Koan

One of the best-known (and least understood) tools of **Zen Buddhism**, the essential *koan* is a brief statement in the form of a question or puzzle, the answer to which can only be discovered by direct perception rather than common sense or logical deduction.

Examples of koans are:

Two hands clapping make a sound. What is the sound of one hand clapping?
Should a tree fall in the forest with no-one and nothing to hear it, what noise does it make?

A goose is trapped in a narrow-necked bottle. How do you free the goose without killing it or breaking the glass? Answer: There – it's out!

Koestler, Arthur

The late Arthur Koestler was a significant political and scientific thinker. His books and numerous newspaper articles profoundly influenced intellectual opinion and were instrumental in popularizing what was essentially a mystical viewpoint.

Koestler was born in Budapest in 1905 and educated at the University of Vienna. He took up journalism as a career and became foreign correspondent for a number of German and British publications. During the Spanish Civil War he was captured by the Fascists, imprisoned and condemned to death.

During a lengthy incarceration, with his execution a constant threat, he underwent a mystical conversion which changed the entire course of his life. Part of his new insight was expressed in his essay, *The Yogi and the Commissar*, in which he argued that there were two essential psychological types: the 'Commissar' who believed the world should be changed by influencing others and the 'Yogi' who believed the world should be changed by influencing oneself.

British protests saved Koestler from execution and on his release he came to settle in Britain where he became one of the most interesting and dynamic personalities on the world literary scene. His novel *Darkness at Noon* was translated into 32 languages and possibly ranks with Orwell's *1984* as the most widely-read political novel of the century.

Alongside his work as a popularizer of science, Koestler became in later years profoundly interested in psychical research and anomalous phenomena, as testified by works like his *Roots of Coincidence* and the fact that on his death he endowed a Koestler Foundation established to encourage investigation of these areas.

Koran

Islam was based on the inspired readings which were revealed to Mohammed by the Archangel Gabriel while he was meditating in a cave on Mount Hira and which became the Koran.

Krishna, Gopi

In the winter of 1937, while meditating on his crown **chakra** in a small room of a little house on the outskirts of Jammu, Kashmir's winter capital, Gopi Krishna suddenly experienced a strange, intense and pleasant sensation at the base of his spine.

The sensation crept erratically upwards, disappearing when his attention went towards it, reappearing when he concentrated on the chakra above his head. Then suddenly, 'with a roar like that of a waterfall, I felt a stream of liquid light entering my brain through the spinal cord.' Although he did not know it at the time, Gopi Krishna had awakened **kundalini**.

It was an experience that came close to killing him.

> The illumination grew brighter and brighter, the roaring louder, I experienced a rocking sensation and then felt myself slipping out of my body, entirely enveloped in a halo of light . . . I felt the point of consciousness that was myself growing wider, surrounded by waves of light . . . I was now all consciousness, without any outline . . . I was no longer myself . . . but instead was a vast circle of consciousness in which the body was but a point, bathed in light and in a state of exaltation and happiness impossible to describe.

The exaltation did not last. When Krishna returned to normal **consciousness** he found himself weak and depressed, his thoughts out of control. After repeating the experience and triggering a permanent eruption of energy from the base of his spine, he found normal food had become toxic to him. Over a period of weeks he weakened and fell into a delirium from which he was convinced he would not recover.

At the point of death, a dream suggested the type of food he might eat – milk and a little well-boiled meat – but he discovered more importantly that it was the timing of his meals which mattered. His wife fed him each hour until gradually he regained his strength.

Gopi Krishna was unable to find any **guru** or yogi throughout the whole of India who could advise him on his condition. The pandits he visited quoted ancient texts but obviously had no real understanding of the situation. Everything Krishna discovered about the phenomenon was based on personal experience so that his book *Kundalini: the Evolutionary Energy in Man* is one of the most useful, not to say fascinating, accounts of kundalini.

Recently there has been more attention to the crises that can sometimes form part of spiritual awakening, and in the USA the Spiritual Emergence Network was set up in 1980 by Christina and **Stanislav Grof**.

Krishnamurti

In 1910, Jiddu Krishnamurti, the 15-year-old son of Brahmin parents, was in Adyar, India, when the strength of his **aura** caught the **psychic** eye of **C.W. Leadbeater**, the noted Theosophist. Leadbeater was so impressed that he persuaded his friend and colleague **Annie Besant** to join with him in adopting the boy.

Krishnamurti was carried off to England where he was intensively groomed as the next incarnation of Lord Maitreya, the new World Teacher. His own mystical organization, the Order of the Star of the East, was established for him and, as a teenage **guru** he quickly attracted thousands of followers.

The lifestyle did not agree with him. In 1929, he threw his hat at the whole sorry business, dissolved the Order and told his followers bluntly to find another guru since he had no spiritual authority whatsoever.

In its own way, this move was a genuine vindication of Besant and Leadbeater's conviction that they had found a most remarkable personality. Having repudiated **Theosophy**, Krishnamurti went forth with the message that all beliefs are mental and spiritual strait-jackets and all religions a convenient way to offload responsibility for one's personal state. The road to freedom and enlightenment was simply self-observation and the only difficulty to be overcome was the age-old problem of actually getting down to it.

He died in 1985 aged 91.

Kundalini

Often referred to as the 'serpent power', kundalini is likened in esoteric **yoga** to a serpent coiled at the base of the spine. Either naturally or, more often, as the result of specific yoga practice, the energy is aroused to travel upwards along the spine and 'strike', again like a serpent, into the brain.

What happens when the 'serpent' strikes depends on how kundalini has been aroused. If the properly prescribed exercises have been followed and the energy has travelled through the correct spinal channel, enlightenment results. If not, then the result is a psychospiritual crisis. (*See also* **Krishna, Gopi.**)

L

Laing, Ronald David

Born in Glasgow in 1927, R. D. Laing was both a psychiatrist and a psychoanalyst who is best known for his depiction of the process of going mad. In his many books he challenged science's emphasis on objective data. He valued human experience above all and was therefore an important figure in **humanistic psychology**. He died in 1989. His books include *The Divided Self*, *Sanity, Madness and the Family* and *The Voice of Experience*.

Lao Tzu

Lao Tzu was the Chinese sage who founded **Taoism** and wrote the 81 poems of his holy book, the *Tao Te Ching*, but while he is believed to have lived in the sixth century BC, contemporary with **Confucius**, very little is actually known about him.

In such circumstances, inevitably, numerous legends have grown up. According to these, Lao Tzu was the product of an immaculate conception, the result of a liaison between his mother and a shooting star. His gestation lasted 82 years, so that he was born an old man with white beard and hair. Although among the wisest of his age, he did not found a church, refused to preach and spread his ideas only through his poetry. After working as Keeper of the Archives of his native province, he rode away westwards on a water buffalo. Fortunately he did not neglect to leave a copy of the *Tao Te Ching* with a frontier guard, so that his insights were not lost.

Lazaris

Lazaris channels through Jach Pursel. The wisdom, techniques and concern for psychological and spiritual growth evident in the teachings channelled seem to have affected the lives of many people all over the world. (*See* **Channelling**.)

Leadbeater, C. W.

A man destined to become one of the more disreputable leading lights of the Theosophical Society, Charles Webster Leadbeater was born in 1847 and entered the Anglican Church as a curate before his interest in the occult led to his joining the Theosophical Society in 1884.

A man who greatly enjoyed travel, he visited Ceylon, the United States and Australia where he founded a Theosophical commune. In India, helping to establish the society's headquarters at Adyar, he concluded with Mrs **Annie Besant** that a 15-year-old Brahmin boy, Jiddu **Krishnamurti** was the next World Teacher and actually became the boy's adoptive father.

In a career marred by accusations of homosexual pederasty, Leadbeater was a founder member of the Liberal Catholic Church (an institution which continues to flourish) and subsequently became its second Bishop. He claimed, almost certainly with some justification, to be a **psychic** with the ability to see **aura**s and other inner structures of reality, including Nature **spirit**s and similar entities. Many of his books, notably *Man, Visible and Invisible* and *The Chakras*, remain well worth reading. One work, *The Science of the Sacraments*, describes the inner workings of the magical Mass and is still in use in the Liberal Catholic Church.

Leek, Sybil

Although born in England (in 1923), Sybil Leek has been resident in the United States since 1964 where she has attracted widespread media attention on account of her practice of **witchcraft**.

Ms Leek has never been coy about this practice. She has written several books including *Diary of a Witch* and *Cast your Own Spell*, taken part in numerous radio programmes on witchcraft and even opened her own witchy restaurant, 'Sybil Leek's Cauldron'.

Lemuria

The legendary lost continent which preceded **Atlantis**. Supposedly located in the Indian Ocean and said, by the German biologist Ernst Haeckel, to be 'the probable cradle of the human race'. Both **Blavatsky** and **Steiner** believed in its existence and wrote about it.

Lethbridge, T. C.

When Tom C. Lethbridge, a powerfully-built Cambridge don, retired to Devon at the age of 56, he left behind a busy, distinguished and somewhat controversial career in archaeology which included many years as Honorary Keeper of Anglo-Saxon Antiquities in the University Museum of Archaeology and Ethnology. He might have been forgiven for hoping for a rest. But if so, he did not get it.

For one thing, his nearest neighbour turned out to be an old lady who practised **witchcraft**. She became friendly with Lethbridge and told him about **astral projection** and 'throwing pentagrams'. (*See* **Pentagram Ritual; Psychic Self Defence**.) Most important of all, she reawakened his interest in **dowsing** by means of a **pendulum**.

At the time Lethbridge moved to Devon in 1957, most pendulum dowsers used a heavy weight and a short string so their instruments would not blow about in the wind, but Lethbridge had the idea that it might be interesting to find out whether pendulums of different lengths would react to different things. To test his theory, he made a long pendulum using a ball of hazelwood and wrapped the string around a pencil so that the length could easily be varied.

Following his neighbour's instructions, Lethbridge put a silver dish on the floor and swung his dowsing pendulum over it. Carefully he varied the length of the string until the pendulum suddenly started to circle. He measured the length of the string (22 inches) and concluded that a 22-inch long pendulum was 'tuned' to the 'wavelength' of silver.

Over a long series of experiments, he discovered lengths for a wide variety of different things: copper was 30 inches, grass 16 inches, apples 18 inches and so on. He even discovered it was possible to tune the pendulum to abstract emotions (like anger) simply by visualizing them clearly. He and his wife Mina picked up stones and threw them against a wall. The pendulum could be tuned to detect which stone was thrown by the man and which by the woman.

By the time his experiments were finished, Tom Lethbridge was convinced he had made a fundamental discovery about pendulum dowsing. He wrote a number of books in which he gave the precise pendulum lengths for various substances, but subsequent investigations have strongly suggested that the lengths are not absolutes, but need to be varied in relation to the individual who is using the pendulum. In other words, dowsing pendulums need to be individually tuned.

Alongside dowsing, Lethbridge had a considerable interest in ghosts. (He had seen one at Trinity College, Cambridge, in his early twenties.) His investigations in this field convinced him that many **apparitions** were not **spirits** of the dead, but natural 'recordings' somehow impressed on their surroundings and 'replayed' when conditions were suitable. Noting that ghost sightings were often associated with damp and dismal places, he postulated that the recording might be a field phenomenon generated in the presence of water. He coined a special usage of the word 'ghoul' to describe 'cold spots' and other areas associated with hauntings in which witnesses felt uncomfortable.

Lévi, Eliphas

Alphonse Louis Constant, who later achieved fame under the name Eliphas Lévi, was born the son of a Parisian shoemaker in 1810. Although his family were poor, the local parish priest recognized Constant's intelligence and arranged for his education – with a view to his taking up the priesthood – in Saint-Sulpice.

At first things went smoothly, for he went into minor Orders and eventually became a deacon. But he was a heretic at heart and was subsequently expelled from the seminary. It was the start of several brushes with authority. He embarked on a mission to the poor and published several socialistic pamphlets which proved so unpopular with the courts that he was fined and jailed.

His marriage proved a mistake. Constant selected for his bride the 16-year-old Noemie Cadot, who left him when the two children she bore him died. The marriage was subsequently annulled on the curious grounds that he had been pledged to celibacy when he contracted it. Noemie married again and achieved fame as a sculptress. Constant plunged into the dark world of **occultism**.

At this period he first took the name Eliphas Lévi and published several books on **magic** – a number of which are still in print (and in English translation) today. They did not, however, sell all that well during his lifetime, so that he was forced to supplement his income by giving private lessons in the mystic arts. His rates were high. He once charged 40 francs for a one-minute exposition of the **Tarot**.

Lévi does not appear to have been a particularly pleasant man. His personal hygiene left much to be desired and he was something of a glutton. But his disciples fawned on him and even today he retains a considerable following. As a magician, he was largely a theorist, avoiding actual practice of the occult arts. This may have been due to his reconversion to Roman Catholicism, some time between 1854 and 1860.

Despite the theoretical bent, Lévi did lend himself to one spectacular operation of practical magic while on a trip to London in 1854. Lévi's sponsor on the trip was Baron Lytton of Knebworth, the novelist Bulwer-Lytton, who was himself an occultist. Lytton asked Lévi to demonstrate his powers before a small gathering of friends. Lévi declined and withdrew to immerse himself in the **Qabalah**. But if he had withdrawn from England's occultists, not all of England's occultists had withdrawn from him. He returned to his hotel one day to find waiting for him a piece of card with the pencilled note, 'Tomorrow at three o'clock, in front of Westminster Abbey, the second half of this card will be given to you.' On the card was a section of the Seal of Solomon, the interlaced triangles now seen on the flag of Israel and long believed by occultists to be a glyph of power.

Lévi duly presented himself at the Abbey. A carriage drew up and a footman emerged. After signalling to Lévi, he opened the carriage door to reveal a mysteriously-veiled woman. She motioned Lévi to enter the coach and at the same time showed him the other half of his card.

As the carriage drove off, the lady unveiled and told Lévi she had heard of his reluctance to produce phenomena and wondered if it might be for lack of the proper magical equipment. Consequently she had decided to show him a complete magical cabinet, providing he pledged himself to secrecy. Lévi, who considered the woman a high initiate, agreed.

At the woman's home, Lévi was loaned several rare books, shown a collection of magical robes and instruments and persuaded to try to raise the **spirit** of Apollonius of Tyana by using a **ritual** drawn from the *Magical Philosophy* of Patricius. In accordance with the ritual instructions, Lévi devoted 21 days to **meditation**. For 14 of them he maintained a strictly vegetarian diet, for the final seven he fasted.

On 24 July, he bathed, put on a white robe and crown of vervain leaves intertwined with a gold chain, took up sword and book and entered the turret room where the evocation was to be carried out. The room had been furnished in black and equipped with four concave mirrors and a spectacular altar surrounded by a chain of magnetized iron. Lévi lit fires in two chafing dishes and began to read the ritual evocation in a voice at first low, but rising by degrees.

Eventually he got results.

> I seemed to feel a quaking of the earth, my ears tingled, my heart beat quickly . . . I beheld before the altar the figure of a man of more than normal size, which dissolved and vanished away . . .

Lévi promptly stepped inside a protective circle he had drawn and continued with the ceremonial. A wan form appeared in the mirror behind the altar, then a man appeared in front of him, wrapped head to foot in a shroud. Lévi experienced an abnormally cold sensation and lost the feeling in his sword arm when the **apparition** touched it as Lévi sought to drive it away again. It was the end of Lévi's short career in practical magic. Afterwards he wrote, 'I regard the practice as destructive and dangerous . . .'

Levitation

The supposed ability to defy gravity, levitation should properly be divided into two categories: 1) The levitation of objects, animate and inanimate; and 2) Self levitation.

The first of these categories is closely associated with **psychokinesis** (*see also* **Bacheldor, Kenneth**) and has been the object of extensive investigation since Victorian times, with considerable evidence for its reality, even under stringent test conditions.

Self levitation, traditionally associated with the ecstatic experience of saints, is rather more controversial, although there is a vast body of anecdotal accounts (including that concerning St **Teresa of Avila** who used to rail against God for causing her to fly about in such an undignified manner) reaching far back into history.

One of the most interesting manifestations of self levitation in comparatively modern times is that of **Daniel Dunglas Home**, a Spiritualist **medium** who managed to float out of one upstairs window and back in through another before a startled group of witnesses. The most highly-publicized contemporary investigation into self levitation is currently being carried out by the **Transcendental Meditation** movement, which claims to be able to train its adepts in the art and has issued photographs of cheerful, cross-legged meditators apparently floating a foot or more above the floor. Some observers remain unconvinced, claiming that the technique is closer to hopping than levitation.

Ley Lines

In the summer of 1921, the 65-year-old brewer and magistrate, Alfred Watkins, was horse-riding in the Bredwardine Hills of Hereford when he was struck by the sudden insight that a whole variety of ancient sites, churches, mounds, standing stones, etc., appeared to be aligned in straight lines. It occurred to him that the entire countryside was criss-crossed by a network of such lines. He called them 'leys', a word derived from the 'lea' or 'leigh' often found in place names, which Watkins believed meant a grassy track.

Watkins theorized that leys were remnants of ancient roads, mainly associated with the salt trade. He argued that in heavily wooded country, workable routes would have to be charted from hilltop to hilltop and marked in the valleys with standing stones, mounds, crosses or what have you.

Surprisingly, Watkins' innocent suggestion, which he expounded at length in his *The Old Straight Track*, first published in 1925, provoked a violent reaction in the archaeological establishment. (The magazine *Antiquity* actually refused an advertisement for the book on the grounds that it was a crank work.) But the controversy did nothing to diminish the book's popularity or halt the spread of Watkins' theory. A 'Straight Track Postal Club' was formed to which members reported their own observations of ley lines. It soon became evident that Watkins' initial observations could be widely confirmed. Straight-line alignments were found throughout the country.

But if Watkins was correct about the existence of leys, there was growing doubt about his theory of their nature. By the late 1930s, Major F. C. Tyler had noted that leys often consisted of two parallel tracks. If they marked prehistoric roads, why should the old travellers have felt the need of two, both going in the same direction? And when ley-hunting moved out of the countryside and onto the Ordnance Survey map, it soon became evident that the old straight leys often combined to form exact geometric figures.

Worse was to follow. Larger-scale maps soon showed that certain major British leys actually carried across onto the continent of Europe. Whatever the lines were, it was very evident they were not roads.

But what then were they? Many objectors insisted they were nothing at all. If you make an arbitrary decision to join up a number of random sites on a map, then some, quite by chance, will arrange themselves in a straight line. Ley-hunters responded by tightening their criteria. A ley was not a ley unless it joined a minimum of five sites; and the sites themselves had to be shown to be genuinely ancient. This lengthened the odds against chance to a degree where they could be safely ignored. But the leys refused to go away.

The author John Michell pointed out the close similarities between the ley lines of Europe and the *lung mei* or 'dragon paths' of China, which were supposed to carry mystical energy to the Emperor. (*See* **Feng Shui**.) Closer to home, other investigators were discovering for themselves that there was a definite energy aspect to certain ancient sites. The dowsers Robert Boothby and Reginald Smith discovered, for example, that long barrows typically had underground streams running along their length. Another dowser, Guy Underwood, not only confirmed this but detected a whole spectrum of energy effects – some associated with underground streams, some not – at stone circles and other megalithic sites. That such effects were genuine was confirmed by the physicists Professor John Taylor and Dr Eduardo Balinovski of London University, who used a gaussmeter on a South Wales megalith and found it surrounded by a spiroform magnetic field phenomenon.

Lilly, John

In 1972 the neuroscientist Dr John Lilly published a remarkable book entitled *The Centre of the Cyclone*, subtitled 'An Autobiography of Inner Space'. It was one of the more unusual autobiographies issued in the twentieth century for it was concerned, almost exclusively, with Lilly's personal experiences of altered states of **consciousness** produced by **hypnosis**, **meditation** and even psychedelic drugs.

Lilly has also become well-known because of his work in communicating with dolphins. His work with the isolation or **flotation tank** was Lilly's attempt to understand his own mind through sensory deprivation.

Lodge, Sir Oliver

Evidence provided by the **medium** Mrs Gladys Leonard persuaded the British physicist Sir Oliver Lodge that his son Raymond, killed in the First World War, still survived in a post-mortem state. Henceforth, Lodge enthusiastically championed belief in life after death and became a prestigious addition to the Spiritualist cause.

Born in 1851, Lodge became principal of Birmingham University in 1900, a post he held with distinction for 19 years. He was knighted in 1902 for his services to science. Against this hard scientific background, he developed a profound interest in the **paranormal** and was elected president of the **Society for Psychical Research** in 1901. The touching story of the post-mortem communications with his son is told in one of his many books, *Raymond: or Life After Death*.

Lovelock, James

The British scientist who, in 1979, first propounded the theory of the Earth as **Gaia**, a living entity, in his book *Gaia: A New Look at Life on Earth* and in so doing confirmed the insights of generations of mystics.

Lull, Ramon

Ramon Lull (the name often Anglicized as Raymond Lully) is one of the more romantic figures of thirteenth-century **occultism**. According to legend, as a young cavalier he fell in love with a married woman. When she attempted to let him down gently by suggesting his passion was such that it would require an eternity to contain it, Don Juan became Faust and dedicated his next 30 years to the alchemical search for the elixir of life.

The legend states that Lull found this magical potion and drank it, becoming immortal. But when he sought out his beloved to share the elixir with her, she revealed she was in agony from cancer and sought only death as a relief.

At this point, the grief-stricken Lull converted to **Christianity** and wandered the world deliberately provoking the **Islam**ic faithful in the hope that they would kill him. Many attempted to do so, but Lull, protected by his elixir, always survived. Eventually, at a great age and with a substantial reputation as an evangelist, Lull was stoned to death after the Lord took pity on him.

The reality of Lull's life is more difficult to discover. He was born in 1235 and died in 1315. He seems at one period of his life to have been Seneschal of Majorca and he certainly practised **alchemy**. His alchemical works were popularized by Sir George Ripley, who claimed Lull transformed large quantities of mercury, tin and lead into gold for Edward III.

M

Mabinogion, The
A rare collection of 11 medieval tales, written in Welsh in the
eleventh century and clearly containing a profusion of elements
drawn from the old pre-Christian myths of Celtic Britain. The
tales, which hold their fascination even today, contain some of
the earliest surviving material relating to **Arthurian legend**.

Macrobiotics
An Oriental dietary system based on the ancient Chinese
philosophy of **yin** and **yang** and designed to promote health and
longevity through a diet largely based on whole grains.

Macumba
Common term for the Brazilian form of **Voodoo** and **Santéria**,
both of which came to North and South America with West
African slaves. It involves the worship of African deities through
magic and possession of the **spirit**.

Magic
'Magic' is one of those words everybody understands, but
nobody seems able to define. **Aleister Crowley** attempted to do
so with the insight that 'Magic is the art of causing change in
accordance with Will', a definition so wide that it would cover the
drinking of a cup of tea. **Dion Fortune** modified Crowley's
expression to produce her famous statement, 'Magic is the art of
producing changes of consciousness in accordance with the Will.'
This is the definition most widely accepted by occultists, even
though plainly it could be taken to refer to the act of going to
sleep. J.H. Brennan has suggested in his published work that
magic should be seen as the art of generating synchronistic effects
(i.e. meaningful coincidences) to order.
    Magic is, in fact, slightly easier to describe than define. In its
modern form, it almost always involves:

1) Communication with or entry into alternative states of reality (*see* **Astral Plane**) and/or
2) Manipulation of subtle energies associated with the cosmos or the human body. (*See* **Ch'i**.)

Mahabharata

An epic poem of ancient India, the *Mahabharata* is 100,000 stanzas long, or 15 times the size of the Bible. It is around 3,000 years old and means 'The Great History of the Bharatas (or Mankind)'. It is a repository of myths, fairy tales and archetypal characters and source of spiritual wisdom. Central to *Mahabharata* is the *Bhagavad Gita*, Arjuna's famous dialogue with Krishna on the eve of the great battle between the Pandavas and the Kauravas over the succession to the kingdom. The war threatens to destroy mankind.

Maharaj Ji, Guru

Prem Pal Singh Rawat was born in Hardwar, India in 1957 and declared a 'Perfect Master' only eight years later. He completed his schooling in 1971 and, as the Guru Maharaj Ji, began a world tour as spiritual leader of the Divine Light Mission in order to spread knowledge of inner peace.

Although branches of the Mission now function in Europe, Britain, Africa, the United States and Australia, the Guru has received a bad press for his alleged fondness of secular pleasures, including Rolls Royce motor cars.

Maharishi Mahesh Yogi

Sometimes referred to as the 'Giggling Guru' on account of his perpetually sunny disposition, the Maharishi Mahesh Yogi achieved considerable prominence in the West during the 1960s on account of two unrelated factors. The first was his national television appearance in Britain when he charmed millions of viewers during a debate with the Archbishop of Canterbury. The second was his adoption by the Beatles as their personal **guru**.

The Maharishi worked for a time in the West under the full glare of media publicity before returning to his native Himalayas, leaving behind the flourishing structure of **Transcendental Meditation** which continues to recruit followers to this day.

Maharshi, Ramana

Ramana Maharshi was one of the greatest Indian saints of modern times, also known as the Sage of Arunachala.

While still a schoolboy in the closing years of the Victorian era, Ramana Maharshi died . . . or at least underwent a death-like experience that convinced him of the reality of **spirit**. Determined to find out more of spiritual things, he left home to become a wandering mystic and eventually attracted a following, some of whom, like Dr **Paul Brunton**, recorded his doctrines.

Ramana, who lived from 1879 to 1950, essentially taught that the true self was identical to God while the demands of the ego, or false self, had to bow to a higher truth if enlightenment was to be achieved.

Mandala

An intricate symbolic design, usually circular, with an inscribed square, widely used in the East, particularly in pre-invasion Tibet, as an aid to **meditation**. Typically, such pictures show a harmonious balance of elements, often with a fourfold subdivision and multiple mirroring of individual segments. **Carl Jung** considered mandalas to be diagrams of the integrated psyche, hence their intrinsic power. They are sometimes painted, sometimes pictured in the mind, and sometimes traced in coloured sand upon the ground.

Manichaeism

A new religion of the third century which combined **Zoroastrianism** with certain Gnostic ideas (*see* **Gnosticism**). Mani established his teachings in many parts of the Persian empire. St Augustine was a Manichaean before he became a Christian and brought some of his old beliefs with him. Mani accepted the Zoroastrian beliefs in God and a devil, heaven and hell, the concept of history, individual judgement and **reincarnation**. But his teaching was essentially dualistic, regarding matter as evil and advocating asceticism and celibacy.

Manning, Matthew

Matthew Manning's mother had a severe electric shock three weeks before his birth on 17 August 1955, but there were no problems with the birth itself and he grew up to be a normal, healthy, intelligent and outgoing boy. Then, on the morning of 18 February 1967, the **poltergeist** activity started . . .

Over the next three years, poltergeist manifestations continued intermittently in the environs of the Manning family. Then, in 1970, they became noticeably focused on Matthew. They even followed him to boarding-school the next year. He began to hear **spirit** voices and eventually saw a full-blown **apparition**.

It was the start of a process that was to make Matthew Manning one of the most powerful **psychic**s in Britain. Soon he was demonstrating the same abilities as **Uri Geller** and bending metal objects by means of concentration. Like Geller he volunteered for scientific testing, travelling widely to meet scientists. The Toronto Society for Psychical Research concluded his abilities were associated with an unknown form of electro-magnetic phenomena, the manifestation of which was accompanied by changes in Manning's brain-wave patterns.

The broadly-based nature of Manning's talents – he could see **auras**, create psychokinetic effects and produce **automatic writing** alongside many other phenomena – attracted the attention of the Press, who mounted a media circus so intense that Manning felt compelled to escape on a pilgrimage to India. While meditating in the Himalayas, he decided to dedicate his life to psychic **healing** and has done so ever since.

Mantra

A good deal of confusion surrounds the subject of mantras, which are sometimes confused with spells, or the 'words of power' of **ritual** magic. In fact, a mantra is simply a word or phrase which, when repeated, influences the human mind. By this definition, a good many advertising slogans and jingles are mantras, but the term is more generally used to describe those chants used in **yoga** and Oriental esoteric and/or mystical practice in order to still the mind.

Transcendental Meditation is essentially a mantric art since, on initiation, its practitioners are given a personal mantra, attuned to their individual vibrations. But individual 'tuning' is unnecessary, to judge by the millions of Orientals who use 'off-the-peg' mantras in their **meditation** practice.

Of these, perhaps the most widely known is the mantra *Aum mani padme hum*, associated with **Buddhism** and usually translated as 'Hail to the Jewel in the Lotus'. Another, equally well-known in the Middle East, is the **Islam**ic mantra *Hua allahu alazi lailaha illa Hua* ('He is God and there is no other God than

He'). An example of an ancient mantra is the Egyptian *A ka dua, Tuf ur biu, Bi aa chefu, Dudu ner af an nuteru* ('I adore the might of thy breath, supreme and terrible God, who makest the Gods and Death to tremble before Thee').

For practical purposes, the meaning is of little importance. Mantras became popular because of their usefulness in creating changes in **consciousness** or mentation. The common denominator of a great many of them is that they swallow their tails. No sooner has the last word of the mantra been pronounced than the practitioner begins it again from the beginning.

You can gain some insight into the use of mantras by experimenting with the mantra *Aum mani padme hum*. Try chanting it aloud at first. Make it sonorous and run the final *mmm* of *hum* into the beginning of *aum*. Rhythm and pronunciation are as follows:

> *Aw-um mah-nee padmeh hummmmm um mah-nee padmeh hummm* . . .

After you have listened to it aloud for a few cycles, lower the volume progressively until you 'withdraw' the sounds into your mind and continue pronouncing the mantric circle mentally. Experiment with speed until you find a rhythm which grips your attention so that extraneous thoughts are thrown out by the spinning mantra. The effect is very similar to getting a tune into your head that will not go away. The mantra spins and expands to fill your consciousness until there is no room for anything else. Even if you are aware of the meaning of the phrase you are using, that meaning is soon lost, in the same way that your mind blanks out the meaning of a word you repeat too often.

Once the spinning mantra is firmly established, it will continue with no conscious effort, leaving you free to relax more fully with an untroubled mind. When you wish to return to your normal mode of consciousness, slow the spin rate of the mantra, then 'externalize' it by pronouncing it aloud a few times before stopping altogether.

Martial Arts

Despite the best efforts of the Hong Kong movie industry to project an image to the contrary, the Oriental martial arts are as much spiritual disciplines as fighting techniques. Their fundamental philosophy tends to be Taoist in essence, with emphasis on efficiency derived from harmony with the universe and usage of the cosmic energy known as *ch'i* or *prana*.

Although generally associated with China and South East Asia today, historians believe it likely that the martial arts were actually developed in India and subsequently exported more than 1,000 years ago. They may have come into being within monastic communities whose religious convictions forbade the use of weapons, but whose environment was sufficiently dangerous to require that they protected themselves.

The spread of the martial arts into our Western culture began in the early years of the twentieth century with the introduction of jiu jitsu. This was quickly followed by the arrival of judo, karate, aikido and many more. Judo was officially adopted as the preferred unarmed combat technique of Western armies as long ago as 1908. In their Western expression, however, the martial arts tend to emphasize the physical at the expense of the spiritual and almost no use is made of the subtle energy aspects which characterize the Oriental practice.

Maslow, Abraham

One of the founders of humanistic psychology, Abraham Maslow was born in 1908 in New York, the son of a Russian Jewish immigrant. His early research work was on monkeys. Going on to study Native American culture, he then taught psychology at Brooklyn College and then Brandeis, where he did his major work on peak experiences and self-actualization. He was an intuitive, interdisciplinary thinker and knew many of the leading intellectuals of his day – **Aldous Huxley**, Gregory Bateson, Margaret Mead, Ruth Benedict, Alfred Adler, Erich Fromm, Karen Horney and Max Wertheimer. He was also one of **Esalen**'s principal mentors between 1962 and 1970.

Maslow's work and thought has powerfully affected the way we think about ourselves. Unlike most psychologists of his day, he did not study neurosis and human weakness. What he was fascinated by were 'self-actualized' people – the exceptional, healthy, fulfilled and successful individuals. His ideas about self-fulfilment and emotional well-being have influenced the fields of psychology, counselling, education, health care, business, management, marketing and theology. A great visionary and inspiration to many in his lifetime (he died in 1970), he has helped change long-standing popular values about how to lead a worthwhile life.

Mathers, S.L. MacGregor

One of the most intriguing and influential figures in the entire **Western Esoteric Tradition**, Samuel Liddell MacGregor Mathers remains one of the most mysterious. He still lacks a definitive biography and only the broad details of his life are easily accessible.

Mathers was born in 1854 and grew up to be a scholarly individual fascinated by the world of the occult. He spent a great deal of his time in the British Museum Reading Room consulting ancient esoteric texts. His lasting achievements include translations of a great many *grimoires* and magical works, including *Armadel*, the *Key of Solomon* and the fascinating *Book of the Sacred Magic of Abra-Melin the Mage*.

He was a key figure in the establishment of the **Golden Dawn**, having been consulted to decode the famous cypher manuscripts discovered by **Wynn Westcott** which provided the impetus to found that influential magical Order. Mathers also wrote most of the Order **rituals** in the forms they were used and quickly became head of the organization under the guidance of the Secret Chiefs.

Mathers married Moina Bergson, sister of the French philosopher, and spent the latter part of his life in Paris, apparently supported by contributions from Golden Dawn members. He took the side of **Aleister Crowley** in the vicious disagreement with **W.B. Yeats** which eventually destroyed the Order.

MacGregor Mathers died in 1918, a victim of the influenza epidemic, a transcendental encounter with the Secret Chiefs or a magical attack by Aleister Crowley, depending on which source you elect to believe.

Matter of Britain, The

According to **Arthurian legend**, the words *Hic jacet Arthurus, rex quondam, rexque futurus* ('Here lies Arthur, the once and future King') appear on Arthur's tomb, indicating that Arthur will rise again one day to lead Britain back to glory.

For many modern occultists, this legend and, indeed, the whole Arthurian mythic cycle, lies at the heart of the Matter of Britain, the spiritual destiny of the British Isles. To this end, various esoteric organizations have devoted a great deal of time and energy to investigating the inner aspects of the myths and attempting, through **pathworkings** and similar techniques, to make contact with the spiritual energies of the Grail Quest.

Maya
A term from Hindu philosophy meaning illusion, in the sense of mistaking appearances of things for their intrinsic nature.

Medicine Wheel
A Native American concept of a sacred circle which is the focal point of the ceremonial life of the community as well as being used in everyday life, in forms such as the tipi, or the sweat lodge, the circular Council (where everyone is equal), dancing in a circle, etc. The Native Americans see life as a circle from birth to death to rebirth, and the constant movement around the wheel teaches people to change (to become static is to cease to grow). The Medicine Wheel has four Directions (North, East, South and West) with special qualities and lessons to learn. North = winter, the time of resting for ourselves and the Earth Mother, the place that represents old age and the time of changing worlds and forms. East = spring, the place of birth and awakening, representing mankind's birth. South = summer, the time of fruitfulness and growth. West = autumn, when we reap our harvest and have found the knowledge needed to be at peace in ourselves. Each Direction has a Spirit Keeper, a Spirit Being responsible for teaching the power of the Direction. Used in a proper manner, this Native American concept helps in our own **healing** and in the healing of the planet.

Meditation
Meditation is an umbrella word which encompasses a multitude of techniques aimed at achieving a state of enlightenment or ecstasy or both. But despite the variety of approaches, almost every form of meditation tends to fall into one of two basic categories.

The first, on which most Christian, Sufi and **yoga** meditation techniques are based, is heightened concentration. The practitioner gives his/her undivided attention to a single idea or perception, seeking the total absorption which leads to understanding. If successful, a trance-like state ensues in which

193

external awareness dims and the effects of competing stimuli die away. Experts believe this to be the oldest form of meditation and its advanced practice can lead to ecstatic states.

The second, traditionally credited to the **Buddha** for its development, involves the passive examination of the changing content of individual awareness, taking care neither to select the content nor to cling to any aspect of it once another aspect arises. The aim of this type of meditation is obviously increased awareness, but it also creates a very effective channel through which previously unconscious contents may present themselves to the conscious mind.

Medium

A Spiritualist term denoting an individual with the talent necessary to act as intermediary between the living and the **spirits** of the dead.

There are a great many different types of medium. Some receive only 'impressions' of messages from the 'Other Side', some hear and even produce voices, some are taken over by the deceased spirit in a process of temporary benign possession, some are actually claimed to cause spirits to materialize in physical form.

A (fairly) common denominator among mediums is the presence of a spirit **guide** who acts as a sort of gatekeeper – and sometimes bouncer! – in relation to spirits who wish to use the medium for communication.

Although **Spiritualism** itself is a relatively recent movement – it began in the nineteenth century – there are clear parallels between mediumistic phenomena and certain **shaman**ic practices dating back to prehistory.

Megaliths

From the Greek *megas*, 'great', and *lithos*, 'stone'. Standing stones exist around the world and are believed to have had sacred, astronomical or burial purposes. Many are said to possess **healing** and magical powers or to be repositories of electromagnetic energy. Megaliths are either dolmens, which are tombs of one or more chambers, or menhirs, which are single standing stones or groups of standing stones that are arranged in circles and called cromlechs or henges. Carnac, in Brittany, is the site of the greatest and oldest megaliths, while Stonehenge is the best known in England.

Meher Baba

Born in Poona in 1894, Meher Baba was taught by various spiritual masters of different traditions. He himself taught for over 40 years, and what was unusual about this and what he is best known for, is the fact that he kept silent. For him the daily practice of love was all that was necessary and his work was an expression of this. He died in 1969.

Mencius

The great successor of **Confucius** was the contemporary of Plato. Unable to obtain a fair hearing for his views among the rulers or professional philosophers of his day at the great centre of Chinese learning, Chi-hsia in present Shantung, Mencius retired and wrote seven books called the *Mencius*. According to Mencius, human nature is originally good, and this idea formed the basis for his entire philosophy. He believed that an individual 'can develop his mind to the utmost', both serving God and fulfilling his own destiny.

Merlin

The archetypical British magician, once thought to have been a Druid, now appears largely a fictional creation, although with some basis in fact. If there was ever a real Merlin at all, he seems to have been a sixth-century bardic seer named Myrddin, living in the Cymric borderland near the Solway Firth.

It is not impossible for the historical Myrddin to have met with the best historical candidate to form the basis of the legendary King Arthur, but in so doing, Merlin would have been a child and Arthur an old man. The mythic Merlin, however, combining two old Welsh traditions, first created by Geoffrey of Monmouth and richly embellished by later authors, presents a very different picture.

In its most developed form, the legend describes Merlin's birth as the result of the powers of Hell attempting to bring about the conception of a Satanic child. Something went wrong and the selected mother gave birth to a colourful and somewhat ambiguous individual who insisted on going his own way.

But while refusing to serve Satan, the boy retained substantial mystic powers and even as a child was frequently moved to **prophecy**. At the age of five, for example, he visited King Vortigern's court and foresaw a battle between red and white dragons which would lead to the king's death. Some years later, he used magic to transport the Giant's Dance (Stonehenge) from Ireland to its present site on Salisbury Plain at the request of King Aurelius. He aided the next king, Uther Pendragon, on a rather more personal matter when he changed the king's appearance to that of the husband of the Lady Igerna so that Uther might seduce her. The exercise was a rollicking success and Arthur was conceived.

Merlin played an important part in the education of the young Arthur. He was instrumental in providing him with the sword Excalibur, which Arthur withdrew from the stone in order to establish his claim to the throne. In later years, it was Merlin who suggested the use of a *round* meeting table so that Arthur's knights would not fight over the most important position, and it was Merlin's prophetic powers which aided Arthur in battle and helped establish his kingdom. (*See also* **Arthurian Legend**.)

Eventually, Merlin met his magical match in the sorceress Nimuë (the archetypal Vivian la Fey) with whom he fell in love. She overcame him, apparently with the aid of one of his own spells, and imprisoned him within a cave where, immortal, he languishes to this day.

Merton, Thomas

Thomas Merton was born in 1915. Both at Cambridge and Columbia universities he led a fairly profligate life, but a growing restlessness in his early twenties resulted in his conversion to Catholicism. He joined the Abbey of Our Lady of Gethsemani, a Trappist monastery, where silence, white robes, prayer and strict ascetic discipline prevailed. Here he wrote *The Seven-Storey Mountain* (the image is from Dante), which is a unique spiritual document. Crucial to Merton's thought is the idea that self-will and desire must be renounced for spiritual development to take place. Life's task is to discover our real identity. Familiar with the mystical literature of Catholic theology, Merton was also well-versed in Eastern religious thought. He died in a mysterious accident in Bangkok in 1969.

Mesmer, Franz Anton

The German healer and physician who postulated that there was an all-pervading force or magnetic fluid which linked all beings. He called this 'animal magnetism' and it was not so different from

Hindu *prana* or Chinese *ch'i*. Mesmer's method of laying on of hands and giving suggestions to patients led to the development of therapeutic **hypnotism**.

Metamorphic Technique
A form of spiritual and physical therapy identical in technique, if not in theory, to **zone therapy**.

Milarepa
Today known as Tibet's greatest yogi, Jetsun Milarepa practised black magic as a young man, but later achieved a profound mystical **initiation** under the guidance of the Lama Marpa.

Milarepa, who lived between 1052 and 1135, underwent the transcendent unity typical of the mystical experience and developed powers commensurate with **yoga** practice. The name 'Milarepa' is partially a title derived from proficiency at **tumo**, the Tibetan yoga of body heat which allows adepts to survive in the snows while wearing only a thin cotton robe, or *repa*.

Ming Shu
Chinese **astrology**, literally 'the reckoning of Fate'. It involves both character and personality delineation, as well as **divination** and prediction. In Chinese astrology, the hour, day, month and year are known as the Four Pillars of Fate, and it is the year that is most significant. Other factors too are relevant, particularly the interaction of the Five Elements – Wood, Fire, Earth, Metal and Water, which exert influence at different times in an individual's life.

Originally Chinese astrologers had reckoned the years by the 'Twelve Earthly Branches', supposedly to mark the 12 years it takes the planet Jupiter to complete its orbit of the sky. About 1,000 years ago, when **Buddhism** was the dominant religion in China, the monks exchanged the Twelve Branches with more memorable names of 12 animals: Rat, Ox, Tiger, Hare, Dragon, Snake, Horse, Sheep, Monkey, Rooster, Dog and Pig. These are regarded in popular Chinese astrology as direct indicators of personality, although the Five Elements help to provide a deeper personality portrait.

Moksha
The state of freedom from the need to reincarnate as the result

of enlightenment. The term is very similar, possibly even identical to, the better-known Buddhist term **nirvana**.

Monroe, Robert

Robert Allen Monroe studied commerce, engineering, journalism and drama at Ohio State University. In 1937, he went into broadcasting as a writer/director.

He moved to New York, where he made his living writing features and screenplays before breaking into network radio with a long-running dramatized documentary. At the end of the Second World War, he formed his own production company and embarked on a highly successful business career.

In 1958, he had his first **out-of-the-body experience**.

Monroe had a very hard time with it. Long before it occurred, he began to experience painful cramps and rigidity of the upper abdomen. This was followed, over a period of weeks, by bouts of temporary paralysis during which his entire body would seem to shake violently.

He considered the possibility of epilepsy, but dismissed it on the grounds that epileptics had no memory of their seizures while his own recollection of the experience was clear. He suspected a brain disorder, possibly a tumour, and sought medical advice. His doctor suggested he was simply working too hard and should lose a little weight.

On one occasion when a seizure struck, his arm was draped over the side of the bed, fingers just brushing the rug.

> Idly, I tried to move my fingers and found I could scratch the rug. Without thinking or realizing that I could move my fingers during the vibration, I pushed with the tips of my fingers against the rug. After a moment's resistance, my fingers seemed to penetrate the rug and touch the floor underneath. With mild curiosity, I pushed my hand down further. My fingers went through the floor and there was the rough upper surface of the ceiling of the room below . . .

Monroe has survived more than 25 years of projection experiences (*see* **Astral Projection**; **Etheric Projection**), produced two interesting books on his experiences, set up his own training centre in the art of leaving the body and taken out at least two patents on devices which are a proven aid to the process.

Montgomery, Ruth

A widely-syndicated newspaper reporter, Ruth Montgomery turned to **automatic writing** on the suggestion of the well-known Spiritualist **medium**, Arthur Ford, and has brought through a substantial body of communications from a variety of **spirit guide**s.

Now in her middle sixties, Ruth Montgomery has published more than a dozen best-selling books, including *A Search for Truth*, which explores the mystery of life after death.

Moreno, Jacob L.

See **Psychodrama**.

Morphic Resonance

A term coined by **Rupert Sheldrake** to describe the explosive acquisition and spread of certain behaviour patterns among wild animals.

Experimental support for the idea of morphic resonance began to be established at Harvard University as long ago as the 1920s when the celebrated psychologist William McDougall began putting laboratory rats into a tank of water which had two gangways, one brightly lit but leading nowhere, the other a dimly lit escape route.

The first rats tested took up to 300 soakings before they learned the right way out. Later generations – McDougall kept up the experiments for 15 years – learned progressively more quickly. Evaluation of the test series indicated that the average number of mistakes make by first generation rats was 200. In the last generation tested the number had fallen to 20. Understandably, McDougall concluded the knowledge was inherited: somehow passed on cumulatively, generation by generation, in the genes. But reasonable though the conclusion was, it transpired he was wrong.

Some years later an attempt was made to duplicate the McDougall experiments in Australia. But the scientists there quickly discovered two fascinating facts. The first was that the rats they tested were substantially better at finding the correct exit *right from the start*. The second was that it did not matter whether you tested actual offspring from the original rats or took rats from the general population which had never been tested at all: all second-generation test subjects did better than the first.

Commenting on the experiments, Sheldrake produced a clear definition of morphic resonance. 'If rats are taught a new trick in Manchester,' he said, 'then rats of the same breed all over the world should show a tendency to learn the same trick more rapidly, even in the absence of any known type of physical connection or communication. The greater the number of rats that learn it, the easier it should become for their successors.'

The most exciting aspect of morphic resonance is that it may apply to humanity as well as rats and other animals, explaining such historical phenomena as the accelerating development of technology in recent centuries and the fact that today's generation of children have a higher average IQ than their grandparents.

Sheldrake decided to test this possibility experimentally and hit on the ingenious idea of using nursery rhymes. If morphic resonance was a fact of human life, he reasoned that it should be easier for children to memorize strange, even meaningless, words from a foreign language if they had already been memorized before by millions of people.

For his test series, Sheldrake used three short Japanese rhymes of similar structure. The first was in fact meaningless, a jumble of disconnected words. The second was a newly-composed verse. The third was a traditional rhyme, learned by generations of Japanese children. Although it was a 'blind' experiment in which Sheldrake did not know which rhyme was which, he quickly discovered one was learned far more easily than the other two by English schoolchildren with no knowledge of Japanese. At the end of the test, he was able to confirm the easily-learned rhyme was that which had already been learned by millions of Japanese.

Moxibustion

An ancient variation on the Chinese system of **acupuncture** in which heat is applied to the acupuncture points for therapeutic effect.

In modern practice, the heat source may be electrical, but traditional moxibustion makes use of 'moxa punk', a substance vaguely like cotton wool made from the dried fibres of the plant *artemesia vulgaris*. The punk may be formed into small cones which are then burned directly on the points, or used in cigar-shaped rolls.

In ancient times, moxibustion often involved scarring the patient, but this is no longer the case.

Mu

Supposedly the inhabitants of **Lemuria**, according to **Madame Blavatsky**, but there is also a theory that Mu was itself a lost continent in the Pacific Ocean. Colonel James Churchward wrote several books on the subject, but they are generally regarded as romantic science fiction.

Muktananda, Swami

Swami Muktananda was born in 1908 in Mangalore, India, and initiated at the age of 39 into Kashmir Shaivism by his **guru**, Bhagwan Sri Nityananda. In 1956 he attained *samadhi*.

Peculiar to siddha **yoga** taught by Muktananda is the idea that the power of **kundalini** can be aroused in an individual not through his own efforts, but through the grace of the guru. This is known at *shaktipat* and is bestowed in the form of touch (with peacock feathers!) or even a thought transmission.

Muktananda travelled widely and attracted an international reputation. He wrote several books including his spiritual autobiography, *Play of Consciousness*. His teaching is summed up in the words:

> Meditate on your Self
> Honour your Self
> Worship your Self
> Understand your Self
> God dwells within you as you.

Muktananda died in 1982 and nominated Swamis Nityananda and Chidvalasananda, a brother and sister who had spent all their lives with him, as successors.

Murphy, Bridey

Perhaps the most widely publicized example of **reincarnation** research in the twentieth century was embodied in Morey Bernstein's work in uncovering the past-life personality of a Colorado housewife named Virginia Tighe. The story was told in Bernstein's book *The Search for Bridey Murphy*, which became an international best-seller in the early 1950s.

Although the experiments were originally designed to test hypnotic **regression** within the subject's present lifetime, Mrs Tighe quickly recalled a past life as an Irishwoman, Bridey Murphy, born in County Cork in 1798.

' The regression sessions provided an enormous amount of detail about Victorian Ireland. Mrs Tighe talked about coinage, food, furniture, books, popular songs, farming methods and a good deal more. She was able to give the names of shops – Caden House, Farr's and John Carrigan's among them – and frequently used words like 'flats' (meaning platters) which, though current in the nineteenth century, were no longer a part of modern usage.

Much of the information checked out. In one intriguing instance, she actually confounded experts who were convinced iron bedsteads were not in use in Ireland prior to 1850. Bridey claimed to have slept in one as a child and subsequent investigation showed that such bedsteads were advertised as early as 1802.

Yet not everyone was satisfied that the information originated in a past life. It was eventually discovered that Mrs Tighe had an Irish nurse in her own childhood and the assumption was made that much of the information had really been drawn from her. Although the discovery allowed the Bridey Murphy case to be tidily closed, there remain investigators who consider the explanation glib and insist there are still many aspects of the experiments which provide genuine evidence that Virginia Tighe had lived before.

Music of the Spheres

A concept developed by **Pythagoras**, which still retains considerable power to fascinate, relating planetary orbits to the mathematical relationship between the tones of the musical scale. In his day, the relationship appeared close, but the validity of the concept has weakened progressively as science produced increasingly accurate astronomical measurements.

Mystery Cults

'Mystery' derives from the Greek *myein*, 'to close', and refers to the closing of the lips or eyes. The preservation of the secrets of the cult was required of an initiate.

Many cults flourished during the Hellenistic period, the

Eleusinian mysteries and the Dionysian mysteries being the best known. As well as the Greek mysteries, the mystery tradition can also be traced back to the **Egyptian mysteries** of Isis and Osiris and the Mithraic mysteries in Persia. Later there were the Qabalists, the Gnostics, the Neoplatonists, the Alchemists, the **Rosicrucians** and the Freemasons.

At the heart of all mystery schools is the idea of salvation and resurrection to eternal life.

Mysticism

A system of behaviour, belief and practice which derives ultimately from personal experience of universal unity and, generally, seeks to achieve that unity again.

The central mystical experience, in which the individual persona is absorbed into a greater whole, is interpreted in differing ways by differing cultures. Thus the Christian might see it as union with the Godhead, the Buddhist as achievement of **nirvana** and the atheist as a transcendent recognition of the essential nature of reality.

Reports of the experience itself are widespread and do not rely on any particular belief system. It can and frequently does arise spontaneously, but can also be triggered by specific exercises such as **meditation** and **yoga**.

N

Nag Hammadi Gospels

In 1945, on the west bank of the Nile, a jar was found containing 13 leather-bound papyrus codices. These comprised 52 Coptic documents of the fourth century, almost all Gnostic in character. The Gospels include the Gospel of Thomas.

Nagarjuna

The second-century Buddhist sage who first propounded the doctrine of the Middle Path followed by devotees of Mahayana **Buddhism**. Curiously, Nagarjuna's expression of *sunyata* or 'void' has much in common with the picture of the universe held by modern astrophysicists.

Naturopathy

An holistic system of medicine which emphasizes the need to assist the body in resisting disease rather than attempting directly to attack the disease itself. Such assistance relies on what Hippocrates referred to as 'the healing power of nature', advocating a wide range of non-toxic and non-suppressive methods like exercise, massage, fasting and unprocessed wholefoods, **osteopathy**, and psychological counselling.

Nazca Lines

Believed to have been created between 500 BC and AD 500, the Nazca lines are giant lines, geometric figures and human and animal drawings in the Peruvian desert. The Nazcas preceded the Incas, but neither culture left behind any written explanation of the lines. Various theories have been put forward about their purpose, ranging from the theory that they were meant for astronomical purposes to the idea that they were created by extraterrestrials to guide the landing of their spacecraft. It is more likely, however, that they were used for ancient religious ceremonies to worship the mountain gods associated with the weather, forces of nature and fertility, or were used by ancient **shaman**s, who ingested hallucinogens in sacred rites.

Near Death Experience (NDE)

Maureen Cowan died on the operating table of a Northern Irish hospital in 1959. She remained dead so far as all clinical signs were concerned for two-and-a-half minutes before the medical team revived her. Thereafter she made a complete recovery.

Journalists hearing of the incident interviewed Mrs Cowan and found she had a very clear memory of what it was like to die. She had passed through a gloomy tunnel to emerge in a pleasant, sunny parkland with shadowy figures in the background. But what seized her attention was a far from shadowy figure waiting to meet her, a tall, handsome, bearded man wearing sandals and long white robes. He exuded an **aura** of kindness and peace and she knew at once he must be Jesus Christ. She badly wanted to go with him, but a strong pull drew her back after a short time into the tunnel. She blacked out briefly and awoke to find herself in the recovery room.

On the face of it, the experience appeared a fairly predictable example of wish fulfilment. As a good Christian, Mrs Cowan confidently expected to meet Christ in Heaven and thus, on the point of death, hallucinated doing just that. The only problem with the theory was that Mrs Cowan was not a good Christian. She was Jewish.

Investigation of near death experiences, which first began to gain momentum in the late 1960s, has produced a number of puzzles of this type. Doctors prepared to correlate the reported subjective perceptions of individuals who died briefly, then revived, or simply passed close to death through accident or illness, have discovered striking similarities in the experiences.

Common denominators seem to be the sensation of passing through a tunnel, an **out-of-body experience**, a perception of light and meetings with spiritual or Biblical figures and/or dead friends and relatives. Individuals tend to interpret the experience in the light of their own cultural background. (In this Mrs Cowan was unusual in that Jews meeting with a bearded white-robed figure during a near death experience are more likely to assume they have met with one of the Biblical patriarchs than with Christ.)

Interestingly, near death reports garnered across a spectrum of cultures are not only internally consistent, but seem to agree remarkably well with the essential features of the post mortem state as described in the *Tibetan Book of the Dead*. There is also a marked similarity to the reported inner 'journeys' of **shaman**ism and certain **astral projections**.

Nei Ching

The Yellow Emperor's Classic of Internal Medicine, or *Nei Ching*, is the world's oldest existing medical textbook . . . and one full of surprises. Even conservative estimates place its composition at 1000 BC and it may well date from 2700 BC or even earlier. Yet the book makes it clear that ancient Chinese doctors were aware of blood circulation, differentiated between arteries and veins, accurately described the position, composition and function of every major internal organ and were quite capable of differential diagnosis of many diseases which baffled Western medicine for centuries.

The *Nei Ching* itself lays the foundation for the systems of Chinese **acupuncture** and **moxibustion** and describes a variety of techniques like pulse diagnosis still in common use today.

Neopaganism

A return to pre-Christian ideals and religious practices characteristic of several branches of recent thought, notably in the development of modern **witchcraft** and aspects of the burgeoning movement of **women's spirituality** which tends to regard Judaeo-**Christianity** as patriarchal, hence anti-feminist.

Neoplatonism

The philosophy developed from the third century onwards by Plotinus, Iamblichus and Porphyry, which holds that all manifestation, material and spiritual, emanates from a single transcendent godhead through the action of divine will.

An amalgamation of Platonic philosophy and Eastern **mysticism**, it is not surprising to find echoes of Neoplatonism in the **Qabalah** and other esoteric systems. The philosophy was banned in 529 by the Emperor Justinian I, but enjoyed a considerable revival amongst Renaissance mystics.

Neuro-Linguistic Programming (NLP)

NLP began in the early 1970s. The originators were John Grinder, then an Associate Professor of Linguistics at the University of California, and Richard Bandler, a mathematician, computing student and Gestalt therapist. They studied three exceptional therapists, both in person and on videotape: **Fritz Perls**, the originator of **Gestalt Therapy**, Virginia Satir, the very successful family therapist and Milton Erickson, the well-known hypnotherapist. The object of their studies was to identify the patterns used by outstanding therapists and pass them on to others.

They found that there were indeed similar underlying patterns, then went on to refine them, building a model which can be used for effective communication, personal change, accelerated learning and greater enjoyment of life. Gregory Bateson described NLP as the first systematic approach towards learning to learn.

NLP therapeutic techniques include mirroring and matching, reframing, pacing, anchoring; and tend to be used and taught in a group setting. NLP is now one of the fastest-growing developments in applied psychology and has practical applications in personal development, counselling, education and business.

New Age

'New Age' is an umbrella term, but as with all such general terms it has both advantages and disadvantages. It is useful because it describes an emerging world-view, but controversial because of some of the more trivial, even dubious, activities that are associated with it. 'New Age' is used to denote a whole range of interests, including health and well-being, the many forms of therapy or self-help, the practice of an esoteric or spiritual tradition, concern for the rest of humanity and the environment, and respect for nature and feminine wisdom.

Those who subscribe to the New Age philosophy of a changing world-view share an understanding that science, technology and a higher standard of living for many in the Western world do not necessarily produce happier human beings or make the world a better place. They believe that there is a different way of being which is life-enhancing and empowering; that we have far more potential than we are realizing; and that only in changing ourselves can society as a whole be transformed.

In many respects there is nothing at all new about the New Age. What is new is the accessibility of New Age ideas to all those who wish to know about them. With modern technology and increased travel, enabling the rapid transmission of ideas to all parts of the globe, that has all changed.

Astrologically, we are deemed to be moving from the Piscean Age to the Aquarian Age, and there have been many psychic and mystical predictions of the dawning of a new age at this time. The New Age has its roots deep in human history, though the current phase has its immediate prelude in the 1960s and 70s. The 1960s saw experimentation with mind-expanding drugs and **meditation**; the 1970s the growth of the **human potential movement**. Prior to that there have been many significant individuals and movements who have played their part, many of whom are included in this dictionary.

Alongside the old have been the new theories in science which have challenged the western mechanistic paradigm. The New Age is with us now as the pace of change accelerates and the new world-view emerges, one that is holistic and ecological, androgynous and mystical, fostering self-realization.

Nichirenism

Nichiren **Buddhism**, unlike its better-known counterpart **Zen**, which was imported from China, is a purely Japanese development. Named for its thirteenth-century founder, the militant prophet and saint Nichiren, it remained a minor sect until the end of the Second World War when it increased dramatically in popularity and influence and began to spread abroad. It is now reputedly one of the fastest-growing schools of Buddhism in the West.

Nichirenism is characterized by simple practices, a clear-cut philosophy which avoids subtlety and paradox and a success-orientated ethic.

Nirvana

The blissful state of union with supreme godhead which is the characteristic goal of Hindu, Buddhist and **yoga** practice. Achievement of nirvana obliterates ego and self, discharges all karmic debt and removes the need to reincarnate. (*See* **Karma**; **Reincarnation**.)

Nostradamus

In a secluded backroom of a house in the French town of Salon de Craux on a day in 1550, a doctor and astrologer – the two were usually combined in those days – began for the first time a very curious magical ceremony, the ultimate results of which were to echo down through the centuries.

Michel de Nostredame, destined to achieve fame under the Latin version of his name, Nostradamus, was a smallish, heavily-bearded man with a broad forehead and grey eyes. There was a faintly fanatical air about him. Historical sources tell us he had been in a fever of enthusiasm for several weeks before embarking on the operation.

Like most magicians, Nostradamus believed in a spiritual borderland, peopled by its own inhabitants. He also believed that somewhere in the northern wilderness there were areas where the two worlds overlapped and beings from one could meet and communicate with beings from the other. But if no-one had yet found the exact location of the overlap, it did not matter, for there were age-old magical techniques which allowed communication almost anywhere. Nostradamus was about to use one of them now.

He carried a special divining wand of laurel. Set up before him was a tripod brazier on which was a vessel filled with water. Full details of the ceremony were not recorded, but it seems probable he used one of the ponderous Judaeo-Christian rituals preserved in the *grimoires* of his day, now resting in our museums. It is known, however, that at the climax of his evocation, he struck the brazier with his wand, then dipped first the fringe of his robe, then one foot in the water.

At this point, the form of a **spirit** appeared in the vapour above the bowl. Nostradamus convulsed violently and his body shook under the impact of the experience. It seemed to him the spirit dictated a four-line verse and Nostradamus carefully wrote it down. It was the first of a thousand he was to write down and they were to make him famous for centuries.

Nostradamus was born in St Rémy, a town in Provence, on 14 December 1503. His father was a notary, his mother a member of a well-known medical family. Both were Jewish.

Young Michel's early education was at the hands of his great-grandfather, who gave him an interest in **astrology**. Later he attended school at Avignon, then university at Montpellier, which contained the most famous medical school in all France.

When he was 22 years old, plague struck in Montpellier and Nostradamus moved out, first to Narbonne, then Toulouse and finally Bordeaux. He began to practise medicine in these towns even though it was not until four years later that he returned to Montpellier to take his doctor's degree. He settled for a time in Agen, but left again after his wife died. By this time he was building up a considerable reputation, for the Parliament of Provence invited him to make his home in Aix and granted him a salary when he agreed.

Plague ravaged the town in 1546. Prospects of a cure seemed so remote that the modest women of Aix took to sewing themselves up in their winding sheets at the first sign of infection so that their bodies would not be exposed naked after death. But Nostradamus did develop a treatment which proved so effective that a grateful town voted him a sizeable pension for several years after the plague died out.

From Aix, he went to live in Salon de Craux, midway between Avignon and Marseilles. There he married again, raised children, and began the magical operation which led to the series of verses he later collected and published under the titles of *Centuries* and *Presages*. The verses were predictive, outlining a massive sweep of future history until the end of the world.

With the revival of interest in the works of Nostradamus, considerable credence has been given to the belief that he set the end of the world in 1999. In fact, Nostradamus' prophecies continue for some thousands of years after that date. What *does* seem to be predicted for 1999 is the aerial bombardment of Paris and the fall of Rome. Curiously, the Prophecies of Malachy, an Irish saint and seer, sets the end of the Papacy around the year 1999 as well. As a good Catholic, Malachy could not envision the world continuing after so catastrophic an event.

With 1999 approaching a great deal faster now than it did in 1550, other good Catholics, or perhaps just those of a nervous disposition, may draw some comfort from two facts.

The first is that while many of Nostradamus' predictions were accurate up to and including the time of the French Revolution, the accuracy percentage has dropped considerably since then, as if his perceptions of the future grew dimmer the farther ahead he looked.

The second is that while some of his verses are clearly stated, others are couched in such obscurity of language and symbol that they have become a sort of prophetic Rorschach Test into which interpreters can read almost anything they wish. Because of this, there is no shortage of modern pundits who can show conclusively that Nostradamus predicted something after the event has occurred. Far fewer have gone on record with accurate predictions based on his prophecies before the event to which they are supposed to point.

Numerology

It is a curiosity of Hebrew (and several other ancient alphabets) that its letters have numerical counterparts. This meant that words could be expressed as numbers and led to the development of Qabalistic *gematria*, a (now somewhat discredited) system whereby hidden correspondences between unrelated things and events were sought out through analysis of the numbers produced by the spelling of their names.

Essentially the same thinking lies behind the occult art of numerology which, in any recognizable modern expression, seems to draw on the speculations of **Pythagoras** for its inspiration. Since the English alphabet has no numerical equivalents, these are assigned to it. In its simplest form, the assignments are A = 1, B = 2, C = 3 and so on as far as I = 9, after which the sequence is repeated with J = 1, K = 2 etc.

To analyse the hidden meaning of a word, its assigned numbers are added together then 'reduced' (by adding together the individual digits of any number larger than 9) so that a single figure number is eventually obtained. This figure is then interpreted according to traditional associations.

Unfortunately, there are many different assignments of figures to letters, not all of them stopping at 9. Furthermore, the 'traditional' interpretations of the reduced numbers can often vary widely, with the result that numerology is not always taken seriously, even among occultists.

O

Occultism

The term 'occult' means simply 'secret' or 'hidden' (and is used in this sense in orthodox medicine) but has clearly been extended to imply a secret tradition of magical and mystical knowledge followed by initiates down the ages. Unlike the very similar term 'esotericism' which suggests a theoretical knowledge of such subjects, 'occultism' conveys the idea of practice as well as study.

Om

A Sanskrit term pronounced 'A-U-M', which is the most important and sacred sound in Vedic and Hindu tradition. It is a mystical **mantra** which is used to symbolize the trinity of Brahma, Vishnu and Shiva, rulers of the manifested universe.

Oracle

Throughout history various cultures have referred to oracles for advice on the best course of action. Deities or supernatural beings are consulted, usually through a human **medium** or channel. One of the most famous oracles was the one at Delphi, where a priestess called Pythia was the oracular medium.

Orr, Leonard
See **Rebirthing**.

Osteopathy

Osteopathy is a manipulative therapy. It was formulated by Dr Andrew Taylor Still, who was trained in both engineering and medicine. Hardly surprising, then, that whilst he was developing his technique he approached the human body rather as if it fitted together like a machine. He discovered that disease was caused by the spinal vertebrae slipping out of position. This could result in the disturbance of the nerves or blood supply that runs

212

through the vertebrae. Correction is by manipulation, and although osteopaths are generally thought of as treating back pain, they can also treat successfully such complaints as migraine and painful joints.

Ouspensky, P.D.

One of the few disciples of **G.I. Gurdjieff** to stand out as an original thinker in his own right, Peter Demianovich Ouspensky was a Russian-born mathematician who devoted much of his time to an attempted synthesis of mathematics, **mysticism**, science and religion into a coherent system of thought.

At the age of 37 in 1915, he met Gurdjieff in St Petersburg and studied under him for about eight years before a quarrel sent them their separate ways. Although he describes his time with Gurdjieff in his *In Search of the Miraculous*, which was published after his death in 1948, his best-known books, *Tertium Organum* and *A New Model of the Universe* seem to owe little enough to the Gurdjieff system.

Out-of-Body Experience (OBE)

See **Astral Projection; Etheric Projection**.

P

Pagan

A sometimes derogatory term applied to those who do not profess the Christian, Jewish or Islamic faiths. The label has, however, been voluntarily espoused by many groups bent on a revival of **witchcraft**, Nature worship or devotion to the **Goddess**.

Palmistry

A system of character analysis cum **divination** based on the study of the creases, pads, skin texture and colour of the human hand. Some of the traditional systems of palmistry link the art with **astrology** in giving astrological linkages to certain parts of the hand, e.g. the fleshy root of the thumb is known as the Mount of Venus.

Although often associated in the public mind with fairground fortune-telling, there are some indications that palmistry should be taken seriously. Certainly its best-known twentieth-century exponent, Count Louis Hamon, who adopted the professional name Cheiro, was noted for the accuracy of his predictions and managed to convince many eminent clients that his abilities were genuine.

Paracelsus

Born Theophrastus Bombastus von Hohenheim in .1493, Paracelsus changed his name in adult life to underline his claim that he was the greatest physician of his, or any other, age – greater even than Celsus, the Roman physician revered in ancient times.

There was actually something to his claim. He developed amazing skill in medicine and in 1527 he was appointed city physician of Basle and Professor of Physic, Medicine and Surgery at the university there. But he was an arrogant, intemperate man with little understanding of the feelings of others, so that it took him only a short time to irritate the authorities.

This he did by announcing that his lectures would not be drawn from the works of Galen (as was the tradition in the universities of the time) but from his own knowledge and experience. Then he emphasized the point by burning Galen's texts. He insisted on writing in German, rather than the traditional Latin, and demanded laws to regulate the work of apothecaries. Eventually he went too far by abusing a magistrate who found against him in a court case and had to flee the city.

For all his pomposity and inflated ego, Paracelsus was father to several theories which might be viewed quite sympathetically today. He believed that the stars and other bodies, especially magnets, influenced patients by means of a universal force he called *munia*, which seems very similar to the Hindu *prana* or the Chinese *ch'i*. Paracelsus stated that the force was 'not enclosed in man, but radiates within and around him like a luminous sphere', an obvious allusion to the human **aura**. He also believed that mineral, plant and animal substances could be purified and intensified in order to produce active principles, which might then be used in **healing**. Two centuries later, his **intuitions** were confirmed with the development of **homoeopathy**.

Paracelsus died in 1541.

Paradigm, New/Emerging

The term 'paradigm', which derives from the Greek *paradeigma*, or pattern, was used by Thomas Kuhn in his book *The Structure of Scientific Revolutions* to denote a conceptual framework shared by a community of scientists and providing them with a convenient model for examining problems and creating solutions.

Since the book was first published, a broader definition of the term has emerged from the work of individuals like **Fritjof Capra** who interprets paradigm as 'the totality of thoughts, perceptions, and values that form a particular vision of reality'. Capra adds it is this vision that is the basis of the way a society organizes itself.

There can be little argument that there has been a dramatic and continuing shift in the paradigm as defined by Capra. This is discernible in economics, with an increasing acceptance of the need to place people before profit, in medicine, with its move towards a holistic approach and more broad-minded acceptance of alternative therapies, in psychology, with the development of the experiential schools of the **human potential movement**, and in science, with the emergence of Chaos Theory and a host of new ways to examine and structure the world around us.

If an emerging paradigm is evident, the reasons for its emergence are not altogether clear. To some it is simply the result of a perfectly predictable process in the history of human thought. When certain ideas can take us no further, they are naturally abandoned for fresh approaches with greater potential. To others, it may be humanity's way of demonstrating **morphic resonance**, with the spread of ideas through the general population now reaching a sort of critical mass and exploding in new directions.

One school of thought links the new paradigm with both esoteric (and **Jung**ian) notions of cyclical changes in the dominants of the group psyche which follow the arrival of the Aquarian Era.

Paranormal

A term used to describe any phenomenon which cannot be explained by the laws of nature as currently understood by science. As a noun, it is often loosely used as synonymous with psychical phenomena.

Parapsychology

The scientific study of **paranormal** phenomena relating specifically to the human mind. Thus parapsychology would normally encompass the study of telepathy, **precognition** and such talents as **astral projection**.

Past-Life Therapy

See **Regression; Reincarnation**.

Past Lives

See **Regression; Reincarnation**.

Patanjali

An Indian sage of the third century BC, noted as author of the *Yoga Aphorisms*, a series of sutras on which almost the whole body of Indian **yoga** is now based. Patanjali is not, however, regarded as the founder of yoga, which was practised in his homeland for almost 1,000 years before he was born, but rather as its codifier. As such, he has been of considerable influence, since entire yoga sub-systems have evolved from a single verse – sometimes even a single word – taken from his *Aphorisms*.

Pathworking

The foremost modern exponent of the art, **Dolores Ashcroft-Nowicki**, has defined pathworking as 'a journey between this side of the mental worlds and the other side . . . [which] offers a path, a map through the landscapes of the mind . . . [Pathworkings] are Doorways between the known and the physical and the unknown and the non-corporeal. They accomplish their work through the medium of the creative imagination . . . They can and do cause actual physical effects in the everyday world . . .'

Although the term 'pathworking' is derived from Qabalistic practice, the technique itself is not specifically Qabalistic and appears under a variety of names, ancient and modern, including 'guided **meditation**', 'active imagination', 'thought building' and even 'fantasy role play'. When used as esoteric tools, such workings serve a variety of purposes, from **initiation** to the **channelling** of power. Some make use of visual symbols, others rely on detailed verbal instructions to paint pictures in the mind.

Pathworkings are not new. They were used in early Egypt and Sumer, the first known human civilization, and are believed to have formed an important part of Chaldean star **magic**. But while hints and aspects of pathworking leaked out to some degree from age to age, a full esoteric exposition remained the exclusive prerogative of initiate occultists until the early 1980s when **Dolores Ashcroft-Nowicki** decided to go public with the technique.

Her decision created a furore among her fellow-occultists, many of whom disapproved deeply of what she was doing. But she felt that the time was right for the method to reach a wider audience and persevered with her controversial approach. From public expositions before large, but necessarily limited, audiences she then went into print to reach the largest public possible.

Her first book on the subject was *The Shining Paths*, a collection of verbal pathworkings centred on the Qabalistic Tree of Life. Four years later, she was in print again with *Highways of the Mind*, an even more detailed exposition of the art and one which contains a fascinating history of its development.

Peak Experience

A moment of intense feeling when we are in touch with the whole universe. Communing with Nature, sex, a religious **ritual** or listening to music can give rise to a peak experience. **Abraham Maslow** studied peak experiences and believed that they are within the reach of us all.

Pendulum

A suspended weight used in **dowsing**, radiesthesia diagnosis and certain types of psychical activity.

The archaeologist **T.C. Lethbridge** believed differing lengths of string produced pendulums specifically 'tuned' to various substances and even to emotional states. One of the most peculiar usages of the pendulum is in map dowsing where water courses, minerals and even archaeological finds can be pinpointed by the behaviour of the instrument when held over a map of an area. During the Second World War, a Pendulum Institute in Berlin sought to determine the location of Allied convoys by pendulum dowsing sea charts. The information was then passed on to U-boat commanders.

Map dowsing has similarities with radiesthesia diagnosis in that practitioners hold the pendulum above a chart on which is placed a patient's blood sample in order to determine the nature of the illness.

Penry-Evans, Violet Mary

See **Fortune, Dion**.

Pentagram Ritual

One of the most common methods used by Qabalists to prepare a place of magical working, the Lesser Banishing Ritual of the Pentagram was developed, or at least popularized, by the Order of the **Golden Dawn** and is even now used as a major method of **psychic self defence**.

The **ritual** itself is actually a composite, incorporating a sub-ritual called the Ritual of the Qabalistic Cross. It acts rather like the astral equivalent of disinfectant in an operating theatre and is designed to clear the atmosphere before magical operations are carried out. When this is done, it acts as a barrier against all astral intrusions until the next sunset or sunrise. The ritual can also be used to seal an individual's **aura** temporarily, to guard against energy loss or repulse **psychic attack**.

Perennial Philosophy

The idea that underlying all the great religious traditions runs an essential truth: there is one divine reality which cannot be directly and immediately understood, except through the practice of love, i.e. by a mind in a state of detachment, charity and humility. **Aldous Huxley**'s classic work, *The Perennial Philosophy*, was published in 1946.

Perls, Fritz

Born in Germany in 1893 and trained as a psychiatrist before the Second World War, Fritz Perls became internationally renowned at **Esalen** for **Gestalt therapy**, which he developed with Paul and Laura Goodman in the mid-1950s.

Philosopher's Stone

In alchemical theory, the Philosopher's Stone was the original substance from which all metals derived and consequently could be used in the transformation of lead and other base metals into gold.

Many alchemists devoted lifetimes to searching for literal, physical examples of the substance, but when it proved elusive, the theory arose that it was non-material, possibly even spiritual, in essence and could be recognized only by initiates.

Arab **alchemy**, an advanced form of the art, may actually have discovered the non-material Stone in the form of electricity as the uncovering in June 1936 of artefacts later identified as earthenware, copper and bitumen batteries dating from the Parthian period (248 BC–AD 226) in Iraq showed. Experiments in the United States using reconstructions of the batteries showed each capable of producing a ½ volt current for up to 18 days, with the possibility of higher voltages still if the batteries were linked sequentially. This was more than enough for electroplating, which may well have accounted for stories of the ancient alchemists turning base metals into their 'noble' counterparts of gold and silver.

PK

See **Psychokinesis**.

Polarity Therapy

Randolph Stone was the originator of polarity therapy and he studied **osteopathy, naturopathy** and **chiropractic**. A variety of techniques are used, including manipulation, stretching postures and diet, all with the aim of removing the blocks in the flow of energy through the body.

Poltergeist

Colin Wilson, a well-known writer on esoteric themes, estimates there are probably more than 1,000 recorded cases of poltergeist hauntings.

The word *poltergeist* derives from the German and means 'noisy ghost'. A typical case reported was in America's *Harper's Magazine* in 1962.

The article told how a middle-aged couple rented an isolated house in Cape Cod for the summer. On the evening of their arrival, the husband was sitting up working on a manuscript when his wife Helen, who had gone to bed earlier, called down 'Was that you?' She had heard a noise like someone tapping with a cane on the brickwork by the front door.

Neither of them paid much attention to the incident. But the following night the sound came again. The husband ran outside with a torch. As he opened the front door the tapping stopped. From then on, night after night, the sound came again, but every attempt to catch the person who was tapping failed.

During the second week, on three successive nights, the husband was awakened by other noises. The first was a sound like a box of matches falling on the floor. He switched on the light at once, but could find nothing. The second was a noise like a sheet of newspaper swishing across the room. The third was a sound was like that of something heavy rolling across the floor and coming to a stop against the wall. There was no explanation for any of the noises.

By the end of the second week, the haunting was getting worse. The couple began to hear a mysterious clicking noise from the walls. During the time they remained in the house, they were to hear it several hundred times.

The third week of their stay introduced the sound of footsteps. These were clear, loud and heavy like those of a large man wearing leather shoes with solid heels. When the couple were downstairs, the sounds would come from the rooms above them. When they were upstairs, the footsteps roamed around below. Each time they went to investigate, the rooms proved empty.

Midway through their stay, there was a crash in the garage so loud that it shook the whole house. It sounded like a grand piano dropping through the roof. They raced out to find the cause. But the garage, which they used to store books, was empty.

The couple were not the only ones to hear the noises. They were visited during their stay by a lawyer friend, his wife and daughter. On the first evening of the visit, the women went out to a play while the two men remained to work on a contract. In the course of the evening, the lawyer remarked that he would certainly like to hear from the ghost they had been telling him about . . . and at once there was a click from the wall.

The lawyer suggested it might be drying wood, but 20 minutes later the footsteps started. Unable to believe it was a ghost, the lawyer ran upstairs and investigated bedrooms and attic with a torch. He found nothing. That night, the lawyer and his family heard the shattering crash in the garage, although on this occasion the two other occupants of the house heard nothing.

The story is fairly representative of poltergeist phenomena, which are spectacular, noisy, usually lacking any visual element, and, while certainly frightening, usually harmless. Poltergeists present a pattern of behaviour that is typically mischievous rather than evil. Windows and ornaments may be broken, but people are seldom actually injured or even hurt. A haunting often gives the impression of a house occupied by an invisible, but hyperactive, child.

This pattern, coupled with the observation that poltergeists will often haunt people rather than places, has led some investigators to conclude that the noisy ghost is not a ghost at all, but rather an externalization of psychic energy from the subconscious of someone in the house – usually an emotionally repressed child or adolescent.

The theory has gained widespread acceptance among psychical researchers, but some investigators are moving towards the conclusion that it may not fit all the facts and a **spirit** hypothesis cannot, after all, be ruled out in certain cases.

Prana

In Hindu **yoga**, a universal energy associated with the breath, absorbed into and used by the human body to maintain health and fitness.

Prana, which is generated by the sun and occurs naturally in the atmosphere (and beyond), is absorbed into the body through a series of subtle centres known as **chakras**. The **asanas** of Hatha yoga direct the flow of pranic energy to promote fitness.

The concept of *prana* appears to be virtually identical to the Chinese *ch'i*.

Pranayama

The Indian **yoga** of breath control which is used to produce an altered state of **consciousness**.

Precognition

The ability to obtain information, by extra-sensory means, about future events, precognition has now been well established via tests using a variation of Dr **J.B. Rhine**'s famous experiments in telepathy using Zener cards. Unlike the telepathy tests where subjects were required to guess the card currently under examination by a 'sender', the statistical analysis for precognition related to guesses which predicted symbols one or two cards ahead in the sequence. (*See also* **Prophecy**.)

Pribram, Karl

According to Pribram, a Stanford neuroscientist, the brain in many ways resembles a hologram. (*See* **Holographic Theory**.)

Prigogine, Ilya

Belgian chemist and winner of the 1977 Nobel Prize in chemistry for his theory of **dissipative structures**.

Primal Therapy

Founded by Arthur Janov, primal therapy is concerned with re-experiencing and giving physical expression to the pain and hurt of childhood through screaming and crying. This is done in order to dissolve neurosis. The therapy is carried out in a sound-proof, softly-lit room with plenty of cushions to curl up on. The role of the therapist is to be supportive in this process and help in the **healing** of pain.

Prophecy

A divinely inspired vision or revelation which is a form of **precognition**, or knowledge of the future. Throughout history, prophecies have been made through **oracle**s or prophets/ prophetesses. The Old Testament contains numerous prophets and prophecies. In **Islam** Mohammed was chosen as the last of all the prophets. In the sixteenth century, **Nostradamus** published his famous prophecies, in which there continues to be enormous fascination today. The most famous prophet of the twentieth century has been **Edgar Cayce**.

Psi

An umbrella term used by parapsychologists to describe **paranormal** phenomena such as **ESP**.

Psychic

Used as a noun, the term denotes one who possesses such paranormal abilities as telepathy, **precognition**, **clairvoyance,** etc. As an adjective, it is used as an umbrella term to describe the essence of the abilities themselves.

Psychic Attack

One of the earliest **Huna** techniques to be demonstrated to the Christian missionaries who landed in Hawaii in the early nineteenth century was the notorious 'death prayer'. Kahuna sorcerers using this technique would typically dispatch **spirit**s to penetrate the body of the victim and absorb his *mana* or life force. This was experienced as a numbness starting at the feet and gradually travelling upwards. When the numbness reached the heart, the victim died.

Almost every primitive culture has its techniques of psychic attack, from the pointing bones of the Australian aborigine to the **Voodoo** dolls of Haiti. Early anthropologists assumed that when such **magic** worked, it worked through suggestion and it was often claimed that the scientifically advanced white man was immune to psychic attack while the superstitious native could be expected quickly to succumb. Unfortunately, it was soon shown that the advanced white man was no more immune to psychic attack than the tribal native and the technique worked on a variety of domestic animals which would not normally be expected to react to suggestion.

Occultists accept the reality of psychic attack and while admitting that suggestion may in certain instances play a (small) part in it, insist the true technique operates via the **astral plane**.

Dion Fortune claimed that shortly after she established the Society of the Inner Light, which leeched members from the dying Order of the **Golden Dawn**, she was subjected to psychic attack by the widow of **MacGregor Mathers**. The astral entity dispatched was in the form of a gigantic cat, which Dion Fortune fought off only with difficulty. When she emerged from her trance battle, she was covered from neck to waist by scratches.

Psychic Healing

A therapeutic technique which involves the **channelling** of **psychic** or spiritual power through the healer into the patient, often involving a laying on of hands and/or prayer. It may be that certain examples of this type of **healing** involve a transfer of personal or universal *ch'i*.

Psychic Self Defence

It is a curious fact that methods of psychic self defence are a little more difficult to discover than the techniques of **psychic attack**. But it is probably true to say that an understanding of the fundamentals of psychical attack makes defence relatively straightforward.

Most forms of psychical attack work through the **astral plane**, making contact with the intended victim and manifesting, usually undetected, in his/her subconscious mind. Because of the astral association, effective defence will normally involve the **visualization** of a defensive structure which, it is hoped, is then established sufficiently strongly on the astral plane to stop external influences coming in.

Perhaps the simplest structure involves imagining oneself surrounded by a spinning wall of light. But the principle remains the same whether or not one adopts this technique or opts for a more elaborate approach like the banishing **pentagram ritual** which can be used to safeguard an individual or group as well as clearing a space for working.

Psychic Surgery

Often performed in a trance state, sometimes without touching the physical body, but more dramatically by psychic surgeons in the Philippines and Brazil involving physical operations followed by immediate **healing** of the wounds.

Psychical Research

Although investigation of psychical phenomena has been carried out for centuries, systematic, structured scientific research really only dates back to the foundation, in Britain, of the **Society for Psychical Research** in 1882. An American society, based on the same stated principles, came into being shortly afterwards.

At the time these societies opened, the Spiritualist movement was at its peak so that it was perhaps understandable that early investigations concentrated almost exclusively on mediumship and séance-room phenomena. With a decline in public interest in **Spiritualism** following the First World War (**medium**s, by and large, failed abysmally to predict the outbreak of hostilities and many had reassured clients that all would be sweetness and light despite a manifestly threatening political situation), psychical research began gradually to broaden its field of interest.

In the late 1930s, Dr **J.B. Rhine** of Duke University in North Carolina added a new dimension to the research by developing methods by which statistical analysis could be applied to psychical talents like telepathy, **precognition** or **pyschokinesis**. The statistical approach tended to dominate professional psychical research over the next two or three decades and continues to dominate it today, although to a much lesser extent.

But this relates only to the Western situation. In the Soviet Union, where scientific interest in the **psychic** survived even Stalinism, the emphasis was always much more on qualitative research than statistical analysis or the production of phenomena under laboratory conditions.

As a result, it became widely acknowledged in the sixties and seventies that the Soviets led the world in their understanding of such oddities as dermo-optic vision (eyeless sight), bio-plasmic energies and the whole gamut of **psi** abilities from telepathy to **prophecy**. Inspired by the **paradigm** shift, Western scientists began to narrow the gap in the eighties.

Psychical Research, Society for

The Society for Psychical Research was founded in 1882 by a small, distinguished group of Cambridge scholars interested in **paranormal** phenomena and determined that it should be investigated in an unbiased, scientific manner.

It proved a remarkably successful move, for in the century or so of its existence, the society has attracted some of the finest minds in Britain. Past presidents include philosophers C.D. Broad and Henri Bergson, Prime Minister A.J. Balfour, the psychologist William James and Nobel Prize-winning physiologist Charles Richet.

Psychodrama

Psychodrama was developed by Jacob Moreno in Vienna in the 1920s and 30s. He set up a psychodrama school in New York but it was not until the 1960s and 70s that Moreno's work was taken up and finally used more extensively.

Moreno believed that we tend to adopt rigid roles and act them out. In psychodrama theatre and make-believe, situations are used to free spontaneous expression.

Psychokinesis

The ability to influence physical matter through mental concentration. In Britain, the most spectacular psychokinetic experimentation has been carried out in a group context by **Kenneth Bacheldor** and his followers. In the Soviet Union, the emphasis was on individual manifestations of the talent. Russia's most famous PK medium, Nelya Mikhailova, is reported to have caused a reporter's sandwich to crawl across a table and fall off the edge. Tests using **Kirlian photography** suggest that Madame Mikhailova produced such phenomena by creating a rhythmic pulsing of her personal energy field. (*See* **Aura**; **Ch'i**.)

Psychometry

Defined as the ability to gain intuitive impressions of an object's history and associations merely by handling it, psychometry is possibly a much more widespread **psychic** talent than is generally imagined. The fact that it rarely manifests may have more to do with the fact that few people have heard of it, let alone seen it demonstrated, than with any difficulty in stimulating the talent itself.

The technique of psychometry is very simple and open to personal experimentation. The easiest way to test yourself for the talent is to obtain an object – a watch or piece of jewellery would be ideal – the history of which is known, but not to you.

Fondle the item loosely in your hand, or press it against your forehead, while allowing your mind to go blank. Then watch for any mental pictures that may arise. Describe these pictures to the individual who knows the story of the object you are holding. Very often the two will tally.

Psychometry is a talent which strengthens with self-confidence and practice. In its fully manifested form, it has been used successfully in archaeology (to indicate the location and provenance of artefacts) and in police work where a psychic can provide vital clues to a crime by obtaining impressions from, for example, the clothing of a murder victim.

Psychosynthesis

Developed by the Italian psychiatrist, **Roberto Assagioli**, between 1910 and the 1950s, psychosynthesis only became known in the 1960s. It is a transpersonal or spiritual psychotherapy. The process of psychosynthesis is to synthesize the different and contradictory aspects of the psyche, and various techniques have been developed to do this. A therapist may use guided fantasy or voice dialogue, drawing or painting to clarify feelings about a particular issue. Techniques from other therapies like **Gestalt** or **psychodrama** may also be used.

Pursel, Jach
See **Lazaris**.

Pyramid
See **Great Pyramid**.

Pyramid Power

When Press reports in the 1960s highlighted the fact that the Czech radio engineer, Karel Drbal, had been granted a patent on his discovery that cardboard pyramids could be used to sharpen razor blades, an explosion of interest soon led to a host of investigations into and not a few published books about what quickly came to be called 'pyramid power'.

Although patent protection requires no theoretical explanation of why an invention works (merely the demonstration that it does), it would appear that the fundamental shape of the pyramid generates a hitherto unsuspected energy which affects the blade. The molecular structure of the edge is crystalline in nature and is susceptible to quite subtle influence. (Polarized light, moonlight for example, is enough to dull a razor's edge over a period of a few hours.)

Whatever energy or energies exist within a pyramidal structure, they also appear capable of dehydrating and preserving organic matter, a process of mummification, in fact, made all the more interesting by the ancient Egyptian fascination with death.

But as the interest in pyramid power began to snowball, claims for the phenomena it was supposed to generate became wider and wider. At the height of the fad, pyramids were sold as **meditation** aids, generators of visionary experience, anti-biotic machines, wound healers, boosters of the immune system and vehicles of mystical illumination. Pyramidal cloches were supposed to make plants grow better. Pyramidal tents were used to communicate with the **spirit**s of the dead.

A useful antidote to the growing hysteria about pyramid power was provided by the Irish wit and scholar, the late P.N.N. Synnott who, on being told that pyramids were being used to sharpen razor blades, remarked that a neighbouring family of aristocrats had been buried in a pyramidal crypt for four generations without much indication of its having sharpened *them*. But despite understandable cynicism about the wilder claims, it seems beyond doubt that some curious phenomena are associated with the pyramid shape, and in particular the pyramid shape which is a scale model of the **Great Pyramid** of Cheops.

Pythagoras

The author of the geometrical theorem taught to every schoolchild, the Greek philosopher and mathematician Pythagoras was also a mystic.

Pythagoras was born in Samos about 572 BC, but travelled to Egypt before settling in southern Italy where he established a religious brotherhood. He taught the importance of contemplation and **meditation** and believed in **reincarnation**. One of his most interesting (although essentially inaccurate) ideas concerned the **music of the spheres**, a theory by which he attempted boldly to divine the innermost secret of the creation of the solar system.

Q

Qabalah

According to Rabbinical tradition, the Qabalah was first taught to Adam in the Garden of Eden by the Archangel Gabriel and passed on 'from mouth to ear' a phrase embodied in the name itself through a long chain of select initiates ever since.

Whatever the truth of this engaging fable, there is little doubt that the body of esoteric doctrines which contain the heart of the Jewish mystical and magical traditions is very old indeed. Internal analysis shows definite Gnostic influence and it seems reasonable to assume some at least of the teachings may be rooted in the prophetic **mysticism** of the Old Testament.

But the Qabalah remained a strictly oral tradition until the late thirteenth century. Sometime around AD 1280, a Spanish **Qabalist** named Moses ben Shemtob de Leon issued a lengthy commentary on the first five Books of Moses. This work, known as the *Zepher ha Zohar* or 'Book of Splendours', was not exactly Moses de Leon's own composition. He claimed it represented the work of another Rabbi, the learned mystic Simeon bar Yohai, who had died in an ecstatic trance, leaving his followers to record the information he had received through his visions.

The *Zohar* departed substantially from orthodox **Judaism** in that it taught the ultimate godhead to be the Ain Soph, a limitless undifferentiated 'being' beyond all description or speculation. (The concept is not unlike the Brahman of the Hindus, the undifferentiated background state from which all manifestation has sprung and to which it must one day return.)

The Ain Soph 'condensed' (the word is necessarily inexact) a somewhat lesser being, the Yahweh or Jehovah of the Hebrews, who nevertheless had the prime characteristic of manifest unity. Since the name of Yahweh was too holy to be spoken aloud, Qabalists preferred to use the term *Tetragrammaton*, which means 'Name of Four Letters' and refers to the fact that Yahweh is spelled, in Hebrew, YHVH.

In attempting to describe the essence of this god, Qabalists conceived of manifestation as ten interlinking states or spheres of activity, called Sephiroth. The first Sephirah, Kether, the state of unity, encompassed all the rest and was clearly associated with Yahweh. The remaining nine, culminating in Malkuth, the physical world, provided a sort of map of manifestation which was called by Qabalists the **Tree of Life**.

This was all heady, profound, mystical stuff and the *Zepher ha Zohar* was a long and difficult book (which may explain why so few modern Qabalists have actually read it). But much of the historical interest generated by the Qabalah centred not so much on its philosophical doctrines as its practical application. The Qabalah, and in particular the Tree of Life, was considered to be an exceptional tool for the evocation of spiritual powers. The inverse Tree, associated with the Qlipoth or Shells, could be used to call up demons.

Such notions have not been entirely abandoned in modern times. Since the establishment of the **Golden Dawn** in the Victorian era, the Qabalah has become a pivotal point of the entire **Western Esoteric Tradition**. But it is a Qabalah the old Hebrews might have had difficulty in recognizing. The original tradition has become heavily encrusted with Christian and even Far Eastern elements, attention is focused almost exclusively on the Tree and emphasis placed firmly on such practices as **meditation** and **pathworking**.

Today, the typical Qabalist is a manipulator of symbols. In her magnum opus on the subject, *The Mystical Qabalah*, **Dion Fortune** wrote that the formulation of the image and the vibration of the Name was designed to put the student in touch with the forces behind each sphere of the Tree. The Name was the particular (Hebrew) Name of God associated with a specific Sephirah. Vibration was a specialist magical pronunciation. The image was one of many associated with the sphere.

Students learning the Qabalah will typically spend a considerable amount of time and effort on building in to their minds traditional associations with the Sephiroth and the Paths of the Tree, then go on to formulate their personal associations on this basis. The end result is that the Tree becomes a sort of organizational filofax which can be applied to unknown mystical systems in order to make sense of them. It can also be used as the basis for operations of **ritual magic**.

Qabalistic training, offered by, among others, the **Servants of the Light** and the Society of the Inner Light, takes some three or four years to complete to any worthwhile standard and can become thereafter a lifetime occupation.

Qabalist

The Qabalist is an individual, who may or may not be Jewish, trained in a practical system of **magic** based largely but by no means exclusively on traditional Hebrew Qabalistic doctrines about the **Tree of Life**.

Qi Gong

See Ch'i Kung.

Quakers

See **Society of Friends**.

R

Rabi'a

Rabi'a al-Adawiyah was the first and one of the very few women in **Islam** to be elevated to Sufi sainthood. She was born in Basra and became the first known individual to formulate the basic Sufi ideal of the perfected love of God. This love was conceived as total, excluding person or personality, and disinterested, neither seeking paradise nor fearing hell. So strong was her dedication to the ideal that many stories told of her sitting on her roof all night under the stars, completely absorbed in God. It was through Rabi'a that the early asceticism of the Sufi movement transformed itself into **mysticism**. She died about AD 801.

Radionics

The term 'radiesthesia' denotes the medical use of **dowsing**, pioneered in France during the nineteenth century. Radionics is the mechanical counterpart of radiesthesia, originally developed by the San Francisco neurologist, Dr Albert Abrams.

Dr Abrams theorized that since the human body was known to emit radiation, it should be possible to detect changes in this energy field due to tissue damage or illness. After years of experimentation, he developed a 'reflexoscope' which he claimed could differentiate between cancer, tuberculosis and syphilis.

The reflexoscope was a diagnostic tool, but Dr Abrams surmised it should be possible to design therapeutic instruments which would act on the body's radiation. Eventually, with the aid of an engineer, he built one which became known as the 'oscilloclast' or, more popularly, 'Abrams' Box'. Perhaps surprisingly, it worked. In 1925, a British Commission of Inquiry set up to examine results obtained by the Box, subsequently reported, 'The fundamental proposition underlying the so-called ERA (Electronic Reaction of Abrams) is established to a very high degree of probability.'

Other practitioners followed in Dr Abrams' footsteps and constructed radionic devices of their own, including the 'black box' of George de la Warr, which was the subject of a court action during the 1960s. Despite the fact that they could find no scientific explanation for its effect, the judges decided that the box actually worked and produced cures as claimed.

Despite such favourable decisions, radionics has traditionally been bedevilled by two problems. One is the inconsistency of the method, which seems to rely as much on the practitioner's sensitivity and well-being than on the machinery involved. The other is the established fact that radionics can diagnose and treat patients in their absence, using no more than a small blood or urine sample – something which has so far defied a rational explanation.

Rajneesh, Bhagwan Shree
See **Rajneesh, Osho**.

Rajneesh, Osho
Osho (1931–90), formerly known as Bhagwan Shree Rajneesh, was the most fashionable Indian **guru** of the 1970s. His **ashram** in Poona was a mecca for the counter-culture, combining Western psychotherapy techniques with Hindu and Buddhist **meditation**s. He also became famous for teaching that sex could be a path to enlightenment. His daily discourses on life, love and meditation have been published in over 300 books.

In 1981 he moved to Oregon, USA, and set up the community of Rajneeshpuram, an ecospiritual experiment which attracted much hostility in Oregon. The movement was taken over by an autocratic group whose leaders were later convicted of various crimes and imprisoned. Osho was also arrested and deported in 1985, after which Rajneeshpuram was disbanded.

Osho spent his remaining years back in the Poona commune, which is still flourishing after his death with a year-round programme of **New Age** and psychospiritual groups and meditations.

Ramakrishna, Sri
While playing the part of the Hindu god Shiva in a play, little Paramahamsa Ramakrishna suddenly fell into trance and remained in an ecstatic state for three whole days. The childhood experience was an indication of things to come.

Ramakrishna, who was born in Bengal in 1836, became at the age of 20 chief priest of a temple of the goddess Kali. Although married (a traditional Indian arrangement involving a child bride) he came to believe that sexuality was a bar to mystical **consciousness** and embraced celibacy for the remainder of his life.

Sri Ramakrishna, who is still venerated as a **guru** inside and outside India, died in 1886.

Ramayana

One of the earliest extant epics of ancient India, the *Ramayana* is a 24,000-couplet poem describing the fabulous adventures of its hero Rama who managed, among other things, to rescue his beautiful wife Sita from Sri Lanka where she was imprisoned by the demon king Ravana.

Rampa, Lobsang

Readers in the 1960s were fascinated by the publication of a book entitled *The Third Eye*, written by a Tibetan lama named Tuesday Lobsang Rampa and describing how, as a novice, Rampa had undergone a surgical operation during which a sliver of wood had been inserted into his skull to awaken the fabulous **third eye** and give him a wide range of psychical and mystical powers.

The book became an international best-seller, but was based more on the writings of **Blavatsky** than the reality of Tibet. Lobsang Rampa's real name was Cyril Hoskin, and far from being a 'Tibetan monk', he was actually an Irish plumber!

Hoskin (or perhaps 'Hoskin') responded to the subsequent exposés by claiming that the **spirit** of the real Lobsang Rampa had now taken over his body as part of a deal they had made and went on to publish a whole series of books under the Rampa name.

Whatever the reality of the claim, there is no doubt that Rampa had a genuine literary talent and the ability to popularize esoteric concepts so that they attracted a remarkably wide audience. Not all Tibetan experts would agree that his description of the opening of the third eye was particularly accurate, but overall his picture of Tibetan monastic life was evocative in the extreme.

Possibly to escape from unwelcome Press attention, Hoskin moved first to Dublin, then to Canada and in the process produced more than a dozen books on esoteric subjects, all but one resting on his authority as a lama. (The exception was a work he claimed to have ghosted for his Siamese cat.) It is probably not too unfair to suggest his later works lacked the power of his first three books, but all – including that dictated by the cat – are well worth reading.

Ramtha

Ramtha is the **spirit** entity of J.Z. Knight, a former housewife now living in Tacoma, Washington State. Since 1977, when Ramtha first appeared to her in a vision in her suburban kitchen, many people have flocked to hear her talk. Mrs Knight goes into a deep trance, claiming to leave her body so that Ramtha can enter. Ramtha proclaims himself to be a 35,000-year-old warrior from **Atlantis**.

Rebirth

See **Reincarnation**.

Rebirthing

Rebirthing, or conscious connected breathing, aims at releasing physical and psychological tension through relaxation and the release of the breath. The technique is often taught in combination with an emphasis on the power of thought.

Rebirthing involves a series of 'breathing sessions', usually weekly, designed to re-establish the natural, unrestrained breathing pattern with which we are born. This pattern is easy, deep, relaxed and connected in a rhythm which is natural and unique for each person. Such breathing has the effect of building up energy in the body, in much the same way as physical exercise. Since the energy is not used up, it has a vitalizing and relaxing effect on the body and psyche. The increased physical and psychological relaxation tends to facilitate the release of memories from the subconscious which often date back to birth or earlier. This effect of rebirthing was initially the main focus of the technique and has also given it its name.

First developed in America in the 1970s by Leonard Orr, rebirthing has many similarities to Eastern breathing exercises such as **yoga** and *ch'i kung*. Rebirthing is taught within various contexts, ranging from **meditation** to intense psychotherapy. The main schools of rebirthing today stem from Leonard Orr, Sondra Ray (the LRT-training) and Phil Laut (Vivation), all of whom were part of the initial American rebirthing group in the early 1970s.

Reflexology

A form of therapy, commonly linked with **acupuncture** but in fact based on somewhat different principles, in which pain relief and the alleviation of certain ailments is achieved by pressure on specific areas of the feet. It originated in China, but was first used in the West by Dr William Fitzgerald, an Ear, Nose and Throat specialist interested in acupuncture.

According to reflexology theory, specific foot zones, notably on the soles, are linked to every important organ, gland and muscle group in the body. When a physical disturbance occurs, this is reflected in the relevant foot zone which produces crystalline deposits beneath the skin. Reflexology works the zone in order to break down the **crystals**, which then brings relief to the afflicted part.

Whatever crystalline structures may or may not be present, there is no doubt at all that reflexology works and in some instances can achieve very worthwhile results where more orthodox approaches have failed. There are no known negative side-effects to reflexology, which appears to have a normalizing or harmonizing effect on the body, but the treatment itself can be painful.

Regardie, Francis Israel

Over the period 1937 to 1940, Israel Regardie embarked on one of the most controversial ventures of his life. He published, in four volumes, the complete **ritual**s and other magical workings of the **Golden Dawn**, of which he had once been a member.

His action caused a furore among occultists, who pilloried him as a dangerous oath-breaker, but by the time of his death in 1986, Regardie had become the world's acknowledged authority on ceremonial **magic**.

Born in England in 1907, Regardie was heavily influenced by **Aleister Crowley**, whose secretary he became for a number of years. He joined Crowley's magical order, the *Stella Matutina*, but managed to avoid the type of excesses that made Crowley notorious.

Regardie spent much of his life in the United States, where he worked as a body therapist. Along with his four-volume *Golden Dawn*, he published numerous books including *The Middle Pillar* and *The Art of True Healing*, both of which are better known to practising occultists than to readers of Regardie's more popular works.

Regression

In various forms of psychotherapy, patients are required to explore memories of events which have contributed to current emotional problems. A great many such events occur in childhood, but memories of childhood are not always easy to regain. Consequently psychiatrists may elect to make use of drugs or techniques like **hypnosis** in order to produce the material required for analysis.

The process of pushing back towards childhood is known by the psychoanalytic term of 'regression'.

Within the overall phenomenon of hypnosis, the reality of regression is well established. Even Professor H.J. Eysenck, who dismisses certain of the more extreme claims for the technique as 'absurd', wholly accepts the evidence of remarkable memory improvement presented by regression subjects.

Such evidence is, in fact, extremely interesting. When regressed to an early age, the subject will typically adopt the limited vocabulary of that age and may even begin to speak in a childlike tone. Personality changes occur. Behaviour patterns become those of the suggested age level. If a drawing is requested, it shows a childlike technique. Most interesting of all are the handwriting changes, which often conform precisely to handwriting samples produced by the subject when he was actually of the age suggested.

In one experiment, a 20-year-old woman switched the chalk to her left hand when it was suggested she was six years old. She had been born left-handed, but forced to switch to her right hand once she entered the educational system. The phenomenon of changed handedness has been seen quite frequently in regression experiments and has arisen spontaneously in cases where the subject had no conscious memory of ever being left-handed. In such cases, parents or older relatives would confirm the regression results.

Another experiment involved a 30-year-old male subject who was seated in a special chair psychologists use to stimulate emotional reaction. (It has a catch which causes it to fall backwards abruptly into a horizontal position.) When regressed to the age of one year, the chair was triggered and the man flung back. As an adult, he would have been expected to extend his arms and legs in a reflex compensatory action. In his regressed state, he screamed, fell back and urinated in his trousers.

Examination of eye movements indicates that when subjects are regressed to an early age, their ocular co-ordination degenerates. In two specific cases, ophthalmic examination produced even more remarkable results. With one subject, who had worn glasses since the age of twelve, regression to the age of seven produced a measurable improvement in vision – a development most opticians would insist was impossible. The second subject had actually suffered blindness in the left half of the right eye, due to the presence of a colloid cyst in the third ventricle. When the cyst was surgically removed, his sight returned to normal. But when regressed to a time before the operation, the visual defect reappeared.

Some psychoanalysts have theorized that the most troublesome experiences might actually be the very earliest: the moment of birth, for example. Such analysts pushed regression to extremes. Their patients reported recall of cradle events and even the birth trauma itself. A few claimed to be able to remember life within the womb. A handful of patients produced more distant memories still. They presented apparent recall of lives beyond the womb.

Analysts wondered if the respectable process of regression had gone rogue and was producing fantasies or hallucinations. It seemed a likely explanation. Because if the reports of these few patients were correct, it would mean they had actually lived before – and that opened up a whole series of scientific and philosophical difficulties.

It is probably fair to say the psychiatric community dealt with these difficulties by ignoring past-life regression altogether. The technique was taken up and carried forward largely by individuals outside the medical profession with an interest in **reincarnation** and/or **psychical research**. From their work, a substantial body of literature has built up.

From this literature, it is clear that different subjects react to regression in different ways, but many actually *relive* past-life experiences in a manner they find indistinguishable from physical reality.

In his *Encounters with the Past* (with Peter Moss), researcher Joe Keeton tells of a subject who, when regressed, found herself 'at the Assizes' and accused of **witchcraft**. It was the start of a 20-minute session marked by steadily growing tension. The trial was held at Chelmsford Assizes in 1556. Keeton's subject, a 23-year-old businesswoman, was reliving the experience of an accused 17-year-old, who was stripped and pricked as part of an interrogation which left her screaming in terror. (*See also* **Reincarnation**.)

Reich, Wilhelm

Wilhelm Reich was a man with an enormous talent for getting on the wrong side of people. It began at the age of 14 when it appears he told his father that his mother was having an affair with his tutor. His mother promptly killed herself.

Reich, who was born in Galacia in 1897, studied medicine after the First World War, then joined **Freud**'s psychoanalytic movement in Vienna. In 1927 he sought analysis from the master himself. Freud refused. Reich had a breakdown and sought refuge in a Swiss sanitorium. When he emerged, he became a Communist.

At this period of his life, Reich was beginning to formulate the ideas for which he was subsequently to become famous. Never a man to do anything by half, he took Freudian sexual doctrines to the extreme and insisted that orgasm was the ultimate key to physical and psychological health. In 1930, in Berlin, he founded the German Association for Proletarian Sexual Politics, which actually went beyond his own orgasmic doctrines to advocate the abolition of laws against homosexuality and abortion, and the publication of birth-control information.

It was explosive stuff – too explosive for the age he lived in. In 1933, he was expelled from the German Communist Party. The International Psychoanalytical Association stuck it a further year, then edged him out too.

An autocratic and difficult man, Reich was perfectly prepared to go it alone. By the end of the decade, he was claiming to have discovered a fundamental energy, called *orgone*, which, while it seems to have similarities with *prana* or *ch'i*, he believed to be the specific basis of love and orgasm. It was not a metaphysical concept. Reich said he had found fundamental biological entities, called *bions*, which carried the energy. More to the point, he invented orgone accumulators, special sorts of batteries in which the energy could be stored for therapeutic purposes . . . or even to influence the weather.

By now an emigrant to the United States, Reich founded an Orgone Institute in Maine from which issued increasingly extravagant claims for his discoveries. He began to market his energy accumulators, claiming they could cure serious diseases like cancer. The US Food and Drug Administration stepped in with an injunction restraining him from distributing accumulators and further instructing that he disassemble those he carried in stock and destroy all printed matter dealing with orgone energy.

It is unlikely that the FDA move would have survived in court, but Reich refused to fight it. Instead he simply elected to ignore it. As a result, he was arrested and jailed for two years for contempt. He died in prison in 1957.

Reich was, however, very much the pioneer of **bodywork**, and his concepts of sexual energy and body armouring have been very influential in contemporary bodywork practices.

Reichian Therapy

Whatever the response to **Reich**'s ideas on orgone energy and accumulators, Reichian therapy has contributed to contemporary **bodywork**, particularly **bioenergetics**, **Rolfing** and **Feldenkreis**. It is based on Reich's concept of 'bioenergy flow' through the body. When emotions and sexual instincts are repressed, the flow of energy is impaired. The body holds these repressions as 'body armour'. The aim of Reichian therapy is to dissolve the body armour and release the blocked physical and emotional energy. Several approaches are used, including deep breathing, deep massage, working with facial expressions to express true emotions, chest work, convulsive reflex-work, maintaining stress positions and active movements such as kicking and stamping.

It can be both physically and emotionally painful, but there is little doubt that it achieves results. Those who can stay the course report substantial improvements in their levels of awareness and general well-being, with a notable enhancement of their sex lives.

Reiki

A Japanese form of laying on of hands involving an energy transfer which catalyses the **universal life force** to promote **healing** and well-being, reducing stress and alleviating the symptoms of serious illness.

Reincarnation

When the late Sir Winston Churchill threatened to lodge a protest should he be reborn a Chinese coolie, he was referring to a process accepted as a fact of life by all the major religions of the Orient and now under serious investigation in the West both by occultists and some few of the more imaginative scientists.

As a religious belief, the doctrine of reincarnation is intimately connected with ideas about **karma**, the concept of cosmic balance echoed in the Christian precept that 'Whatsoever a man soweth, so also shall he reap.'

But it is the scientific evidence for reincarnation rather than the religious theory which has caught public imagination. To provide such evidence, researchers like Professor **Ian Stevenson** have investigated cases such as those of Bishen Chand and Shanti Devi.

Bishen Chand, the five-year-old son of railway clerk Ram Ghulam Kapoor, stunned his father when he suggested he (the father) should take a mistress and then, although he had never been taught the facts of life, explained precisely why.

Bishen lived in the Indian town of Bareilly, Uttar Pradesh. His precocious knowledge of human sexuality stemmed from an eruption of 'memories' which corresponded eerily to the life of a wealthy reprobate named Laxmi Narain. Laxmi had died in 1918 at the age of 32. A feature of his life was his passion for a prostitute named Padma.

The revival of Bishen's bizarre memories at the age of five did not end the story. Eighteen years after he first remembered her, the prostitute Padma walked into the office at Tenakpore where he was working. Bishen was so overcome by emotion that he fainted. That night he went to her home carrying a bottle of wine and determined to take up the old relationship where it left off. But Padma would have none of it. She pointed out that even if he was Laxmi reincarnate, she was now old enough to be his mother, and sent him home.

The experience of meeting someone from a past life has been shared by a number of those who suddenly began to experience memories of a pre-birth existence. One of the most widely publicized and investigated was that of Shanti Devi. The facts of the case were this:

In 1929, the three-year-old daughter of a middle-class couple' in Delhi, India, began to tell her parents about her husband and children. At first little Shanti Devi's parents paid scant attention. Many children create imaginary companions and if Shanti's fantasies were a little adult, they still thought it was nothing to worry about.

But the problem did not go away. Four years later, Shanti was still insisting she had a husband . . . but now she was claiming his name was Kedarnath and that she had borne him three children whom she also named and described. They had lived together, she said, in a town called Muttra where she had died in 1925 giving birth to a fourth child.

Muttra actually existed. It was a town not far from Delhi. But since claims to have died in childbirth sounded morbid, Shanti was taken to a doctor. To the consternation of her parents, he concluded her 'fantasy' of childbirth contained medical details a seven-year-old could not possibly know. On the credit side, he could find no reason to conclude she was ill.

For Shanti the memories were no problem at all. She had, she believed, simply lived before. Her name in her past life had been Ludgi and the details she had given her parents were as she remembered them.

Then a business acquaintance of Shanti's father called at the house. Shanti opened the door and recognized him at once as a cousin of her past-life husband. Incredibly, the man did indeed live in Muttra and had a cousin named Kedarnath. Worse still, Kedarnath had had a wife named Ludgi, who died in childbirth.

Without telling Shanti, her parents arranged a test. Before long a stranger called at the door. Shanti recognized him without hesitation. She had once again met Kedarnath, the man she claimed as her husband from a previous life.

Eventually the Indian government set up an investigative committee and scientists appeared, determined to discover whether her experiences were genuine. For the first time, Shanti visited Muttra. To the astonishment of all concerned, she was so familiar with the town that she was able to lead the researchers through it blindfold. When the bandage was removed, she had no trouble finding her former home. There she recognized and correctly named Kedarnath's father, mother and brother. Kedarnath's children by his deceased wife Ludgi were brought out. Amid scenes of intense emotion, Shanti recognized three of them. The fourth, whom she did not know, was the child born as Ludgi died.

Shanti Devi then took the scientists to the home of Ludgi's mother where she pointed out structural and decorative differences to the house as she remembered it. Ludgi's mother confirmed the changes had all taken place since Ludgi's death.

As final proof, Shanti insisted Ludgi had buried some rings before she died and volunteered to show the investigators where they were hidden. The scientists dug where she indicated and did indeed discover a small bag of rings. Ludgi's mother identified them as having belonged to her daughter.

It is difficult to read anything into this case other than the genuine recall of a past incarnation. Certainly none of the many experts who investigated it has ever suggested trickery or fraud. But if reincarnation was a fact in Shanti Devi's case, this does not necessarily mean it is a widespread phenomenon.

At the same time, investigators in the field of reincarnation research have perfected a technique of hypnotic **regression** which has helped literally thousands of subjects to produce what certainly appear to be past-life recollections. The phenomenon is intriguing in itself. If the 'memories' are actually fantasies, some explanation is required for the fact that so many people whose whole religion, upbringing and culture deny reincarnation appear to believe in it at an unconscious level.

But beyond this is the even more disturbing fact that in certain cases, research has shown an historical validity to the memories – so much so that in a number of instances it is difficult to accept any explanation of the facts other than past-life memory.

Rhine, J.B.
The father of experimental **parapsychology**, the science that investigates **psi** and **paranormal** abilities such as telepathy, **clairvoyance** and **precognition**. His experiments at Duke University in the 1930s resulted in a storm of controversy.

Right-Hand Path
A concept widely popularized in the occult novels of Dennis Wheatley, who equated the Right-Hand Path with all that was good and benign in mystical practice while relegating its counterpart, the Left-Hand Path, to the Satanic disciplines of black **magic**.

While both terms are still widely used in precisely this sense today, even among occultists, their derivation is rooted in

Oriental Tantric practice where the essential difference was that adepts of the Left-Hand Path used sexual techniques in their pursuit of enlightenment, while those of the Right-Hand Path did not.

Ritual

Strictly speaking, the term 'ritual' describes any frequently repeated sequence of actions (like checking the doors and windows before going to bed), but has developed into a description of religious and/or magical ceremonial, characterized by a set sequence of actions and (usually) special dedicated clothing and equipment.

Although the fact was successfully kept secret for centuries, magical ritual is now known to have an inner as well as an outer aspect – that is to say, its practitioners engage in a series of very specific visualizations in tandem with the visible physical actions.

Roberts, Jane
See **Seth**.

Rodegast, Pat
See **Emmanuel**.

Rogers, Carl

The American psychologist and educationalist Carl Rogers was the pioneer of person-centred principles in counselling. He was the first person to use the **encounter** group and his particular form is known as 'basic encounter'.

Rolfing

A muscular realignment therapy developed by Ida Rolf to eliminate chronic back and neck pain by releasing muscles frozen by stress. Rolfing is sometimes called 'structural integration'.

Rosary

Although generally associated in the West with Christian and specifically Roman Catholic practice, the bead string known as a 'rosary' is found in a number of religions where it is used as an aid to **meditation** and prayer.

A rosary can serve as a convenient guide to the number of times a **ritual** action or prayer should (or must) be repeated and fulfils this function almost exclusively in Catholicism. Oriental rosaries, however, often have differently shaped or coloured beads which have symbolic meanings in their own right. The contemporary Western occultist, **Dolores Ashcroft-Nowicki** has published a series of meditations, *The Sacred Cord Meditations*, describing a rosary system believed to date back to the fabulous lost continent of **Atlantis**.

Rosenkreutz, Christian

The mythical founder of the Brotherhood of the **Rosy Cross**, Christian Rosenkreutz was claimed to have been the son of poor but noble parents who was born in 1378 and entered a monastic Order as a child and travelled widely throughout the Middle East absorbing mystic wisdom. On his return to his native Germany, he was joined by three monks from his old monastery who, under pledges of secrecy about anything they might learn, formed with him the nucleus of the Rosicrucian Order. They studied **magic**, healed the sick and eventually produced a considerable library of mystical lore before extending their numbers and going their separate ways in the world, vowing to keep the existence of their Fraternity secret for 100 years. Rosenkreutz himself died at the age of 106, with an inscription on his tomb promising that he would reappear again in 120 years.

Rosicrucians

In 1614 a slim pamphlet printed in Kassel and entitled *Fama Fraternitatis* began to circulate throughout Germany. It claimed to have been issued by a hitherto unknown occult Brotherhood called 'Rosicrucians' and sought to stimulate a general improvement of the world by fusing the Reformation with advances in scientific knowledge. The pamphlet then went on to tell the story of the founding of the Order by the legendary **Christian Rosenkreutz**.

Although obscure in style and difficult to understand, the publication created such widespread interest that it was actually reprinted three times in 1615 and again in 1617. It went into two Dutch editions almost immediately and an English translation followed some years later.

The *Fama* was followed in 1615 by a second publication on the subject, the *Confessio Fraternitatis R.C.*, spelling out 37 of the Order's aims, which included bringing an end to sectarianism

245

and political strife, and expressing the Fraternity's opposition to the papacy, **Islam** and quack alchemists. The publication sought to recruit members to the Rosicrucian movement, without, however, telling readers how to join.

In 1616 an eager public was treated to the final book in the series, the *Chymische Hochzeit Christiani Rosenkreutz*, subsequently rendered into English as *The Hermetick Romance: or the Chymical Wedding of Christian Rosenkreutz*. It was a lively story full of esoteric symbolism and one which has since been interpreted as representing an alchemical process.

Although the publications were a great mystery in their day, it is now known that their author was almost certainly the Württemburg theologian Johann Valentin Andreae and the works may have reflected the ideals of a small circle of scholars close to Christoph Besold, a Professor of Law at the University of Tübingen. At the time, however, those (many) who wished to join the newly-proclaimed Rosicrucians had no means of doing so and their frustrations generated a considerable volume of secondary literature, speculating on the Order or claiming membership of it.

By 1620 the original interest was burning itself out and discussion of the Rosicrucians died away in favour of other fashions. But the whole thing revived again in 1710 with the foundation by Sigmund Richter of the Order of the Gold and Rosy Cross, an alchemical fraternity which drew, albeit loosely, on the original legend. The terms 'Rose Cross' and 'Rosicrucian' found their way into **Freemasonry** without, however, having very much to do with their originals. But the Victorian Order of the **Golden Dawn** revived the Rosicrucian tradition to such an extent that the legend of Christian Rosenkreutz was taught to members and a representation of his 'vault' or tomb was used in Golden Dawn **rituals**.

There are several institutions which claim descent from, or at least links with, the original Rosicrucians. Perhaps the best known of these is the American Ancient and Mystic Order Rosae Crucis (AMORC), founded by H. Spencer Lewis, which teaches a substantial body of esoteric doctrine and technique and advertises itself widely in publications throughout America and the United Kingdom.

Rosy Cross, Brotherhood of the
See **Rosicrucians**.

Rumi

Generally regarded as Persia's greatest mystical poet, Jalal'al-Din Rumi was certainly its most prolific. Born in what is now northern Afghanistan in 1207, he managed over his 66 years to write 2,000 mystical odes, 1,600 quatrains and an almost unbelievable 25,000 rhyming couplets.

Much of his writings concerned love and wine, both of which he considered symbolic of mystical experience. Rumi himself was a **dervish** who, with all his religious prestige, avoided the mistake of taking himself too seriously. 'I was a grave man of formal praying,' he wrote to the Sufi teacher, Shams of Tabriz, who taught him the spectacular whirling techniques of his Order, 'and you made me the sport of children in the street!'

Runes

> I can carve and stain strong runes
> That will cause the corpse to speak
> Reply to whatever I ask . . .

These disturbing lines are taken from *The Words of the High One from the Elder Edda*, one of many ancient Norse sagas which mention the curious occult symbols known in many areas of northern Europe.

According to legend, the Norse god Odin hung from the World Tree for nine days and nights and lost one of his eyes in order to gain a knowledge of the runes. Those today who wish to explore the runes are more fortunate in that they will usually be asked to invest no more than the price of a paperback book and a little of their time.

Today, the 24 basic runic symbols are usually cut into runestones (which may actually be ceramic or wooden) and used for **divination** in conjunction with a twenty-fifth, blank, stone. There remain, however, persistent rumours of a potent system of rune **magic** in which the ancient Nordic powers are used to change the future, not simply forecast it.

Russell, George William

Author of *The Candle of Vision*, one of the most influential books on **mysticism** published in the twentieth century, George William

Russell was a natural mystic, close friend of **W.B. Yeats** and a member of the Theosophical Society.

Russell, who lived from 1867 to 1935, became better known by his pen-name, 'A.E.'. Apart from his writings, he was a talented artist (he actually met Yeats at Dublin Art School) who produced a number of highly evocative mystical paintings.

S

Sadhana

In **Hinduism**, any spiritual or physical exercise leading to enlightenment.

Sai Baba

Although known as a mystic and **yoga** practitioner, Sai Baba seems by any real yardstick to have been far more of a magician than anything else.

Born in Hisderabad in 1856, he moved into a derelict mosque in the village of Shirdi and remained there for most of his life, engaged in esoteric practices like **astral projection** and prediction. He tended a sacred fire until his death in 1918, when the task was taken over by his followers who continue to look after it to the present day, believing the ashes to have curative powers.

Samadhi

The highest state of **yoga meditation** which leads to self-realization and recognition of the mystic unity of manifestation.

Samsara

A Buddhist term meaning the cycle of continuity, the continual round of birth, death and rebirth until **nirvana** is attained.

Sanders, Alex

When June Johns published her biography of Alex Sanders in 1969, she called it *King of the Witches* for that was the title Sanders claimed as head of 107 covens. The jacket blurb described him as 'probably the most powerful witch in Europe'.

Born in 1916, Sanders maintained he was a member of a family which had practised **witchcraft** for generations. He was initiated into the Craft when he disturbed his aged grandmother naked in her kitchen performing a **ritual**. Fearful that he would reveal her secret, she took him into the Craft by cutting into his scrotum with a small sickle-shaped knife.

With the Gardnerian revival of witchcraft well under way (*see* **Gardner, Gerald; Witchcraft**), Sanders achieved considerable media prominence in the 1960s and 1970s along with his attractive wife and High Priestess Maxine who was, if anything, even more photogenic than the saturnine Sanders himself. The supposed rivalry between Alexandrian and Gardnerian witchcraft was widely featured in the Press and did exist to some degree, although the similarities between the two systems have always been far more extensive than the differences. When Sanders died suddenly in 1988, there were the inevitable rumours that he had succumbed to magical attack, but the more likely cause seems to have been a heart condition.

Santéria

A religion which is a mixture of ancient African rites (brought to North and South America by the West African slaves) and Catholicism (the slaves were forced to convert by their Spanish and Portuguese masters). It is related in **ritual** and practice to **Voodoo**.

Satori

The attainment of enlightenment in Zen **Buddhism**, comparable to *samadhi* of **yoga meditation**.

Sri Satya Sai Baba

Sri Satya Sai Baba, who claims to be a **reincarnation** of the first Sai Baba, is one of the best-known **guru**s in India today. At his **ashram** at Prasanthi Nilayam he conducts **darshan**s and materializes sacred ash. He has an enormous following.

Schumacher, E.F.

A seminal thinker in the field of economics, Fritz Schumacher catapulted to international attention in the early 1970s with the publication of his book *Small is Beautiful*. Based on a series of papers written mainly in the fifties and sixties and heavily influenced by Oriental **Buddhism** and Gandhi's doctrine of non-violence, the book mounted a swingeing attack on the materialist, growth-oriented economics of the day, pointing out that it was based, unthinkingly, on an outmoded value system and view of humanity as a whole.

Schumacher proposed replacing the old economics with a brand new non-violent system which took account of ecological factors and was based on the premise that people really mattered.

Schutz, Will

A social psychologist who taught at both Harvard and Berkeley, Will Schutz was an influential figure in popularizing **encounter** groups in the 1960s and 70s. He saw groups as a means of developing self-understanding, and indeed ecstasy. In 1967 he published *Joy: Expanding Human Awareness*, which became a best-seller.

Schwaller de Lubicz

A philosopher, Orientalist and mathematician, R.A. Schwaller de Lubicz spent 30 years studying hermetic wisdom and then 15 years studying the Temple of Luxor. He developed a thesis – which is not popular with orthodox Egyptologists – that the builders of ancient Egypt had a very sophisticated understanding of metaphysics and universal laws. Through Egyptian glyphs, statues and temples, De Lubicz discovered the earliest known source of a Sacred Science, which forms the basis of what has come to be known as the **Perennial Philosophy**. It may even be that the Egyptian **cosmology** and understanding of universal laws was imported by refugees from Plato's sunken continent of **Atlantis**.

Science of Mind

Dr Ernest Holmes (1887–1960) developed the philosophy of Science of Mind, or Religious Science, as it is also called. The techniques he devised, described by him in a number of books including *The Science of Mind*, are based on the idea that what we think, we experience. This works as an immutable law of cause and effect. Negative thinking produces negative experiences, positive thinking produces positive experience.

Scientology

A quasi-religious movement founded by L. Ron Hubbard, scientology has had a bad press over its methods of recruiting and maintaining members. While some of its ideas are preposterous, others have some affinity with **Gnosticism, Buddhism** and other Oriental ideas. Dianetics is one of the main techniques of scientology and aims at self-mastery.

Scrying

Although often considered synonymous with **crystal** gazing, the term 'scrying' is , in fact, considerably wider in its application. It covers any form of **divination** which involves staring at a polished or shiny surface in order to produce visionary experience or trance.

A great many artefacts have, historically, been used for scrying, ranging from the black concave metal mirror once owned by **John Dee** to the blue bowls of water often used by Middle Eastern and Chinese magicians.

In the **Golden Dawn**, the term was widened still further to include visions generated by Tattwa cards and flashing tablets, while 'scrying in the spirit vision', practised by initiates, seems almost identical to what would now be termed **astral projection** or **out-of-the-body experience**.

Second Sight

'Second sight' is an old term loosely used so that it has become almost synonymous with **psychism** or **ESP**. There is, however, some evidence to suggest it was originally coined to describe a very specific psychical ability: the non-ocular perception of energy field manifestations.

By this definition, those exhibiting second sight have, quite literally, an additional physical sense which operates in a manner analogous to normal vision but appears to have more to do with the pineal gland (or **third eye**) than with mundane physical perception.

Second sight will generally permit the perception of **aura**s. It can be demonstrated by the ability to move around blindfold or in darkness, using the energy emanations of physical objects to navigate the environment safely. Occasionally those with the talent will report an awareness of living beings composed only of an energy field. Their descriptions of such beings often tally remarkably with folklore of Nature **spirit**s and fairies.

Secret Doctrine, The

Title of a multi-volume work written by **H.P. Blavatsky** and published by the Theosophical Society which contains a detailed account of the occult evolution of our planet and humanity according to the Eastern Esoteric Tradition.

Blavatsky claimed she had received much of this doctrine at the feet of Tibetan lamas and while it was for some time fashionable to cast doubts on the claim, the increasing accessibility of Tibetan Buddhist doctrines has shown some remarkable similarities.

Self-actualization

A central concept of **humanistic psychology** formulated by **Abraham Maslow**. Self-actualization is a fundamental human need and means discovering one's authentic self and authentic life.

Servants of the Light

When, in the early 1960s, the Society of the Inner Light moved away somewhat from its original role as a **Golden Dawn**-style organization devoted to the practice of **ritual magic**, a number of members, unhappy with the development, voted with their feet and left to further the cause of the **Western Esoteric Tradition** in their own way. Among them were **W.E. Butler** and Basil Wilby (**Gareth Knight**), two skilled occultists with a sound grounding in the **Qabalah** and ritual magic.

Fearing that developments within the Society of the Inner Light might mean that newcomers to esoteric thought could have difficulty finding a source of purely magical training, they collaborated on creating a correspondence course on the subject. The course was known as *The Helios Course in Practical Qabalah*. It was out of this course that the more formalized structures of the Servants of the Light eventually grew.

In establishing SOL, W.E. Butler was guided by an **Inner Plane Adept** he referred to in his books as a 'Master of Magic'. On Butler's death, this contact was passed on to his successor as head of the organization, **Dolores Ashcroft-Nowicki**.

Today, the Servants of the Light continues to function as an esoteric school within the Western Esoteric Tradition offering supervised training in Qabalistically-based magic. The training, at its more advanced levels, makes considerable use of **pathworking** techniques and is linked with the **Matter of Britain** through its use of symbolism drawn from the Arthurian Mythos.

Seth

Seth is the **spirit** entity who was channelled through Jane Roberts and has become probably the best known and most widely published in the twentieth century. From 1963 until her death in 1984, channelling the Seth material was at the centre of Jane Roberts's life. She produced a whole body of literature including *The Seth Material*, *Seth Speaks* and *The Nature of Personal Reality*. The main message of the material is that we each create our own reality through our beliefs and desires. (*See* **Channelling**.)

Shakers

Founded by Ann Lee from Manchester, England, this American religious sect flourished in the nineteenth century. They lived communally with strict adherence to celibacy, Mother Ann, as she was called, believing that celibacy was the only route to ending humanity's separation from God. Shaker worship involved singing, dancing (which often resulted in 'shaking'), shouting and speaking in tongues and trances.

Shaman

The shaman is a follower of a visionary tradition reaching back into the dawn of prehistory and based on animistic ideas about the world. (S)he will typically make use of rhythmic drumming, dance, **chanting**, fasting, drugs, sweat lodges and **vision quest**s to induce trance states which allow the shaman's soul to enter the **spirit** worlds and there enlist the aid of certain allies for **healing**, **divination** and **magic**. There are similarities in techniques whether used by indigenous peoples in Australia, the Amazon or Eastern Europe.

Long looked on as a primitive precursor to religion, we now see the emergence of a new breed of urban shaman, sometimes with impeccable credentials in anthropology, bent on adapting the ancient system to modern needs.

(*See also* **Castaneda, Carlos**; **Harner, Michael**.)

Shambhala

An ancient Tibetan banner shows the mysterious lost land of Shambhala as an oasis surrounded by snow-capped hills. Legend describes it as a hidden paradise. The records of early **Buddhism** suggested it was the source of esoteric wisdom. Myths of China, Russia, Tibet and even Greece and Rome insist it is the home of superhuman beings, rather like **Blavatsky's Hidden Masters**. It is described as a country of valleys surrounded by high mountains where hot springs nourish a rich vegetation which includes many rare plants and medicinal herbs.

But if there is widespread mythic agreement about the existence of Shambhala, there is considerably less of a consensus on where it is and how to get there.

The Theosophists favour the Gobi Desert. The Chinese think it may be in the Kun Lun Mountains. Middle Eastern and Greek sources favour the Altaic Mountains. According to certain Taoist sects it is hidden somewhere between Szechwan and Tibet. A Hungarian source locates it precisely between Latitudes 40N to 50N beyond the Syr Daria River. Russian legend claims it lies in the Belovodye white waters region and in 1923 an expedition set off across the Kokushi Mountains to find it . . . and never returned.

The fate of the expedition would not, perhaps, have surprised the ancient Tibetan abbot who wrote the *Red Path to Shambhala*. In the work he claimed the entrance to the lost land lay in Mongolia, but only those properly prepared spiritually could find it.

The abbot was not the only one to believe there was a non-physical aspect to Shambhala. In 1928, the traveller Nicholas Roerich was told bluntly by another lama that Shambhala had 'nothing to do with our earth' but existed on another dimension altogether, possibly referring to the **Bardo** level or **astral plane**.

Despite these pointers to an inward Shambhala, rumours of its physical existence still persist. There are claims of underground tunnels linking it with the Potala Palace in Lhasa, while other tunnel routes are claimed to be found in Turfan and Turkestan. The same Nicholas Roerich who was told of Shambhala's astral location met up with a mysterious lama on the road between Darjeeling and Ghum and was subsequently told by Ghum monks that this lama was from Shambhala. There is even a flying saucer connection. Both Roerich and the British mountaineer Frank Smythe saw **UFOs** over locations traditionally associated with the lost paradise.

Sheldrake, Rupert

The Cambridge plant physiologist noted for his theories of formative causation and its extension **morphic resonance**. In formulating his ideas on formative causation, Sheldrake suggested that the form and pattern of things depends not so much on physical laws as on habit. In other words, it is easier to do something that has already been done.

Sheldrake extended the concept to include what he called 'morphogenetic fields' independent of space and time. A developing embryo would thus take its final shape not only in accordance with DNA programming, but also in relation to the morphogenetic field in which it found itself – it would, in other words, follow the physical example of other members of its species sharing that field.

Shiatsu

A comprehensive system of massage therapy, developed in Japan (*shiatsu* means 'finger pressure' in Japanese), which achieves results by specific manipulation of **acupuncture** meridians and points. The system is as often applied to induce a sense of well-being and relaxation as to cure specific ailments. (*See also* **Acupressure**.)

Shingon

An esoteric school of **Buddhism**, introduced from China to Japan by the priest Kukai. Shingon's doctrines are tantric (*see* **Tantra**).

Shinto

The state religion of Japan, Shinto is known as the Way of the Gods and was, until 1946, interlinked with the Japanese monarchy. In that year, however, Emperor Hirohito renounced his divinity, effectively disestablishing Shinto from the position it had held since 1868.

The religion itself developed from a type of Nature worship, but merged with **Buddhism** and later took on board many of the precepts of **Confucianism**, notably that which suggested the Emperor was the divine leader of the nation. In fact, the Japanese went further, claiming their Emperor enjoyed direct lineal descent from the sun-goddess. In 1868, the Emperor was confirmed in this status and worshipped as a living god by followers of Shinto.

Shinto remains a thriving religion in modern Japan with numerous shrines throughout the nation. One of these, at Ise, houses a mirror which the sun-goddess gave to the first Japanese Emperor in the seventh century BC.

Silva Mind Control

José Silva was born in Laredo, Texas, in 1914. His family background was poor and got worse when his father died so that by the age of six young José had become the breadwinner, doing odd jobs like shining shoes and selling newspapers.

When he was 15 years old, Silva went into the radio repair business. (He had done a deal with a local barber who subsidized him in a correspondence course on the understanding that Silva would take the exams in the barber's name so the barber would have an impressive certificate to hang up in his shop.) He prospered in this business, but eventually decided money wasn't everything. The decision was reinforced by his experience of being drafted into the Signal Corps during the Second World War. He was asked a series of questions by an army psychiatrist which he considered just about the stupidest he had ever heard.

But the questions set Silva thinking about the potential of the human mind and started him on a lifelong investigation which moved via **hypnosis** to mind control. He developed exercises that raised IQ, improved memory, increased learning speed and even, so his followers now claim, stimulated talents like telepathy.

His system involves **visualization** and has similarities to **autogenic training** and certain esoteric techniques like **pathworking**, but is presented in a non-mystical, down-to-earth manner which has considerable appeal to modern audiences, so that the Silva Mind Control Movement now has a substantial international following.

Silver Cord

A connecting link between the physical body and the **astral body** reported by some (but by no means all) practitioners of **astral projection**.

Sylvan Muldoon, one of the best-known exponents of astral/**etheric projection** described it in these words:

> My two identical bodies were joined by an elastic-like cable, one end of which was fastened to the *medulla oblongata* region of the astral counterpart, while the other centred between the eyes of the physical counterpart. This cable extended across the space of probably six feet which separated us.

During projection, the cord seems to be almost infinitely elastic, allowing the second body to travel many hundreds, indeed thousands, of miles from the first. When the two bodies approach close to one another, however, the cord thickens slightly and creates a pull which tends to draw the second body back into the physical.

There is a passing Biblical mention of a 'silver cord' severing at the moment of death and many occultists take this to be a reference to the cord seen in astral projection.

Society of Friends (Quakers)
Founded in England around 1650 by George Fox, the Society of Friends was nicknamed the Quakers, possibly deriving from the idea that worshippers were so overcome by the Holy Spirit that they quaked. The Quakers believe in a personal knowledge of God, rejecting sacraments in favour of the 'inner light' of Christ in the soul. Worship is largely silent, allowing believers to listen for the 'still, small voice'. Social concern has always been strong and the Quakers practise pacifism. In recent times they have been noted for their tolerance of other religions.

Sogyal Rinpoche
One of the foremost interpreters of the ancient wisdom of Tibet to the modern world. Educated in Tibet and at Cambridge, Rinpoche is a **meditation** master who has more than 20 years' experience of living and teaching in the West. He has developed a unique way of drawing out the vital importance of the ancient wisdom of Tibet, and has established a network of centres and groups in a number of different countries. He is the author of *The Tibetan Book of Living and Dying*, which has been acclaimed as a landmark in bringing together the Tibetan Buddhist teachings with modern research on death and dying.

SOL
See **Servants of the Light**.

Spangler, David
One of the most important definers of the **New Age**. His ideas can be found in three books in particular: *Revelation: Birth of a New*

Age, Emergence: The Rebirth of the Sacred and, with William Irwin Thompson, *Reimagination of the World: A Critique of the New Age, Science and Popular Culture*. David Spangler's vision of the New Age is a positive one – 'an image that can motivate us to act and work for a transformed future, one that is humane, decent and abundant'. Our current civilization is dying, and we are experiencing the birth pangs of the new. This process of the emerging of the new culture is characterized by four stages: self-discovery; self-development; integration with both the environment and with history; and service, work that leads to a meaningful existence.

Spence, Lewis

One of the more sensible authors on the subject of **Atlantis**, Lewis Spence exhibited an interest in the totality of esoteric subjects and his *Encyclopaedia of Occultism* still has much to say on the subject despite the fact it was first published in 1920.

Spirit

Used in two senses. In the singular it denotes a form of being which is invisible, powerful and life-giving. It is the divine spark in each human being, and at the same time the origin of the divine spark.

In the second sense, 'spirit' is the generic term to describe all non-physical entities, whether **angel**, **guide**, master or god. Most cultures, past and present, have accepted the existence of spirits, of a more or less personal kind, able to affect human life in some way.

Spiritualism

The Spiritualist movement dates from 1848 when the Fox sisters in Hydesville, New York State, began to give public demonstrations of communication with **spirits**. It rapidly became fashionable in both America and Europe, but had peaked by the early twentieth century. In Britain Spiritualism established itself more firmly, helped by the endorsement of respected figures such as **Sir Oliver Lodge** and **Sir Arthur Conan Doyle**. The Spiritualist Association of Great Britain and the Spiritualists National Union are the two largest Spiritualist organizations in the world.

Starhawk

Jewish by birth (original name Miriam Simos), Starhawk is a feminist, peace activist, high priestess and a writer on **witchcraft**. As a student at the University of California in the 1960s she came into contact with modern-day witchcraft as part of her research for an anthropology project. Her first book, *The Spiral Dance*, was about the ancient religion of the Great **Goddess**. In *Dreaming the Dark: Magic, Sex and Politics* she dealt with feminism, witchcraft, environmentalism and political change. *Truth or Dare*, her third book, is more about power structures and the effect on our psyches and what we can do using **magic** ('the art of changing consciousness at will') to change this.

Starseed Transmissions, The

See **Carey, Ken**.

Steiner, Rudolf

Rudolf Steiner was born in Austria in 1861, although shifting boundaries have now put his birthplace in modern Serbia. His father was a minor railway official and educational facilities in his district were so sparse that he received little formal education in his early years.

But the man was, quite simply, a genius and, rarer still, a genius who declined to specialize. By the time he had entered secondary school, he had taken to teaching his fellow pupils arts while he himself studied science. He followed both arts and sciences throughout his years at the University of Vienna. At the age of 29, he began work in the Goethe Archives.

Up to this point there was little outward indication of the direction in which his future life would turn. But at some point in his early years, he began a regular routine of **meditation** which was well established by 1897 when he moved to Berlin to edit a literary magazine.

Two years later, Steiner was asked to speak at a meeting of **Madame Blavatsky**'s new Theosophical Society. He accepted and was exposed, possibly for the first time, to the full impact of Theosophical doctrines. He joined the society itself and went on to become general secretary of the German branch.

Steiner broke with **Theosophy** in 1909 to form his own Anthroposophical Society (*see* **Anthroposophy**), propounding doctrines which were not wildly dissimilar to those of Theosophy.

Steiner is one of the very few occultists whose name is known and respected outside the esoteric field: indeed, it is probably fair to say he has modern admirers who are unaware of his esoteric interests. This curious situation is the direct result of his lifelong refusal to specialize. He managed, for example, to develop a new system of teaching and there are Steiner Schools in operation today throughout the world. He was an outstanding architect and many of his basic ideas still find their way into modern buildings. He was a good painter and a brilliant sculptor. His ideas on medicine are still studied with interest. He invented a wholly new approach to agriculture called 'bio-dynamic agriculture', only now really coming into its own. He was also the originator of a new art form, **eurythmy**, or sacred dance.

Stevenson, Ian

The name of Ian Stevenson is today inextricably linked with painstaking scientific research into the supposed phenomenon of **reincarnation**. His book, *Twenty Cases Suggestive of Reincarnation*, first published in 1926, was the end result of years of exhaustive investigation and remains (despite some criticism suggesting an emotional investment in proving reincarnation to be a fact) a classic in its field.

Born in 1918, Professor Stevenson holds the post of Chairman of the Department of Neurology and Psychiatry at the University of Virginia School of Medicine and is a past President of the (British) **Society for Psychical Research**.

Subud

Muhammad Subuh, the founder of Subud, was born in Indonesia in 1901. He was invited to Europe by **J.G. Bennett**, who maintained that Subuh's ability to help others by touching them when they were in a state of deep relaxation to 'open up', was an effective way of opening up the higher **chakras**. Subud is a synthesis of Sufi, Hindu and Indonesian spiritual ideas. The word *Subud* is an abbreviation of three Sanskrit words:

Sushila – right living in accordance with the will of God
Budhi – the inner spiritual force
Dharma – surrender to God.

Sufism

The mystical heart of **Islam**, Sufism insists on total submission to Allah as the road to ultimate truth. The word *sufi* denotes a wearer of wool and indicates a belief in simplicity and poverty. The aim of the Sufi is to be 'in the world but not of it'. There have been many different schools of Sufism which have been attacked by Islamic purists. Sufism has inspired poetry, music and dance.

Summers, Montague

The Reverend Montague Summers, a priest possibly of the Roman Catholic Church (his actual affiliations are uncertain), produced a variety of books on **witchcraft**, demonology and allied subjects, at a time when it was fashionable to take a coolly academic stance on occult matters. Summers shocked his readers by clearly indicating that he considered demons real and accepted that charges levelled during the historical witch trials were well-founded. He even managed to inject a tone of approval into his translation of the horrific *Malleus Maleficarum* ('Hammer of the Witches'), a sort of witchfinder's bible written by the Dominican Friars Kramer and Sprengler.

Aleister Crowley was friendly for a time with Summers, but the library staff of the British Museum, where he did much of his research, are reputed to have found him less personable. The story goes that they were rendered so uncomfortable by his visits that they attempted desperately to find some excuse to revoke his membership. Summers behaved impeccably, unconsciously foiling the moves, and continued to use the library up to the time of his death, at the age of 68, in 1948.

Sun Bear

One of the most famous contemporary Native American teachers, Sun Bear is a Chippewa medicine man and serves as leader of the Bear Tribe Medicine Society located near Spokane, Washington. A teacher, lecturer and editor of the magazine *Many Smokes*, Sun Bear sees his mission in life as teaching others how to find and follow their own paths of power and how to live responsibly on the Earth as they help to heal it. In his book *The Path of Power* he describes his personal path of power and shares his vision of peace and unity for the whole Earth. He has also published *Sun Bear's Book of the Vision Quest* and *The Medicine Wheel: Earth Astrology*.

Suzuki, D.T.

Perhaps the best-known authority on **Zen Buddhism** in the

twentieth century, Daisetz T. Suzuki was also arguably the least obscure and most readable. Born in 1870, he obtained impeccable scholarly credentials, but his interest in Zen was far from academic since he claimed he himself had achieved *satori*, the ultimate Zen enlightenment, through a sudden leap 'from finity to infinity'. Dr Suzuki brought Zen to the West single-handed. He died in 1966, but his numerous books still stand among the best introductions to Zen Buddhism available in English.

Suzuki, Shunryu

Already a deeply-respected **Zen** master in Japan, Suzuki-roshi arrived in America in 1958, finally making his home in San Francisco and establishing the Zen Centre. He was undoubtedly one of the most influential Zen teachers of his time. His one and only book, *Zen Mind, Beginner's Mind*, is one of the most often recommended books on the practice of Zen. Suzuki-roshi died in 1971.

Swedenborg, Emmanuel

The life of Emmanuel Swedenborg represents one of the great U-turns of history. He spent a lifetime as a scientist, then, in his fifties, suddenly became a full-blown visionary and mystic.

Swedenborg was born in Stockholm in 1688, trained as a scientist and was noted for his work in the field of astronomy where he developed a hypothesis to explain the creation of the planets. He was something of a technician as well and produced plans far ahead of his time for an air gun and a submarine.

But having established himself as a scientist, Swedenborg revealed he was in direct communication with **spirit** beings and had frequent visionary experiences which left him convinced of the mystical truth that all things ultimately were contained within a single godhead. He also appears to have exhibited certain **psychic** powers, notably **clairvoyance**, which went some way towards ensuring his visionary experiences were taken seriously.

A Swedenborgian Church (later renamed the New Church) was established in 1788 and is still active throughout the world.

Synchronicity

A scientific theory which arose out of an unlikely collaboration between the psychologist **Carl Gustav Jung** and the physicist Wolfgang Pauli. Synchronicity postulates an acausal connecting principle in nature which gives rise to meaningful coincidences.

Jung illustrated his theory with a story drawn from his professional practice. The wife of one of his patients (a man in his fifties) had once told him that on the death of her mother and grandmother, a number of birds had gathered outside the windows of the death-chamber. When her husband's treatment was nearing an end, he developed minor symptoms which Jung, however, felt might indicate heart disease. Jung referred him to a specialist, who made an examination and concluded there was no cause for concern.

On the way back from the consultation, with the medical report in his pocket, the man collapsed on the street. As the body was brought home, it was met by his wife who already knew – or was at least worried about the possibility that – a crisis had developed, *because a flock of birds had alighted on their house*.

Jung became convinced that synchronicity could provide an explanation for the curious effectiveness of **astrology** and might be involved in the card-guessing experiments by which Professor **J.B. Rhine** tested for telepathy. He even suggested that the precognitive dreams reported by **J.W. Dunne** might have a synchronistic element.

T

Tai Chi Ch'uan

Despite its literal translation as 'supreme ultimate fist', *Tai Chi Ch'uan* is as much a form of spiritual development (hence a valid **yoga**) as it is a **martial art**. Training in the system takes the form of slow, graceful, somewhat stylized movements through which the individual aligns himself with the natural flow of universal *ch'i*. The practice of Tai Ch'i is extraordinarily popular in modern China where it is almost universally used as a means of keeping fit.

Taliesin

The Welsh legend of Taliesin's birth tells how Gwion Bach, fleeing from Ceridwen's anger after accidentally supping from her Cauldron of Rebirth, changes himself into a hare to get away. But Ceridwen changes herself into a greyhound to pursue and so the two undergo a series of metamorphoses which ends when Ceridwen changes herself into a black hen which picks up and eats the grain of wheat into which Gwion Bach had finally transformed himself. After a period of gestation, he was 'reborn' as the bard Taliesin.

The legend is curiously suited to Taliesin, a bard who lived in the latter half of the sixth century and attracted almost as many myths as the wizard **Merlin** whom, to some extent, he resembles. The historical Taliesin composed a number of songs and poems, but many more have been attributed to him. Much of the latter actually predates the man himself and is drawn from the ancient Celtic shamanism which laid the foundations of Druidic teaching.

Talisman

Talismans are used to attract health, success and good fortune. Unlike **amulets** (which are passive), talismans are active.

Endowed with supernatural power, they can bestow magical power on their owners. King Arthur's sword, Excalibur, is an example of a talisman. Precious stones, **magic** wands and holy relics are all regarded as talismans. Although ancient talismans were often inscribed with a god-name or written spell, their modern counterparts are more often artefacts charged with the personal power of their creator through concentration and/or **ritual**.

Tantra

A body of **yoga** doctrines, originating in India in ancient times, which has profoundly influenced the development of sexual **magic** throughout a broad spectrum of differing cultures, including the **Western Esoteric Tradition**.

Tantrics seek to arouse *shakti*, the divine feminine energy, through acts of **ritual** intercourse in which, however, orgasm is withheld in order to stimulate the upward movement of **kundalini**. An important aspect of the process is often the mediation of specific Hindu divinities while intercourse is taking place.

Tao

Although usually translated as 'The Way', the term *Tao* is an embodiment of three aspects of mystical Chinese thought which has no real English equivalent.

It unifies the concepts of:

1) Ultimate reality, inexpressible, ineffable and unimaginable.
2) Universal energy that makes and maintains all manifestation.
3) Wise order in an individual life, which harmonizes with the universal whole.

(*See also* **Lao Tzu**; *Tao Te Ching*; **Taoism**.)

Tao Te Ching

The Book of the Way, a collection of 81 poems penned by the Chinese sage and mystic **Lao Tzu**, which is now the fundamental scripture of **Taoism** and is studied with great interest by those thinkers concerned with spiritual development.

That the *Tao Te Ching* speaks directly to the modern age is clearly shown by the following lines, which mount a potent attack on traditional Western values:

> Those who would take over the earth
> And shape it to their will
> Never, I notice, succeed.

But Lao Tzu's thought did not stop at criticism. He had his own recipe for building a better life:

> There is no need to run outside
> For better seeing
> Nor to peer from a window. Rather abide
> At the centre of your being
> For the more you leave it, the less you learn.

(*See also* **Tao**.)

Taoism

There are two main branches of Taoism. One is esoteric and primarily monastic. The other is a populist movement which concentrates on the magical power which may be achieved by those in harmony with the **Tao**. Neither branch has a great deal to do with the mystical ideas of **Lao Tzu**, the supposed founder of the religion, except in so much as both subscribe to his basic tenet of Tao.

Even then, it is fairly clear that Lao Tzu did not invent the ideas behind the concept of Tao, but rather integrated and named aspects of Chinese thought dating, literally, from pre-history . . . a suitably nebulous beginning to a religion whose founder may himself have been a myth.

The goal of Taoism is the achievement of *wu-wei*, a state of controlled abandonment similar to the **Zen** concept of positive inaction. This goal is based on Lao Tzu's statement, 'The way to do is to be.' His latter-day followers interpret this as the need to achieve harmony with the universal flow, which can then be followed by choosing any one of an infinite number of directions. For those with a more magical than mystical turn of mind, it all comes down to the exercise of power generated by the fusion of opposites.

Taoist Alchemy

A curious system of esoteric **yoga** developed in China. Practitioners believe the individual will not survive physical death unless (s)he has taken the trouble to prepare a 'diamond body' as an immortal vehicle for the **spirit**.

The diamond body seems to be related to the **astral body** of Western **occultism**, but reinforced and strengthened during the adept's lifetime by a mingling of male and female sexual potencies.

The more literally-minded practitioners of Taoist alchemy create a literal 'cinnebar pill' compounded of, among other ingredients, semen and the lubricating fluid of the vagina. A second school of thought within the system insists the real secret lies in mingling male and female *ch'i* energies.

Both types of (male) practitioner practise *karezza* with a multiplicity of partners to achieve their ends. It is commonly believed that orgasm dissipates the vital energy in men, but that women are blessed with an inexhaustible supply. Consequently in Taoist alchemical intercourse, the man rigorously suppresses his orgasm while multiple orgasm is encouraged in the woman.

Tarot

When T.S. Eliot mentioned a 'wicked pack of cards' in his *Wasteland*, he was thinking of the Tarot, a 78-card deck less wicked than its reputation and probably less ancient than its mythology allows.

One esoteric theory suggests antediluvian origins for the Tarot, claiming that at the time **Atlantis** was scheduled for sinking, masters of occult wisdom met in conclave to find a way to preserve the sacred wisdom. They decided that whatever changes the future had in store for humanity, men would always gamble. Consequently they designed a pack of cards which contained, in symbol form, a synopsis of the wisdom of the universe. The cards, painted on leather, survived the cataclysm and were spread throughout the world by gypsies.

Another version of the story sets the conclave in Fez, Morocco, about the time of the destruction of the library at Alexandria. The oldest surviving example of a Tarot card is rather more recent, dating only from about the beginning of the fifteenth century.

The pack is generally regarded as the precursor of modern playing cards and there is indeed a game of Tarot which is still played with enthusiasm in parts of Europe and the Middle East. But the real association with the pack is **divination** and other forms of magical practice.

The 78 cards of the Tarot are divided into a major arcana of 22 trumps, and a minor arcana of 56 cards divided into the four suits of wands, clubs, pentacles and cups. The minor arcana actually equates quite well with the modern deck, although it has one court card extra, accounting for its slightly larger size than the modern 52-card pack.

The major arcana, by contrast, has no parallels in modern playing cards and consists of such archetypal symbols as The Magician, The Fool and The High Priestess. Each is equated with a particular 'path' on the Qabalistic **Tree of Life** and can be used as a meditational doorway to a specific area of the **astral plane**.

Prior to the 1970s there were really only two main Tarot decks in general use – the Tarot de Marseilles and the Rider-Waite deck. In the past 20 years an enormous range of Tarot decks have been developed. The Arthurian Tarot, the SOL Tarot, the Shakespearian Tarot, the Shining Woman Tarot, the Celtic Tarot and the Merlin Tarot have all been recently published. Tarot has proved to be very adaptable.

Tart, Charles T.

The American psychologist who has done a great deal of work on altered states of **consciousness**. His book, *Altered States of Consciousness*, published in 1969, is a classic in its field.

Teilhard de Chardin

Sometimes referred to as the greatest Christian thinker of modern times, the Jesuit priest Teilhard de Chardin combined careers as a philosopher, theologian and palaeontologist. The most fundamental expression of his philosophy came in his *The Phenomenon of Man*, a difficult book which argues that humanity is on the verge of a leap of **consciousness** similar to that which humans must have experienced as primeval entities when they first began to think.

Teilhard believed the new consciousness would be similar to mystical enlightenment in that it was likely to have collective and cosmic elements which would have the effect of drawing individuals closer to God.

His theory was certainly an attempt to reconcile Roman Catholic theology with the findings of modern science. Some critics have been unkind enough to describe the attempt as 'last ditch'.

Teleportation

The supposed ability to transport physical bodies instantaneously to a new location without moving through the intervening space, teleportation has long been considered the exclusive province of science fiction. A whole generation of *Star Trek* enthusiasts adopted the catch-phrase 'Beam me up, Scottie' in imitation of *Enterprise* crew members who routinely teleported from ship to planet (and sometimes safely back) using a high technology 'transporter'. A *Playboy* story later filmed as *The Fly* gave a horrifying twist to the theme when a scientist working on a teleportation machine finds his body reassembled in the receiver with the head of a bluebottle which had flown unnoticed into the transmitter with him.

But for all this, there remain some indications that teleportation may actually be possible. The séance-room phenomena of Victorian **Spiritualism**, for instance, included **apports** in which small items such as flowers, pieces of personal jewellery or stones materialized from thin air during a sitting. Investigation strongly suggested that these items were not *created* by the 'spirits' but were somehow 'taken' from other locations and transported instantaneously to the séance room. Researchers noted they often grew warm in the process.

An even more striking indication of the possibility of teleportation came in 1815 when warders and inmates of the Prussian prison at Weichselmunde witnessed one of the most incredible incidents ever recorded. A prisoner named Diderici was walking chained to other prisoners in the exercise yard when he began to fade. Within seconds he was invisible, then his manacles and ankle irons fell empty to the ground. He was never seen again.

But the most evidential of all pointers towards teleportation came more than 200 years earlier on 24 October 1593 when a soldier reported for guard-duty at the palace in Mexico City. Since his uniform was wrong for the posting, he was taken for questioning. Under interrogation he claimed to be stationed in Manila (in the Philippines) and had been ordered to report to Manila Palace for guard-duty that morning. He had no idea at all how he got to South America.

The authorities did not believe his story and threw him into jail. But the man had given one detail which subsequently persuaded them to change their minds. He mentioned that the night before he had received his orders, the Governor of the Philippines had been killed. Two months later, news finally reached Mexico that the Governor had indeed been murdered and on the night before the soldier turned up in Mexico. He was released from jail and allowed to return to Manila from whence, it seems, he had teleported eight weeks earlier.

St Teresa of Avila

Generally acknowledged as one of the greatest Christian saints and mystics, Teresa of Avila (full name Teresa de Cepeda y Ahumada) actually had to fight the opposition of her father when in 1535, at the age of 20, she became a nun of the Carmelite Order.

During her years in the Convent of the Incarnation at Avila, she underwent a series of mystical experiences which persuaded her to found her own convent of strict observance – something she finally succeeded in doing in 1562. Five years later, the General of the Carmelite Order instructed her to make other foundations and she spent the remaining years of her life (she died in 1582) establishing seventeen convents and two monasteries.

In copious writings (*Life*, *The Way of Perfection* and *The Interior Castle*), St Teresa distinguished two main stages in the process of mystical union: one in which the emphasis is on human effort, the other in which all progress depends on a gift from God.

Thanatology

The study of the psychology of death and dying, very much pioneered in the West (where it has been a taboo subject) by the psychiatrist Elisabeth Kübler-Ross. Ancient Egyptian and Tibetan cultures have a far more enlightened attitude to death and both have their own *Book of the Dead*, designed to be read to the dying to ease their passage into the world beyond.

Theosophical Society
See **Theosophy**.

Theosophy

When the Theosophical Society was founded, somewhat casually, by **Madame Blavatsky** and Colonel Olcott in 1875, its expressed aims were:

1) The expression of the brotherhood of man, regardless of race, creed, colour, or social position.

2) The study of comparative religion to establish a universal ethic.

3) The development of the latent powers of the human soul.

The society adopted as its motto – current to the present day – the adage: *There is no religion higher than Truth.*

The term 'theosophy', generally used to describe the doctrines of the society, derives from the Greek roots *theos* (God) and *sophia* (wisdom) suggesting a mystical knowledge of the divine. As such, it can be and often is used to describe a range of esoteric systems, such as **Gnosticism** and the **Qabalah**, which have nothing to do with the Theosophical Society.

The specific doctrines of the society remain a fascinating mélange of esoteric **Buddhism**, lamaist doctrines from Tibet, Hindu **mysticism** and a romantic picture of world history which postulates a non-physical period of prehistoric evolution with the ecosphere gradually solidifying into matter, and a series of root races stretching all the way back to lost **Atlantis**.

Therapeutic Touch

A method of **healing** developed by Dora van Gelder Kunz, a clairvoyant and **meditation** teacher, and Dolores Krieger, professor of nursing at New York University. The hands are used to identify and balance disturbances in the energy field around individuals. It helps to alleviate and even eradicate pain and accelerates the healing process.

Third Eye

Certain schemes of esoteric evolution insist that in the far reaches of prehistory, the predecessors of humanity were equipped with a third eye in the middle of their foreheads which permitted them to see directly into **spirit** realms. Over millions of years, the occult theory goes, the organ atrophied, was gradually covered and sank into the folds of the brain so that spiritual perception was all but lost.

Remarkably, there is some scientific indication that all this may be more than an engaging fable. The pineal gland, a smallish body buried within the brain at the approximate site of the traditional third eye, has been found to retain a certain degree of light sensitivity, leaving scientists to theorize that it might indeed be an evolutionary remnant of an organ of sight.

Occultists generally believe that the pineal gland is unusually active in **psychics** and many also insist that it can be stimulated in order to produce psychism. In an internationally best-selling book, the esoteric author **Lobsang Rampa** claimed that on his **initiation** as a Tibetan lama, he underwent a surgical operation in which a sliver of wood was inserted into his skull to awaken the third eye. Other authorities believe substantially similar results can be achieved via **acupuncture** by needling a point between the eyebrows known to the Chinese as the 'Gateway of the Precious Square Inch', or even by simply massaging the same area vigorously. For many **yoga** practitioners, physical intervention is unnecessary and the organ is awakened by a regime of concentration and **visualization**.

Until comparatively recently, science was unable to discover the function of the pineal gland, but in recent years it was found to be one of the factors in physical growth and a trigger for the hormonal changes of puberty. The gland secretes a substance known as serotonin which has itself a certain esoteric linkage in that it is found in concentrated quantities in the fruit of the tree under which the **Buddha** sat when he finally achieved enlightenment.

Thought-forms

The shapes assumed by thoughts and emotions, which can be perceived visibly by clairvoyants or sensed on an intuitive level by others.

Tibetan Book of the Dead, The

Also known as the *Bardo Thodol*, *The Tibetan Book of the Dead* is a guide to the soul, charting its expectations in the afterlife state. Oddly, the work describes a succession of inner planes very similar to those described by practitioners of **astral projection**. It suggests that following death, the soul is faced with the possibility of absorption into the pure light of mystical union with the godhead or **nirvana**. But for the average individual, this possibility is terrifying, so that the soul flees through a succession of dream worlds in which the environment is unconsciously created by the expectations of the dreamer.

The unevolved soul eventually begins to pine for the pleasures of the flesh and thus draws closer to the physical world again. Sexual fantasies attract it as a voyeur towards couples engaged in intercourse and it is trapped in the womb for another incarnation.

Tighe, Virginia
See **Murphy, Bridey**.

Touch for Health
Developed by Dr John F. Thie, this **healing** system combines applied **Kinesiology** for diagnosis and **acupressure** touch for treatment of the musculoskeletal system.

Transactional Analysis
A new style of psychiatry developed in the early 1960s by Dr Eric Berne based on his insights into the alternating personality aspects of Parent, Adult and Child which arose in his patients in response to circumstances; and into the ritualized (unconscious) games played by people in their personal relationships.

Transcendental Meditation
Transcendental Meditation, or TM, was introduced to the West by **Maharishi Mahesh Yogi** in the 1960s. It consists of two 20-minute sessions of **meditation** a day during which a specially-given **mantra** is repeated. Research has shown that TM does have beneficial effects, both physically – in the form of lower blood-pressure, slower heart beat and decreased oxygen intake – and psychologically.

TM has contributed greatly to the interest in meditation in the West and making the practice accessible. TM courses are still widely available.

Transcendentalist Movement
In 1836 a group of American intellectuals got together to explore the **Quaker** and Puritan traditions, the German and Greek philosophers and the Eastern religions. They included **Ralph Waldo Emerson** and Henry Thoreau, and were to influence many, including the poets Emily Dickinson and Walt Whitman, the founders of the British Labour Party, Gandhi and Martin Luther King. Transcendentalism was a philosophy which stressed an inner search for meaning.

Transpersonal Psychology

The first force in psychiatry was classical psychoanalytical theory in the **Freud**ian mould. The second force was behaviourism, the third **humanistic psychology**. Transpersonal psychology is now known as the fourth force, a psychological model appropriate to our current era of change in that it concerns itself primarily with transcendent states, mystical and other peak experiences.

The term 'transpersonal psychology' was coined during a lecture by **Stanislav Grof** and taken up by **Abraham Maslow** and Anthony Sutich. It remains closely associated with the **human potential movement** and **Esalen**.

Tree of Life

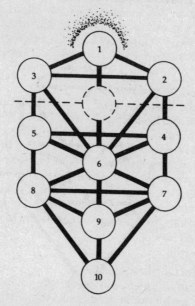

In the **Qabalah** the Tree of Life (see diagram) incorporates ten circles, symbolizing spheres of function in the nature of reality, and the various paths which join them, indicating, among other things, the complex interrelationships of the Tree.

The ten numbered circles, known as *Sephiroth* (singular: *Sephirah*) are usually perceived as energies or states on the physical level, but exist as defined places on the **astral plane**.

The bottom Sephirah (sphere) of the Tree, called Malkuth by Qabalists, signifies the physical aspect of reality, the world in which we live. Directly above Malkuth is the sphere of Yesod, associated with lunar function and symbolizing the astral plane.

The English title of Yesod is Foundation, chosen because the word is indicative of the essential nature of the sphere. To Qabalists, Yesod, the sphere of imagination and astral light, is the literal foundation on which physical reality rests.

As the Qabalist proceeds upwards through the numbered spheres, more and more subtle aspects of reality are reached, including the Christ sphere of Tiphareth (numbered 6 on the diagram) and culminating in the topmost sphere of all, Kether, which symbolizes the essential unity of the universe.

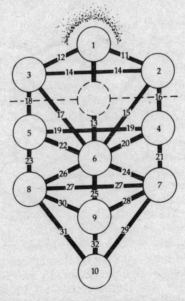

Tree and Paths

There are 22 paths on the Tree of Life. On the second diagram, they are shown as the lines joining the Sephiroth. Each path is a specific astral track and may be investigated using the esoteric technique of **pathworking**.

Trevelyan, Sir George

Sir George Trevelyan has been one of the pioneers of the **New Age** movement, introducing to many the work and ideas of healers, mystics and philosophers through the educational charity which he founded, the Wrekin Trust.

Trigrams

Three-lined figures comprising broken (**yin**) and unbroken (**yang**) lines which are the fundamental building blocks of *I Ching* **hexagrams**.

Trismegistus, Hermes

Literally Thrice-Greatest Hermes, this compound of the Greek Hermes and the Egyptian Thoth is the mystical hero of the **Hermetica**, a prophet with the ability to save the world from evil.

Trungpa Rinpoche, Chögyam

Born in Tibet in 1939 into the Kagyü lineage, Chögyam Trungpa was later to become revered as a **meditation** master, scholar and artist.

With the Chinese invasion of Tibet in 1959, Chögyam Trungpa led a large party of 300 refugees out of East Tibet into India in a dramatic escape, reputedly having to eat boiled leather and to travel by night to avoid Chinese patrols.

In 1963 he arrived in England with a scholarship to attend Oxford University, where he studied comparative religion and philosophy and pursued his interest in art. He went on to establish a meditation centre in Dumfriesshire, Scotland, called Samye-Ling Meditation Centre, after the first Tibetan monastery founded by Padmasambhava in the eighth century.

In 1970 Trungpa arrived in North America, where he was to live and teach until his death in 1987. He attracted an enormous following and centres were set up throughout the country. The main centres were at Boulder, Colorado, and finally at Halifax, Nova Scotia. He was controversial and his appearance and behaviour were puzzling to many. He ate whatever he wanted, drank and smoked, but his students continued meditating and studying with him. No matter how outrageously some nights ended, the next morning Trungpa expected everyone to be back at their practice.

Trungpa wrote numerous books, but his most influential have

277

been *Cutting through Spiritual Materialism, The Myth of Freedom and the Way of Meditation* and *Shambhala: The Sacred Path of the Warrior*. He undoubtedly had a unique ability to express the essence of Buddhist teachings in the language and imagery of Western culture.

Tulpa Creation

When Madame **Alexandra David-Neel** journeyed through Tibet, one of the many mystical techniques she studied was that of tulpa creation. The method, similar in some respects to the mystic adoration of the Tibetan **Yidam**, was virtually unknown outside Tibet until she publicized it in one of her books.

A *tulpa*, according to traditional Tibetan doctrines, is an entity created by an act of imagination, rather like the fictional characters of a novelist, except that tulpas are not written down. Madame David-Neel became so interested in the concept that she decided to try to create one.

The method involved was essentially intense concentration and **visualization**. Madame David-Neel's tulpa began its existence as a plump, benign little monk, similar to Friar Tuck. It was at first entirely subjective, but gradually, with practice, she was able to visualize the tulpa out there, like an imaginary ghost flitting about the real world.

In time the vision grew in clarity and substance until it was indistinguishable from physical reality – a sort of self-induced hallucination. But the day came when the hallucination slipped from her conscious control. She discovered that the monk would appear from time to time when she had not willed it. Furthermore her friendly little figure was slimming down and taking on a distinctly sinister aspect.

Eventually her companions, who were unaware of the mental disciplines she was practising, began to ask about the 'stranger' who had turned up in their camp – a clear indication that a creature which was no more than solidified imagination had definite objective reality.

At this point, Madame David-Neel decided things had gone too far and applied different lamaist techniques to reabsorb the creature into her own mind. The tulpa proved very unwilling to face destruction in this way so that the process took several weeks and left its creator exhausted.

Tumo

The Tibetan **yoga** of body heat which allows practitioners to endure extremes of cold while naked or dressed only in a thin cotton robe. The technique involves a series of vivid **visualizations** at a level with the navel along with some mantric **chanting**. As the heat is generated, it is then channelled outward through the rest of the body.

Prior to the Communist invasion, Tibetan yogis wishing to be known as tumo adepts were required to pass a sort of examination which included the drying off by body heat alone of three blankets in succession soaked in a mountain stream and the melting of a specific circle of snow by tumo heat generated in the backside.

Western practitioners of the art have included **Alexandra David-Neel** and, more recently, the American film actress Shirley Maclaine.

The Turin Shroud

For centuries a 14 ft 6 inch piece of twill linen in Turin cathedral has been venerated as a relic. On the cloth are the seemingly convincing marks of a crucified corpse, bloodstained from a crown of thorns, with what appears to be a lance wound to the chest and scourging on the back. According to the Gospels, 'They took the body of Jesus and wound it in linen clothes', and this, say those who believe in the authenticity of the Shroud, left the image. The image is no ordinary painting, but is like a photographic negative. When photographed originally in 1898 it was discovered that reversing the highlights and shadows gave a far more realistic image.

However, in 1988 an advanced form of carbon 14 dating carried out by three separate laboratories in the USA, Britain and Switzerland revealed the Shroud to be a medieval fake.

u

UFOs

On 17 January 1969, at about 7.15 p.m., the speaker at the local Lions Club in Leary, Georgia, USA, was standing outdoors with some dozen or so members when suddenly they were startled by the appearance of a weird aerial phenomenon.

A UFO (Unidentified Flying Object) was hovering somewhere between 300 and 1,000 yards distant from them, about 30 degrees above the horizon and as bright as, but a little smaller than, the moon. They watched it for ten minutes, during which it changed colours several times.

In October 1973, the club speaker on that night filed a detailed report on the siting with the National Investigations Committee on Aerial Phenomena (NICAP). He signed it *Jimmy Carter*. Much later, attempting to play down the incident in the face of Press inquiries, he suggested lightly that it might have been a star beckoning him towards the White House. Nevertheless, President Carter is on record as saying, 'I am convinced that UFOs exist because I've seen one.'

Most published sources date the UFO phenomenon from 1947 when the civilian pilot Kenneth Arnold reported sighting nine gleaming objects in the vicinity of Mount Rainier near Washington. But there is, in fact, substantial evidence of UFO sightings at much earlier dates. An island in the Hunan Province of China, for example, contains rock carvings not only of UFOs, but of strange, alien beings who might have been their occupants. The carvings have been dated back to 45,000 BC, an era of prehistory when Neanderthals roamed the chill environment of Ice Age Europe.

Flying craft which answer to the description of modern UFOs are also mentioned in the *Mahabharata*, under the name of *vimanas*, in what appears to be a reference to a prehistoric war in India.

In historical times, an Egyptian papyrus from the time of Pharaoh Thutmose III (*c.*1504–1450 BC) describes the appearance of numerous 'fire circles' in the sky, shining with the brightness of the sun. Several authors have suggested the Biblical vision of Ezekiel sounds much more like a description of a rocket landing than a religious experience:

> As I looked, behold, a stormy wind came out of the north, and a great cloud, with brightness round about it, and fire flashing forth continually, and in the midst of the fire, as it were gleaming bronze . . .

Books about UFOs are not new either. Julius Obsequens, a fourth-century AD Roman author compiled one called the *Prodigorium Liber* which reported sightings like the 'round shield' seen in the sky 180 miles east of Rome in 216 BC and the flying disc witnessed by the Tarquinian consuls Murius and Valerius in 99 BC. Even the term 'flying saucer' has an ancient lineage. It was first used by the Japanese to describe a UFO seen over the Kii Province in 1180.

But if UFOs have been around for much longer than people imagine, it is still not possible to say with any certainty what they are. When small discs, nicknamed 'foo fighters', buzzed Allied aircraft during the Second World War, the assumption was they were some sort of German secret weapon. Papers captured when the war ended indicated that Luftwaffe pilots had also seen foo fighters . . . and assumed they were Allied secret weapons.

For the American George Adamski, there was no mystery at all – UFOs were spaceships originating on the planet Venus. He knew this because one landed in the desert near Mount Palomar in the early 1950s and its pilot, a handsome golden-haired and white-robed figure, got out to tell him so.

Adamski's account of the meeting attracted widespread attention when he published it in a best-selling book, *Flying Saucers Have Landed*.

Adamski was neither the first nor the last to claim a meeting with UFO aliens from another planet. On the morning of 24 April 1964, for example, an egg-shaped UFO, 20 feet long by 15 feet wide, landed in a field at the farm of Gary T. Wilcox of Tioga County, New York. Two 4-foot-tall dwarfs appeared wearing seamless suits and hoods covering their heads. They carried trays containing soil samples. In a two-hour conversation (carried out in English) the visitors told Wilcox they wanted some fertilizer and mentioned they had come from Mars – a claim almost as unlikely as that made by Adamski's 'Venusian'.

Although the extra-terrestrial hypothesis is still the most favoured by the general public (encouraged by a great many movies on the subject) it is now well established that no high technological civilization and, indeed, almost certainly no life at all, exists on any planet of our solar system except Earth. This rules out the old science fiction favourites, Mars and Venus, and forces those who favour the hypothesis to look much further afield and postulate an inter-stellar, or even inter-galactic origin for the UFOs.

On the face of it, this seems a much more promising idea. Astronomer Carl Sagan has estimated – admittedly with optimism – that out of the 200 billion stars in our own Milky Way galaxy, as many as a million are circled by planets on which the evolution of intelligent life is likely. All the same, scientists are a long way from believing any of those intelligent life-forms have come calling.

They point out that until the first radio broadcasts less than a century ago, there was nothing to indicate Earth was inhabited. But since the nearest inhabited star system may be many thousands of light years away, the transmissions would not even have reached them yet. Furthermore, any response would surely be in the form of radio broadcasts back. And even if not, a physical visit would take several hundreds, perhaps thousands, of years since the speed of light represents an absolute beyond which no ship could travel.

Sagan and several of his colleagues have also criticized UFO encounter reports as unimaginative.

For those who do not believe in aliens from Outer Space, the multiplicity of UFO contact reports still require an explanation. By far the most popular is that of an *Inner* Space origin that is to say, contactees are suffering from hallucinations which they mistake for physical reality. But there are, however, cases of contact where the psychological explanation does not rest quite so easy. There remains a substantial body of investigators who dislike the extra-terrestrial hypothesis to explain UFOs almost as much as Establishment scientists.

According to this theory, humanity actually shares the planet with one or more alien races. These are normally invisible, but occasionally their representatives make themselves known to selected individuals. In the past, such contacts have been interpreted as meetings with fairies, elves, **spirits** and the like, with abductions described as visits to an Underworld or Elvish Kingdom. Today, it is argued, essentially the same experiences are interpreted within the current cultural milieu as visitors from space. Interestingly, fairy and elvish contacts have long been associated with ancient raths, standing stones and megalithic circles, an association clearly evident in reports of UFO sightings today.

Underhill, Evelyn

A member of **A.E. Waite**'s branch of the **Golden Dawn**, Evelyn Underhill was best known as a writer on mystical subjects. Born in 1875, she had an Anglican background, but converted to Catholicism following a visionary experience in 1906.

She was both a scholar and a spiritual teacher. Her pioneering study, *Mysticism: A Study in the Nature and Development of Man's Spiritual Consciousness*, was published in 1911.

In the last 15 years of her life she explored the spiritual life as lived out by ordinary men and women, working in the slums of North Kensington as well as conducting retreats and acting as a spiritual **guide**. She died in 1941.

Universal Life Force

A vital force or energy which permeates everything. Universally recognized, it is known by many names: *prana* in **Hinduism**, *ch'i* (or *qi*) in China, *ki* in Japan, *Mana* by the **Huna** of Hawaii. **Mesmer** called it 'magnetic fluid', **Reich** named it 'orgone energy' and more recently it has been referred to as 'bioenergy'.

Upanishads

The central scriptures of India's esoteric spiritual tradition, the *Upanishads* form a collection of more than 100 essays extracted from the *Vedas* and dealing primarily with the nature of God and the practice of **meditation**.

V

Vedanta

The dominant philosophy of **Hinduism** which advocates self-knowledge through the practice of **yoga** with the ultimate aim of mystical union with the godhead and release from the necessity of rebirth. It favours a non-dualist (*advaita*) interpretation of existence.

The term *Vedanta* derives from the four *Vedas*, scriptures which, with the *Bhagavad Gita* and the **Yoga** *Sutras*, contain all its basic teachings.

Vedas

A collection of four Hindu sacred texts – the *Rig-Veda*, the *Sama-Veda*, the *Yajur-Veda* and the *Atharva-Veda* – composed somewhere between 1800 to 1200 BC.

The term *Veda* itself is Sanskrit and means 'knowledge'. Collectively, the Vedas deal with **ritual**s, spells, chants, **mantra**s and hymns and form the major canon of the Hindu religion.

Velikovsky, Emmanuel

Dr Emmanuel Velikovsky was born in Vitebsk, Russia, in 1895 and was educated at the universities of Moscow, Berlin, Vienna and Edinburgh. Between the years 1921 and 1924, he partnered Albert Einstein in editing the *Scripta Universitatis atque Bibliothecae Hierosolymitarum* from which the Hebrew University of Jerusalem eventually grew. He emigrated to America in 1939.

Despite his impressive academic credentials, Velikovsky might have ended his days in scholarly obscurity were it not for the fact that in 1950 he published a work called *Worlds in Collision* which caused him to be compared favourably with Newton, Darwin and even **Freud** by New York literati – and dismissed as a dangerous crank by a good many scientists.

The thesis of *Worlds in Collision* was that in the relatively recent history of the Earth, there had been a series of catastrophes triggered by cometary and interplanetary collisions. These disasters were recorded in, for example, Biblical accounts of the sun standing still – a phenomenon interpreted by Velikovsky as neither myth nor miracle, but rather an actual historical account of what appeared to happen when the Earth's rotation temporarily ceased as the planet was in the process of changing its direction of spin.

Velikovsky followed *Worlds in Collision* with *Earth in Upheaval*, which argued essentially the same thesis from a different viewpoint, and *Ages in Chaos*, a companion volume which sought to show that the orthodox chronology of the ancient world – notably Ancient Egypt – was substantially in error. Other major works followed, including *Peoples of the Sea* and *Oedipus and Akhenaton*, the latter of which suggested that the Greek myth of Oedipus, the king who inadvertently married his own mother, was based on the incestuous activities of the heretical Egyptian Pharaoh, Akhenaton.

Although the broad cataclysmic picture of our planetary history presented in Velikovsky's earlier books has now been largely demolished – the astronomer Carl Sagan launched a swingeing attack on many of Velikovsky's most important astronomical claims in his own book *Broca's Brain* – his work retains a mythic fascination and his literary style has a power and accessibility rare among academics.

Vipassana

Vipassana or 'insight meditation' is from the Theravadin Buddhist tradition. It is one of the best-known, popular and practical **meditation** techniques, involving concentration on breathing in and breathing out, and thus stilling the mind and bringing about insight into reality.

Vision Quest

A Native American Indian practice which involves seeking to acquire spiritual power by means of a vision of a supernatural being.

After preparing, by such practices as fasting or the sweat lodge, the individual retires alone to a place of natural power to pray for a vision. A dream or a vision of a guardian **spirit** (usually in animal form) follows and a **talisman** is bestowed as a tangible sign of the power conferred.

Visualization

At its most basic, visualization is the ability to make pictures in the mind, a talent largely devalued in our Western culture, but now coming slowly into its own.

Visualization lies at the heart of almost all modern magical practice, as well as **autogenic training**, **Silva Mind Control**, **pathworking**, and various positive thinking practices.

Vivekananda, Swami

Born in 1863, Vivekananda was the favourite pupil of **Ramakrishna**, whose **ashram** he joined at the age of 20. After Ramakrishna's death in 1886, Vivekananda renounced the world and founded the Ramakrishnan Order, which became the Ramakrishna Mission. He became the first in a long line of Indian **gurus** coming out of the West. In 1893 he represented **Hinduism** at the World Parliament of Religions in Chicago and in 1895 founded the Vedanta Society. He won the respect of such prominent figures as **William James**, Leo Tolstoy and **Aldous Huxley**.

Voodoo

(also Voodoun) Syncretic religion based on ancient African rites and Catholicism. The African slaves transported to North and South America were forbidden to practise their religion and their masters had them baptized as Catholics. Like **Santéria**, Voodoo was a mixture of Catholicism superimposed upon secret native rites and beliefs.

Waite, A. E.

One of the more pompous and tedious of the Victorian magicians associated with the **Golden Dawn**, Arthur Edward Waite was an American, born in Brooklyn in 1857, whose mother brought him to England while he was still a baby.

Waite's intellectual life was influenced by the Spiritualist movement and the writings of **Madame Blavatsky** and **Eliphas Lévi**. His first esoteric work was the codification of the latter's teaching. Waite joined the Theosophical Society for a time, but left because he could not accept the doctrine of the **Hidden Masters**. He entered the Golden Dawn and passed through the grades of the First Order, but resigned in protest at what he considered to be legal improprieties on the part of his superiors.

Oddly enough he rejoined the Order several years later in the aftermath of the **Crowley/Yeats** split, gained control of the mother lodge and rewrote its body of ceremonial from the viewpoint of Christian **mysticism**. Later he turned to **Freemasonry** and attempted to chart a secret tradition underlying various aspects of **occultism**. He produced poetry, now largely forgotten, and a variety of books, many of which are still in print, but marred by an overblown 'scholarly' style.

Watkins, Alfred

The Herefordshire businessman and lover of the countryside who first discovered **ley lines** while out horseback riding in the Bredwardine Hills. Watkins published his discovery in 1925 in a work called *The Old Straight Track*.

Watts, Alan

Holder of a master's degree in theology and a doctorate of divinity, in the 1960s Alan Watts became one of America's best-known interpreters of **Zen Buddhism** and Oriental philosophy in general. It was really Watts who brought Zen, **Vedanta** and **Taoism** to the young American masses.

He involved himself in the **consciousness** expansion movement associated with Drs Timothy Leary and Richard Alpert and among his many books is *The Joyous Cosmology*, which described his personal experience of psychedelic drugs and helped make him a hero of the hippie counter-culture.

Alan Watts died in 1973.

Westcott, William Wynn

There were some odd characters about in Victorian London and none more so than the coroner for north-east London, Dr Wynn Westcott.

Westcott was a plump, grey-haired, grey-bearded man with a tired, doleful expression and bags under his eyes. He had a profound interest in the occult and he was a personal friend of **Madame Blavatsky**. His associates also included the Christian mystics Anna Kingsford and Edward Maitland and his titles included that of 'Supreme Magus of the Societas Rosicruciana in Anglia', indicating his Masonic interests. He was an antiquarian and scholar of distinction, translating the *Chaldean Oracles of Zoroaster* and the Qabalistic *Sepher ha Zohar* into English, but his major claim to fame is the fact that he founded, in 1888, the Hermetic Order of the **Golden Dawn**.

Western Esoteric Tradition

A body of occult knowledge, based mainly on the Jewish **Qabalah**, but incorporating Egyptian, Chaldean, Celtic and mystical Christian elements along with some material from **Gnosticism**, Catharism and the classical Mystery Religions, notably those of ancient Greece.

Modern practitioners often feel free to make use of **yoga** disciplines and Theosophical doctrines which properly form part of the parallel, but separate, Eastern Esoteric Tradition.

White Eagle

A **spirit guide** who communicated through the mediumship of Mrs Grace Cooke, White Eagle gave out a considerable body of spiritual and philosophical teaching which has found its way into print through the good offices of the White Eagle Publishing Trust, established by the Cooke family to disseminate the doctrines.

White Eagle teaches, among other things, that humanity lives in bondage to the body, the limitations of materiality and the lower self. But this bondage is not perpetual since, during the course of many incarnations, individuals undergo a series of **initiation**s by means of which they attain mastery over themselves, their circumstances and, finally, over the substance of matter itself.

White, Ruth
See **Gildas**.

Wicca
See **Witchcraft**.

Wilber, Ken
Widely acclaimed for his work, Ken Wilber has been described as 'the foremost writer on **consciousness** and **transpersonal psychology** in the world today'. With degrees in chemistry and biology, he has also studied widely in the fields of psychotherapy, philosophy and religion.

According to Wilber, there is a hierarchy or spectrum of consciousness incorporating multiple consciousness levels like boxes within boxes, each of which is real at its particular level. These range from the highest level of cosmic consciousness to the lowest, which is purely egoic consciousness. Wilber's ideas are expressed in his books *The Spectrum of Consciousness*, *The Atman Project* and *Up from Eden*.

Wilhelm, Richard
Translator (into German) of the Chinese *I Ching*, producing what is still the definitive Western language text of the **oracle**. Wilhelm began the work in 1913, in collaboration with one of the foremost Chinese scholars of the period, Lao Nai-hsüan. His finished German version, prepared after detailed discussion, was retranslated into Chinese in order to determine its accuracy before it was finally released. The outbreak of the First World War interrupted the translation, so that the finished text was only released in 1923. Since then, Wilhelm's version of the *I Ching* has been translated into English by Cary F. Baynes.

Wilson, Colin

Colin Wilson sprang into international prominence in the mid-1950s as part of the so-called 'Angry Young Man' movement, when his first published book, *The Outsider*, attracted immense readership and substantial critical acclaim.

The Outsider was largely an analysis of a particular personality type as it appeared in literature and marked Wilson at least to some extent as a well-read intellectual with social concerns and a desire to comment on contemporary society. Born in Leicester in 1931, he left school at the age of 16 and moved through a variety of jobs in a wool warehouse, a laboratory, a plastics factory and a coffee bar until the publication of *The Outsider* in 1956 established his literary career.

The Outsider was followed by works on philosophy, religion, crime, history, music and literature. But as more of his books appeared, it became evident that his mind was moving into unorthodox byways. There was a family history of interest in **Spiritualism** and now Wilson seemed determined to examine the vast body of esoteric thought. At a time when both scientists and academics were still wary of the subject, he published a massive tome entitled *The Occult*, which was described by one reviewer as 'An immensely powerful synthesis of all the relevant indications . . . by a mind from which ideas spurt like exploding lava.'

One of the ideas which had been spurting from Wilson's mind for some time was that the central mystery of human existence was how humans managed to experience boredom while inhabiting a world of infinite interest and variety. Wilson concluded, with **Gurdjieff**, that there was something wrong with human **consciousness** – that most people live a robotic existence far below their real potential.

It was a theme to which he returned again and again. By the time he came to publish *Mysteries* in 1978, he was hot on the trail of a solution to low-grade consciousness by making contact with a sort of 'higher self' which banished the plodding, robotic mindset generally experienced.

Wilson continues to write in this area.

Witchcraft

Kramer and Sprengler, the fifteenth-century Dominican authors of the *Malleus Maleficærum*, had no doubts at all about the nature of witchcraft. They considered it the visible expression of Satan's work in the world. Margaret Murray, the distinguished twentieth-century anthropologist, was not so sure. In her influential *The Witch-Cult in Western Europe*, she argued that it was actually a survival of a pre-Christian religion dating back, literally, to prehistoric times.

For a while, Murray's thesis received academic support (she contributed the article on witchcraft to early editions of the *Encyclopaedia Britannica*) but scholars eventually decided her case was not proven. One man who disagreed was **Gerald Gardner**, who claimed to be the appointed publicity officer of a New Forest coven and insisted Margaret Murray had been right in almost everything she said.

Whether or not Gardner was correct was largely irrelevant to the expression of witchcraft. His books *Witchcraft Today* and *The Meaning of Witchcraft*, aided by intense and largely hostile interest from the Press, sparked a revival of the Craft which shows no sign of diminishing today.

At first, the revival tended to attract a mature age spectrum of middle-class followers until the emergence of **Alex Sanders** who established his own brand of the witchcraft with a greater emphasis on magical ceremonial and attracted a younger, more intellectual following. For a time the Press made great play of the supposed 'battle' for the title 'King of the Witches' which, it was claimed, intensified following Gardner's death in 1964. Eventually the distinction went, for what it was worth, to Sanders, but it is noteworthy that when he too died there was no repetition of the undignified scramble for high-sounding accolades. This was not accidental, for whatever it may have been in the past (and whatever it may still be in primitive communities today) witchcraft has become an expression of feminine awakening in Western culture with a consequent abhorrence of centralization and hierarchical structures.

Modern witches tend to refer to their religion as *wicca*, the feminine form of the Old English *wicce*, which itself means 'witch'. Both male and female followers are known as witches, although the cult itself is decidedly matriarchal, with the High Priestess of each coven looked on as a personification (in some rites even the incarnation) of the Great Mother **Goddess** who is the principal deity of the movement. Consort of the Goddess, personified by the coven's High Priest, is the **Horned God**,

Cernunnos, often quite incorrectly identified with the Devil by those outside the cult.

The major festivals of modern witchcraft are seasonal. They mark the vernal equinox on 21 March, Beltane on 30 April, the summer solstice on 22 June, Lammastide on 1 August, the autumnal equinox on 21 September, Hallowe'en on 31 October, the winter solstice on 21 December and Candlemas on 2 February. Additional sabbats, as these meetings are known, are held at each full moon and esbats, as the less formal meetings are known, might be held weekly.

The working unit of witchcraft is the coven – ideally, but not necessarily, a group of thirteen. (The number is chosen as the optimum for dancing within the nine-foot circle used in many wiccan ceremonies.) Some covens work robed, some 'sky-clad' i.e. naked, and some both, depending on the weather. Despite the fertility aspects of the cult, there seems to be little sexual element in the nudity, which is adopted because of the witch belief that clothes can interfere with the emanation of personal power.

Ceremonial differs from coven to coven, although there are obvious similarities and common elements. The average meet, which might be held outdoors on a Saturday, would typically involve the drawing of a circle and the lighting of four candles to mark the cardinal points. Coven members stand just within the circle with the High Priestess kneeling before a central altar on which might be a number of **ritual** implements, including almost certainly a 'Book of Shadows' containing details of ceremonials and spells. The High Priest, possibly wearing a horned helmet, stands facing South.

A saline solution is used as a sort of wiccan equivalent of 'Holy Water' to purify the circle, the participants, the High Priestess and the High Priest. The Priestess then moves to each of the cardinal points, usually holding a ceremonial sword, and evokes the 'Mighty Ones', the elemental rulers of Earth, Air, Fire and Water.

One of the most interesting ceremonies of modern witchcraft is that known as the 'Drawing Down of the Moon'. This is carried out by the High Priest, but its goal is to create a temporary incarnation of the Goddess in the High Priestess, a result which has obvious similarities to the trance possession rites of many **shaman**ic religions. Another ceremony, known as the 'Great Rite' recalls the cult's fertility foundations in an act of sexual intercourse, either actual or symbolic, between priest and priestess.

Women's Spirituality

A growing movement, women's spirituality has developed out of the feminist movement and has been helped by psychoanalysis and ecology.

Women's spirituality is concerned with the way of the **Goddess**. The way is one of natural law and natural wisdom and is still a living tradition in some parts of the world. Not so in the West, where patriarchy and the monotheistic religions of **Judaism**, **Islam** and **Christianity** denied access to the Goddess.

In the beginning, according to Merlin Stone, the author of the ground-breaking *When God was a Woman*, God was a woman – the prehistoric peoples worshipped a female deity who was the source of both creativity and destruction. The ancient Goddess cultures were woman-centred, peaceful and egalitarian.

The emerging women's spirituality movement acknowledges the sacred dimension of women's experience and empowers women to transform their lives. Women's spirituality sees humanity as part of the whole, part of the cosmos and part of Nature. There is now a burgeoning literature in this field with women's spirituality sections in many bookshops. In addition to Merlin Stone's book, some seminal works include *The Goddesses and Gods of Old Europe* by Marija Gimbutas, *Women's Mysteries* by Esther Harding, Hallie Iglehart's *Womanspirit: A Guide to Women's Wisdom*, Edward Whitmont's *Return of the Goddess*, Barbara Walker's excellent encyclopedic dictionaries: *The Women's Encyclopedia of Myths and Secrets* and *The Women's Dictionary of Symbols and Sacred Objects*. A wonderful visual chronicle of the Goddess is the art historian Elinor Gadon's book *The Once and Future Goddess*. (*See also* **Andrews, Lynn; Starhawk**.)

Y

Yates, Frances

Dame Frances Yates taught at the Warburg Institute of the University of London from 1941 to 1981, achieving a world-wide reputation as a historian. She wrote several books, including *The Occult Philosophy in the Elizabethan Age*, *Astraea* and *The Art of Memory*. Her importance lies mainly in her achievement in unearthing details of the 'Memory Theatre', the esoteric memory training system of Renaissance occultists. This system, still in use today, makes use of an imaginary *locus* (or place) – often a monumental public building – into which items to be remembered are placed by an act of visualization. When the locus is recalled at a later date, the items are remembered too.

Yeats, W.B.

While working on the poetry of **William Blake** in the reading room of the British Museum, William Butler Yeats first noticed an individual who impressed him greatly. This was **S.L. MacGregor Mathers**, who was busily copying old magical manuscripts and **rituals**.

Mathers was to become the co-founder of the **Golden Dawn** and Yeats very willingly followed him into that magical organization. He was initiated in the early summer of 1887, taking the secret name *Diabolus est Deus Inversus* ('The Devil is God Reversed'). Yeats helped Mathers write the various Golden Dawn rituals, drawing on *The Egyptian Book of the Dead*, the Chaldean Oracles and the visionary works of Blake.

If Yeats officiated at the birth of the Golden Dawn, he also, in a very real sense, officiated at the death. He was leader of the movement to expel the notorious **Aleister Crowley**, an action which generated a fragmentation of the Order from which it never really recovered. Yeats himself resigned in 1905.

The Golden Dawn was not Yeats' only esoteric interest. Born

the son of Anglo-Irish parents in 1865, he developed a boyhood interest in fairies which carried through into his adult life. He was a close friend of the Irish mystic **George Russell** (who wrote under the pseudonym 'A.E.'). He took a sober and remarkably critical interest in **Spiritualism**. He studied comparative religion and **Theosophy** and seems rather to have liked **Madame Blavatsky**.

Esoteric symbolism found its way into his poetry, which his contemporaries considered surprisingly good, considering the nonsense Willie took seriously. By the time of his death in 1939, history had already adjudged him a great poet, although still with a distinct tendency to ignore the occult elements of his philosophy and career.

Yidam

While strictly speaking no more than one among many of lamaist Tibet's tutelary deities, the Yidam was central to a ceremony of profound interest. A **chela**, bound to one of Tibet's hermit **gurus**, would often be instructed to meditate on the Yidam and study pictures of this fearsome deity, reading everything the scriptures had to say about it. When the student was thoroughly saturated in Yidam lore, he (and in the Tradition, students were almost always male) would be advised to find a remote cave and there draw a *kylkhor* or magic circle using coloured chalk powders for the purpose of evoking the Yidam to visible appearance.

The evocation did not follow a set magical ceremony, as might have been the case in, for example, the **ritual** magical practice of the West. Rather the chela was instructed strongly to visualize the Yidam within the circle, rather in the manner of a **tulpa creation**. Over a period of weeks, or even months, the pupil would be strongly encouraged to keep at the exercise until a full-scale hallucination resulted and the Yidam appeared within the circle.

At this point, the pupil would be told he had been remarkably successful in evoking the Yidam and was obviously favoured by the god. For his next step, he would have to persuade it to leave the circle. This might have taken several more weeks or months, but eventually the chela would report that the god had indeed stepped out of the kylkhor. He would be congratulated, then told to see if he could manage to get the Yidam to leave the cave altogether and accompany him wherever he went.

Typically, the pupil would redouble his **visualization** efforts until he succeeded. The guru would then tell him he had succeeded beyond his wildest expectations: he had evoked and commanded one of the most powerful gods in the entire pantheon of Tibet. His studies were ended and so was his relationship with the guru, since he now had a teacher far wiser and more powerful than the guru could ever be.

Many pupils would in fact leave at this point and spend the remainder of their lives in the comfortable hallucination of a guardian deity prepared to help and advise them at every turn. A few chelas, however, would express doubt about the reality of the Yidam.

At this the guru would grow angry and demand to know if the Yidam did not look as solid as the mountains. The pupil, who might by this stage have spent years fine-tuning his visualizations, would admit that it was. The guru would ask if the pupil had not touched the god and found it solid as the rocks. Again the chela would be forced to admit this was the case. He was then instructed to go away and meditate alone for several more months to try to banish his doubt.

A very few among the pupils would find that their doubts survived despite every effort they made to resolve them. When they admitted as much to the guru, he would tell them they were favoured above all others, for they had realized that however real and solid the Yidam looked and felt, it was no more than a creation of their mind . . . as was the remainder of the world around them.

Yin/Yang

According to traditional Chinese thought, *yin* and *yang* are the two great complementary principles on whose interaction the whole of the manifest universe depends. Yin is defined as dark, negative and passive; yang as light, positive and active.

The yin/yang concept is by no means purely academic. It is an intensely practical aspect both in the **divination** system of the *I Ching* and the medical system of Chinese **acupuncture**. In the latter, diseases are often classified and treated in relation to the over- or under-abundance of yin or yang in a particular meridian.

Yoga

Although Westerners tend to think of yoga largely as a system of non-violent calisthenics, there are in fact ten different yogas traditionally recognized as valid paths to the goal of spiritual attainment.

Bhakti Yoga is defined as the way of love, devotion and faith. These elements are usually directed towards God, but practitioners believe that love and devotion towards humanity or any living creature will achieve the same results.

Dhyana Yoga comes close to the Western religious practices of contemplation and **meditation**, a purely mental discipline often involving trance states.

Hatha Yoga is the only form of yoga widely practised in the West. It emphasises the development and control of the physical body to such a degree that it no longer interferes in any way with the mind's search for enlightenment.

Jnana Yoga is the yoga of knowledge and calls for an understanding of the sacred **Vedas** of **Hinduism**, notably the **Upanishads** which contain a great number of esoteric doctrines.

Karma Yoga is the way of good deeds, usually expressed as charitable acts and work for the needy.

Kriya Yoga is concerned with religious observance and the proper carrying through of **ritual** acts.

Kundalini Yoga is specifically concerned with arousing the serpent power of **kundalini** at the base of the spine so that it may climb upwards and illuminate the brain.

Laya Yoga is a system specifically concerned with the activation of the **chakras** and, like certain Western magical systems, uses specific sounds (or **mantras**) to awaken them.

Mantra Yoga although sometimes inaccurately described as a yoga of spells, is actually a yoga of sound, using chants and **mantras** in order to drive the mind towards a higher state.

Raja Yoga is known as the King of Yogas (sometimes even the King of Kings of Yogas) and exclusively charts a system of mental and psychical development leading towards enlightenment.

Yogananda, Paramahansa

A disciple of the great Indian saint, Sri Yukteswarji, Paramahansa Yogananda was sent to the West as his emissary. He spent over 30 years in the West, establishing the Self-Realization Fellowship in America, the first great **ashram** in the West. Yogananda's book, *Autobiography of a Yogi*, published in 1946, is an eyewitness account of the lives and powers of modern Hindu saints. It is remarkable in that it is a book about yogis by a yogi and has become recognized as a classic and translated into many languages.

Yuga

Both Hindu and Buddhist doctrines teach that the history of the world consists of a repeating series of four ages, or *yugas*, each of which is of enormous length. The *yugas* are named, in order of their occurrence, as *Krita Yuga, Treta Yuga, Dvapara Yuga* and *Kali Yuga*.

It is believed that each age marks a progressive decline in morals, righteousness and piety, a gradual degeneration from the original Golden Age of the *Krita Yuga*.

Zazen

A **meditation** posture of **Zen Buddhism** found in two forms corresponding with the lotus posture and the perfect posture of Hatha **yoga**.

Zen

When **Buddhism** spread from India, it followed a pattern common to many other religions in that it adapted to the needs and conditions of the countries in which it took root. All adaptation requires change and nowhere was the change in Buddhism so marked as in Japan where Zen, while still ostensibly a branch of the parent growth, might almost be a completely different religio-philosophical system.

Culturally, Japan has for centuries held to the rigid codifications of behaviour necessary for survival in an overcrowded society where privacy has long been at a premium. These codifications range from the elaborate **ritual** of the tea ceremony through stylized artforms like painting, calligraphy and flower arranging, all the way up to a Samurai tradition which today manifests in industrial stoicism and corporate loyalties.

Whatever the social and economic benefits of the Japanese way, Zen philosophers have long believed that the mindset it produces acts as a barrier against enlightenment. Consequently, the thrust of Zen Buddhism is the shattering of the mindset, the breaking down of ritualized patterns of thought so that a more direct perception of reality may become possible.

The methods used to achieve this result are both bizarre and interesting. Almost all are designed either to shock or to drive the mind into such a paradoxical state that it can no longer support itself.

An example of the former approach is the Zen Master's well-known habit of answering a disciple's most profound religious or philosophical question by hitting him with a stick.

An example of the latter is Zen's famous **koans**, briefly stated puzzles which defy logical solution.

Zero Balancing

A scientific, grounded technique, developed by Dr Fritz Smith, for balancing the relationship between a person's physical structure and their energy. By putting the patient into a state of Zero Balance through touch, an expanded state of **consciousness** is achieved. As a system of stress control and internal reprogramming, it brings about a sense of balance and well-being, both physically and emotionally.

Zodiacal Ages

The equinoxes are those (two) periods of the year at which day and night are of equal length. They mark the crossover of the sun from northern to southern hemisphere and back again and since the second century BC the position of the sun in relation to the constellations has been known to regress, i.e. it moves through the constellations in a direction contrary to that of the planets. The phenomenon is known as the 'precession of the equinoxes'.

This precession has led to the concept of Zodiacal Ages, each lasting approximately 2,100 years. About 4000 BC, for example, the sun appeared in the constellation Taurus at the time of the spring equinox. This was followed by the Age of Aries (approximately 2000–0 BC). The Age of Pisces is still with us, but the Aquarian Age is not far off.

Zone Therapy

See **Reflexology**.

Zoroastrianism

The Iranian prophet Zoroaster, called Zarathustra in the holy book of the religion he founded, was born sometime in the seventh century BC probably in an area that now corresponds to the Turkmen Republic in Soviet Central Asia.

He fled from his native land on account of the antagonism he raised in his fellow-countrymen by preaching a revelation they could not accept and found refuge in eastern Iran. The king of the area, Vishtaspa, eventually accepted his teachings.

The teachings themselves referred to **Ahura Mazda**, the Wise

Lord who had revealed himself to Zoroaster as the true God. The message of Zoroastrianism was eerily reminiscent of the Judaeo-Christian tradition in that it stated in essence that God was One, holy, righteous and the Creator of the Universe.

But Ahura Mazda's unity manifested in diversity, a series of aspects referred to as the Bounteous Immortals, personifying Truth, Holy Spirit, Sovereignty, Wholeness and so on. In His aspects of Truth and Holy Spirit, He was opposed by the personification of lies and destruction, the fiend **Ahriman**.

Zoroastrianism has gone through many modifications and extensions in the years since its foundation. The **Islam**ic conquest all but drove it out of its native Persia (there are probably fewer than 10,000 followers of the faith in the whole of Iran today) but it survives among the Parsees of India who are the philosophical and in some cases the physical descendants of 100,000 Persian emigrants centuries ago.

Further Reading and Select Bibliography

Publisher and date of publication refer to editions available to authors. In many instances other editions are also available.

Adler, Margot, *Drawing down the Moon* (Beacon Press, 1976).

Arrien, Angeles, *The Tarot Handbook* (The Aquarian Press, 1991).

Ashcroft-Nowicki, Dolores, *The Shining Paths* (The Aquarian Press, 1983).

—— *The Ritual Magic Workbook* (The Aquarian Press, 1986).

—— *Highways of the Mind* (The Aquarian Press, 1987).

—— *The Sacred Cord Meditations* (The Aquarian Press, 1990).

—— *First Steps in Ritual* (The Aquarian Press, 1990).

—— *The Tree of Ecstasy* (The Aquarian Press, 1990).

—— *The New Book of the Dead* (The Aquarian Press, 1991).

—— *Daughters of Eve* (The Aquarian Press, 1993).

Ashe, Geoffrey, *King Arthur's Avalon* (Collins, 1957).

—— *The Ancient Wisdom* (Macmillan, 1977).

Assagioli, Roberto, *Psychosynthesis* (The Aquarian Press, 1990).

Auken, John van, *Past Lives* (Inner Vision Publishing Co., Anaheim, California, 1984).

Aurobindo, Sri, *The Life Divine* (Pondicherry, India, 1970).

Baba Ram Dass, *Be Here Now* (Lama Foundation, USA, 1970).

Bateson, Gregory, *Steps to an Ecology of Mind* (Ballantine Books, 1972).

—— *Mind and Nature* (Dutton, 1979).

Begg, Ean, *The Cult of the Black Virgin* (Arkana, 1985).

Bek, Lilla, and Holden, Robert, *What Number Are You?* (The Aquarian Press, 1992).

Bell, Charles, *The Religion of Tibet* (Oxford University Press, 1931).

Bernard, Theos, *Hatha Yoga* (Rider, 1971).

Bohm, David, *Wholeness and the Implicate Order* (Routledge and Kegan Paul, 1983).

Bonewits, Isaac, *Real Magic* (Open Gate, USA, 1971).

Brennan, J. H., *Astral Doorways* (The Aquarian Press, 1971).

—— *The Reincarnation Workbook* (The Aquarian Press, 1989).
—— *Nostradamus* (The Aquarian Press, 1992).
Brent, Peter, *Godmen of India* (Penguin, 1972).
Bro, Harman H., *Edgar Cayce on Dreams* (The Aquarian Press, 1989).
—— *Edgar Cayce: A Seer out of Season* (The Aquarian Press, 1990).
Brown, Joseph Epes, *The Sacred Pipe* (Penguin, 1971).
Brunton, Paul, *The Hidden Teaching beyond Yoga* (Rider, 1972).
Budge, Wallace (trans.), *The Egyptian Book of the Dead* (Dover, 1978).
Burckhardt, Titus, *Alchemy* (Stuart & Watkins, 1967).
—— *Introduction to Sufism* (The Aquarian Press, 1990).
Butler, W. E., *The Magician: His Training and Work* (The Aquarian Press, 1959).
—— *Magic and the Qabalah* (The Aquarian Press, 1964).
—— *How to Read the Aura* (The Aquarian Press, 1971).
Button, John, and Bloom, William (eds.), *The Seeker's Guide* (The Aquarian Press, 1992).
Campbell, Eileen (ed.), *A Dancing Star* (The Aquarian Press, 1991).
—— *A Lively Flame* (The Aquarian Press, 1992).
—— *The Unknown Region* (The Aquarian Press, 1993).
Campbell, Joseph, *The Masks of God* (4 vols) (Penguin Books, 1969).
—— *Hero with a Thousand Faces* (Paladin Books, 1988).
Capra, Fritjof, *The Tao of Physics* (Fontana, 1976).
—— *The Turning Point* (Simon and Schuster, 1982).
—— *Uncommon Wisdom* (Fontana, 1989).
—— and Charlene Spretnak, *Green Politics* (Dutton, 1984).
Carey, Ken, *Terra Christa* (Uni-Sun, 1988).
—— *Starseed: The Third Millennium* (HarperSanFrancisco, 1991).
—— *The Starseed Transmissions* (HarperSanFrancisco, 1992).
—— *Return of the Bird Tribes* (HarperSanFrancisco, 1992).
—— *Vision* (HarperSanFrancisco, 1993).
Castaneda, Carlos, *The Teachings of Don Juan* (Ballantine, 1968).
—— *A Separate Reality* (Penguin, 1973).
—— *Journey to Ixtlan* (Bodley Head, 1973).
—— *The Art of Dreaming* (The Aquarian Press, 1993).
Cavendish, Richard, *The Black Arts* (Routledge & Kegan Paul, 1967).
Cayce, Edgar, *Edgar Cayce on Dreams*, by Harmon H. Bro, ed. Hugh Lynn Cayce (The Aquarian Press, 1989).
—— *Edgar Cayce on ESP*, by Doris Agee, ed. Hugh Lynn Cayce (The Aquarian Press, 1989).
—— *Edgar Cayce on Reincarnation*, by Noel Langley, ed. Hugh Lynn Cayce (The Aquarian Press, 1989).

—— *Edgar Cayce on Mysteries of the Mind*, by Henry Reed, ed. Charles Thomas Cayce (The Aquarian Press, 1990).

—— *Edgar Cayce on Remembering your Past Lives*, by Robert C. Smith, ed. Charles Thomas Cayce (The Aquarian Press, 1990).

—— *Edgar Cayce on Secrets of the Universe*, by Lin Cochran, ed. Charles Thomas Cayce (The Aquarian Press, 1990).

Chetwynd, Tom, *Dictionary for Dreamers* (The Aquarian Press, 1993).

—— *Dictionary of Sacred Myth* (The Aquarian Press, 1993).

—— *Dictionary of Symbols* (The Aquarian Press, 1993).

Clover, Dr Anne, *Thorsons Introductory Guide to Homoeopathy* (Thorsons, 1991).

Collin, Rodney, *The Theory of Celestial Influence* (Stuart & Watkins, 1954).

Colton, James and Sheelagh, *Thorsons Introductory Guide to Iridology* (Thorsons, 1991).

Conway, David, *The Complete Magic Primer* (The Aquarian Press, 1988).

—— *The Secret Wisdom* (The Aquarian Press, 1992).

Cooper, J. C., *Taoism* (The Aquarian Press, 1989).

Crowley, Aleister, *Magic in Theory and Practice* (Routledge & Kegan Paul, 1973).

—— *The Book of Thoth* (Samuel Weiser, 1972).

—— *Magic without Tears*, ed. Regardie (Llewellyn Publications, 1973).

—— *The Qabalah of Aleister Crowley* —— *Three Texts* (Samuel Weiser, 1973).

—— *Magical and Philosophical Commentaries on 'The Book of the Law'* (93 Publishing, Canada, 1974).

—— *Gems from the Equinox*, ed. Regardie (Falcon Press, 1986).

Crowley, Vivianne, *Wicca: The Old Religion in the New Age* (The Aquarian Press, 1989).

Da Avabhasa, *The Knee of Listening* (Dawn Horse, 1984).

David-Neel, Alexandra, *Magic and Mystery in Tibet* (The Aquarian Press, 1984).

—— *Initiation and Initiates in Tibet* (Rider, 1970).

Dee, Dr John, *The Rosie Crucian Secrets* (The Aquarian Press, 1985).

Dingwall, Eric J., *Abnormal Hypnotic Phenomena*, (4 vols), (J. & A. Churchill, 1967/8).

Donnelly, Ignatius, *Atlantis: the Antediluvian World* (Sidgwick & Jackson, 1970).

Doyle, Arthur Conan, *The Coming of the Fairies* (Samuel Weiser, 1975).

Drake, Johnathon, *Thorsons Introductory Guide to the Alexander Technique* (Thorsons, 1993).

Duke, Marc, *Acupuncture* (Constable, 1973).

Edwards, Betty, *Drawing on the Right Side of the Brain* (J. P. Tarcher, 1979).

Eitel, E. J., *Feng-Shui: The Rudiments of Natural Science in China* (Trubner, 1873).

Eliade, Mircea, *Shamanism* (Princeton University Press, 1964).

—— *Yoga, Immortality and Freedom* (Princeton University Press, 1970).

—— *Origins and Structures of Alchemy* (Harper & Row, 1971).

Enomiya-Lassalle, Hugo, *The Practice of Zen Meditation* (Crucible, 1990).

Evans-Wentz, W. Y., *The Tibetan Book of the Dead* (Oxford University Press, 1968).

—— *Tibetan Yoga and Secret Doctrines* (Oxford University Press, 1969).

—— *The Tibetan Book of the Great Liberation* (Oxford University Press, 1969).

Fabricius, J., *Alchemy* (The Aquarian Press, 1989).

Feild, Reshad, *Travelling People's Feild Guide* (2 vols) (Element Books, 1986).

Ferguson, Marilyn, *The Aquarian Conspiracy: Personal and Social Transformation in the 1980s* (J. P. Tarcher, 1980).

Ferrucci, Piero, *What We May Be* (The Aquarian Press, 1989).

—— *Inevitable Grace* (The Aquarian Press, 1990).

Fortune, Dion, *The Mystical Qabalah* (The Aquarian Press, 1970).

—— *Psychic Self-Defence* (The Aquarian Press, 1977).

Fox, Oliver, *Astral Projection* (University Books, 1962).

Francis, D. Pitt, *Nostradamus: Prophecies of Present Times?* (The Aquarian Press, 1985).

Frazer, Sir James, *The Golden Bough* (Macmillan, 1963).

Fuller, John G., *The Interrupted Journey* (Dial, 1966).

Gadon, Elinor, *The Once and Future Goddess* (HarperSanFrancisco, 1990).

Gardner, Gerald B., *Witchcraft Today* (Jarrolds, 1954).

Gattey, Charles Neilson, *Prophecy and Prediction in the Twentieth Century* (The Aquarian Press, 1989).

Gauquelin, Michel, *The Scientific Basis of Astrology: Myth or Reality?* (Stein & Day, 1969).

—— *The Cosmic Clocks* (Paladin, 1973).

—— *Cosmic Influences on Human Behaviour* (Futura, 1976).

Gawain, Shakti, *Creative Visualization* (Whatever Publishing, California, 1978).

Geller, Uri, *My Story* (Robson Books, 1975).

Gibran, Khalil, *The Prophet* (Heinemann, 1956).

Gimbutas, Marija, *The Goddesses and Gods of Old Europe* (Thames & Hudson, 1982).

Goleman, *Meditative Mind* (The Aquarian Press, 1989).

Grant, Joan, *Winged Pharaoh* (Ariel Publications, 1989).

Grazia, Alfred de, *The Velikovsky Affair* (Sidgwick & Jackson, 1966).

Green, Celia, *Out-of-Body Experiences* (Institute of Psychophysical Research, Oxford, 1968).

—— *Lucid Dreams* (Hamish Hamilton, 1968).

Grof, Stanislav, *Realms of the Human Unconscious* (Dutton, 1976).

Guiley, Rosemary Ellen, *Harper's Encyclopedia of Mystical and Paranormal Experience* (HarperSanFrancisco, 1991).

Guillaume, Alfred, *Islam* (Penguin, 1973).

Guirdham, Arthur, *The Cathars and Reincarnation* (Spearman, 1970).

Gurdjieff, G. I., *Meetings with Remarkable Men* (Routledge & Kegan Paul, 1971).

Gurney, E., Myers, F. W. H., and Podmore, F., *Phantasms of the Living* (2 vols) (Trubner, 1886).

Haeffner, Mark, *A Dictionary of Alchemy* (The Aquarian Press, 1991).

Hall, Nicola M., *Thorsons Introductory Guide to Reflexology* (Thorsons, 1991).

Hamill, John, and Gilbert, R. A., *World Freemasonry* (The Aquarian Press, 1992).

Happold, F. C., *Mysticism: A Study and an Anthology* (Penguin, 1970).

Harding, Esther, *Women's Mysteries* (1971).

Hardy, Jean, *A Psychology with a Soul* (Routledge & Kegan Paul, 1987).

Harlins, Marvin, and Andrews, L. M., *Biofeedback: Turning on the Power of your Mind* (Garnstone Press, 1973).

Harner, Michael, *The Jivaro* (Doubleday/Natural History Press, 1972).

—— *Hallucinogens and Shamanism* (Oxford University Press, 1973).

—— *The Way of the Shaman* (Harper & Row, 1980).

Harper, George Mills, *Yeats's Golden Dawn* (Macmillan, 1974).

—— *Yeats and the Occult* (Macmillan, 1975).

Harrer, Heinrich, *Seven Years in Tibet* (J. P. Tarcher, 1981).

Harrison, E. J., *Fighting Spirit of Japan* (Foulsham, 1966).

Hawken, Paul, *The Magic of Findhorn* (Fontana, 1976).

Herrigel, Eugen, *Zen and the Art of Archery* (Routledge & Kegan Paul, 1953).

Hesse, Hermann, *Steppenwolf* (R. & W. Holt, 1963).

—— *The Glass Bead Game* (Cape, 1970).

—— *Journey to the East* (Peter Owen, 1970).

—— *Siddhartha* (Peter Owen, 1970).

Heyn, Birgit, *Ayurvedic Medicine* (Thorsons, 1987).

Hitching, Francis, *Earth Magic* (Cassell, 1976).

—— *Pendulum: the Psi Connection* (Fontana, 1977).

Hogue, John, *Nostradamus and the Millennium* (Bloomsbury, 1987).

Holmyard, E. J., *Alchemy* (Penguin, 1968).

Hope, Murry, *Practical Celtic Magic* (The Aquarian Press, 1987).

Houston, Jean, *The Possible Human: A Course in Enhancing your Physical, Mental and Creative Abilities* (J. P. Tarcher, 1982).

—— *The Search for the Beloved* (The Aquarian Press, 1990).

—— *The Hero and the Goddess* (The Aquarian Press, 1993).

Howe, Ellic, *The Magicians of the Golden Dawn* (Routledge & Kegan Paul, 1972).

Huson, Paul, *The Devil's Picture Book* (Abacus, 1972).

Huxley, Aldous, *The Doors of Perception* (Harper & Row, 1954).

—— *The Perennial Philosophy* (Fontana, 1958).

Hynek, J. Allen, *The UFO Experience* (Ballantine, 1972).

Iglehart, Hallie Austen, *Womenspirit: A Guide to Women's Wisdom* (Harper & Row, 1983).

Iyengar, B. K. S., *Light on Yoga* (The Aquarian Press, 1991).

James, William, *The Varieties of Religious Experience* (Fontana, 1960).

Jarmey, Chris, *Thorsons Introductory Guide to Shiatsu* (Thorsons, 1992).

Jung, C. G., *Memories, Dreams, Reflections* (Collins, 1963).

—— *The Collected Works* (20 vols) (Routledge & Kegan Paul, 1978–89).

Karlins, Marvin, and Andrews, Lewis, *Biofeedback* (Abacus, 1975).

Keel, John A., *UFOs: Operation Trojan Horse* (Abacus, 1973).

Keeton, Joe, and Moss, Peter, *Encounters with the Past* (Sidgwick and Jackson, 1979).

Kermani, Dr Kai, *Autogenic Training* (Thorsons, 1992).

Keyes, K., *Handbook to Higher Consciousness* (Living Love Publications, 1985).

Kilner, W. J., *The Aura* (Samuel Weiser, 1973).

King, Francis, *Ritual Magic in England* (NEL, 1970).

Klimo, Jon, *Channeling: Investigations on Receiving Information from Paranormal Sources* (J. P. Tarcher, 1987; The Aquarian Press, 1989).

Knight, Gareth, *A Practical Guide to Qabalistic Symbolism* (2 vols) (Helios Publications, Cheltenham, 1976).

Koestler, Arthur, *The Sleepwalkers* (Penguin Books, 1988).

Krippner, Stanley, and Daniel, Rubin, *Galaxies of Life* (Gordon & Breach, 1973).

Krishna, Gopi, *The Secret of Yoga* (Turnstone, 1973).

—— *Kundalini: The Evolutionary Energy in Man* (Shambhala).

Krishnamurti, J., *First and Last Freedom* (Gollancz, 1954).

—— *Life Ahead* (Gollancz, 1963).

—— *Freedom from the Known* (Harper & Row, 1969).

—— *The Only Revolution* (Gollancz, 1970).

—— *Urgency of Change* (Gollancz, 1971).

Kübler-Ross, Elisabeth, *On Death and Dying* (Macmillan, 1969).

Kuhn, Thomas S., *The Structure of Scientific Revolutions* (University of Chicago, 1970).

La Tourelle, Maggie, *Thorsons Introductory Guide to Kinesiology* (Thorsons, 1992).

Lau, D. C. (trans.), *Tao Te Ching* (Penguin, 1963).

Lefort, Rafael, *The Teachings of Gurdjieff* (Gollancz, 1971).

LeShan, Lawrence, *How to Meditate* (The Aquarian Press, 1989).

Lethbridge, Tom C., *Ghost and Ghoul* (Routledge & Kegan Paul, 1961).

—— *Ghost and Divining Rod* (Routledge & Kegan Paul, 1963).

—— *The Power of the Pendulum* (Routledge & Kegan Paul, 1976).

Lévi, Eliphas, *The History of Magic* (Rider, 1957).

—— *Transcendental Magic* (Rider, 1958).

—— *The Key to the Mysteries* (Rider, 1969).

Lewis, Lionel Smithett, *St Joseph of Arimathea at Glastonbury* (Clarke, 1922).

Lilly, John, *Centre of the Cyclone* (M. Boyars, 1973).

Long, Max Freedom, *The Secret Science behind Miracles* (Huna Research Publications, 1954).

—— *The Huna Code in Religions* (DeVorss, 1965).

Loomis, Roger Sherman, *The Grail: From Celtic Myth to Christian Symbol* (University of Wales Press, 1963).

Lovelock, James, *Gaia: A New Look at Life on Earth* (Oxford University Press, 1979).

Luce, Gay Gaer, and Segal, Julian, *Sleep and Dreams* (Panther, 1969).

Luce, J. V., *The End of Atlantis* (Paladin, 1970).

Lutyens, Mary, *The Penguin Krishnamurti Reader* (2 vols) (Penguin, 1970).

Maclaine, Shirley, *Out on a Limb* (Bantam, 1983).

—— *Dancing in the Light* (Bantam, 1985).

—— *It's All in the Playing* (Bantam, 1987).

Maharishi Mahesh Yogi, *Meditations of Maharishi Mahesh Yogi* (Bantam, 1968).

Mann, Felix, *Acupuncture* (Pan, 1973).

Marcuse, F. L., *Hypnosis* (Penguin, 1971).

Mascaro, J. (trans.), *Bhagavad-Gita* (Penguin, 1970).

—— *The Upanishads* (Penguin, 1970).

Maslow, Abraham, *The Farther Reaches of Human Nature* (Penguin, 1973).

Mathers, S. L. MacGregor, *The Kabbalah Unveiled* (Routledge & Kegan Paul, 1951).

Matthews, John (ed.), *The World Atlas of Divination* (Headline Book Publishing, 1992).

Matthews, John and Caitlín, *The Western Way* (2 vols) (Arkana, 1985, 1986).

—— *The Aquarian Guide to British and Irish Mythology* (The Aquarian Press, 1988).

Matthews, John, and Green, Marian, *The Grail-Seeker's Companion* (The Aquarian Press, 1986).

Michell, John, *The View over Atlantis* (Garnstone, 1969).

—— *The Old Stones at Land's End* (Garnstone, 1974).

—— *The Earth Spirit* (Avon, 1975).

Milne, Hugh, *Bhagwan: the God that Failed* (Sphere, 1987).

Monroe, Robert A., *Journeys out of the Body* (Souvenir Press, 1972).

—— *Far Journeys* (Souvenir Press, 1986).

Montgomery, Ruth, *A Search for Truth*.

Moody, Raymond, *Life After Life* (Bantam, 1975).

—— *The Light Beyond* (Bantam, 1988).

Muhyiddin Ibn'Arabi, *Fusus Al-Hikam* (trans. and commentary Ismail Hakki Bursevi, rendered into English by Bulent Rauf) (4 vols) (The Muhyiddin Ibn'Arabi Society, 1986–91).

Muktananda, Swami, *Play of Consciousness* (SYDA Foundation, 1978).

Muldoon, Sylvan, and Carrington, Hereward, *The Projection of the Astral Body* (Rider, 1968).

—— *The Phenomena of Astral Projection* (Rider, 1969).

Murray, Margaret A., *The Witch-Cult in Western Europe* (Oxford University Press, 1921).

Naranjo, Claudio, and Ornstein, Robert, *The Psychology of Meditation* (Viking, 1972).

Needham, Joseph, *Science and Civilization in China* (6 vols) (Cambridge University Press, 1956–86).

Needleman, Jacob, *The New Religions* (Allen Lane, 1972).

Neihardt, John G., *Black Elk Speaks* (1932).

Nichols, Ross, *The Book of Druidry* (The Aquarian Press, 1990).

Nicholson, Shirley (ed.), *Shamanism* (Theosophical Publishing House, 1987).

O'Connor, Joseph, and Seymour, John, *Introducing Neuro-Linguistic Programming* (Crucible, 1990).

Ornstein, Robert, *The Nature of Human Consciousness* (Freeman, 1973).

Ostrander, Sheila, and Schroeder, Lynn, *Psychic Discoveries Behind the Iron Curtain* (Sphere, 1973).

—— *Superlearning* (Sphere, 1981).

Ouspensky, P. D., *Tertium Organum* (Routledge & Kegan Paul, 1957).

—— *In Search of the Miraculous* (Routledge & Kegan Paul, 1969).

—— *The Fourth Way* (Routledge & Kegan Paul, 1972).

Palmer, Helen, *The Enneagram* (HarperSanFrancisco, 1990).

Patanjali, *Aphorisms of Yoga* (trans. Shree Purohit Swami) (Faber, 1973).

Peck, M. Scott, *The Road Less Travelled: A New Psychology of Love, Traditional Values and Spiritual Growth* (Hutchinson, 1978).

Pennick, Nigel, *The Ancient Science of Geomancy* (Thames & Hudson, 1979).

—— *Practical Magic in the Northern Tradition* (The Aquarian Press, 1989).

Peters, Fritz, *Gurdjieff Remembered* (Samuel Weiser, 1971).

Pirsig, R., *Zen and the Art of Motorcycle Maintenance* (Corgi, 1976).

Plato, *Timaeus and Critias* (trans. Desmond Lee) (Penguin, 1965).

Pollack, Rachel, *78 Degrees of Wisdom*, Parts I and II (The Aquarian Press, 1980, 1983).

—— *The New Tarot* (The Aquarian Press, 1989).

Price, Shirley, *Practical Aromatherapy* (Thorsons, 1983).

Puharich, Andrija, *Uri: A Journal of the Mystery of Uri Geller* (Anchor Press, 1974).

Regardie, Israel, *Art of True Healing* (Helios Publications, Cheltenham, 1966).
—— *A Garden of Pomegranites* (Llewellyn Publications, 1970).
—— *The Philosopher's Stone* (Llewellyn Publications, 1970).
—— *The Golden Dawn* (Llewellyn Publications, 1972).
—— *The Tree of Life* (Thorsons, 1975).
Reich, Wilhelm, *Selected Writings* (Farrar, Strauss & Giroux, 1979).
Reichenbach, Karl von, *The Odic Force* (University Books, 1968).
Ring, Kenneth, *Life at Death: A Scientific Investigation of the Near-Death Experience* (William Morrow, 1980).
—— *Heading towards Omega: In Search of the Meaning of the Near-Death Experience* (William Morrow, 1984).
Riso, Don Richard, *Personality Types* (The Aquarian Press, 1991).
Robbins, Christopher, *Thorsons Introductory Guide to Herbalism* (Thorsons, 1993).
Roberts, Jane, *The Seth Material* (Prentice-Hall, 1970).
Rodegast, Pat, *Emmanuel's Book: A Manual for Living Comfortably in the Cosmos* (Bantam, 1987).
Rogo, D. Scott, *Life After Death* (The Aquarian Press, 1986).
—— *Return From Silence* (The Aquarian Press, 1989).
Roszak, Theodore, *The Making of a Counter Culture* (1968).
Russell, Peter, *The Awakening Earth: Our Next Evolutionary Leap* (Routledge & Kegan Paul, 1982).
—— *The White Hole in Time* (HarperSanFrancisco and The Aquarian Press, 1992).
Sanderson, Ivan T., *More 'Things'* (Pyramid Books, 1965).
Sargant, William, *Battle for the Mind* (Pan, 1970).
—— *The Mind Possessed* (Heinemann, 1973).
Satin, Mark, *New Age Politics* (Delta Books, 1979).
Scheffer, Mechtild, *Bach Flower Therapy* (Thorsons, 1993).
Schul, Bill, and Pettit, Ed, *The Psychic Power of Pyramids* (Coronet, 1977).
Schumacher, E. F., *Small is Beautiful* (Blond and Briggs, 1973).
—— *A Guide for the Perplexed* (Harper & Row, 1977).
Shah, Sayed Idries, *The Secret Lore of Magic* (Frederick Muller, 1957).
—— *The Sufis* (Doubleday, 1964).
—— *Oriental Magic* (Octagon Press, 1970).
Sheldrake, Rupert, *A New Science of Life* (Blond & Briggs, 1982).
Shinoda Bolen, Jean, *Goddesses in Everywoman* (Harper & Row, 1984).

Siegel, Bernie S., M.D., *Love, Medicine and Miracles: Lessons Learned About Self-Healing from a Surgeon's Experience* (Harper & Row, 1986).
—— *Living, Loving and Healing* (The Aquarian Press, 1993).
Simonton, Carl and Stephanie, *Getting Well Again* (J. P. Tarcher, 1978).
Smith, Warren, *The Secret Forces of the Pyramids* (Sphere, 1977).
Spangler, David, *Revelation: Birth of a New Age* (1977).
—— *Emergence: The Rebirth of the Sacred* (1984).
—— and Thompson, Willam Irwin, *Reimagination of the World: A Critique of the New Age, Science and Popular Culture* (Bear & Co, 1991).
Sprague de Camp, Lester, *Lost Continents* (Dover, 1970).
Starhawk, *The Spiral Dance: A Rebirth of the Ancient Religion of the Great Goddess* (Harper & Row, 1979).
—— *Dreaming the Dark: Magic, Sex and Politics* (Beacon Publishing, 1983).
Steiger, Brad, *Project Blue Book* (Ballantine, 1976).
Stone, Merlin, *When God was a Woman* (Dial Press, New York, 1976).
Storr, Anthony, *Jung* (Fontana, 1973).
Strunckel, Shelley von, *The No-Nonsense Guide to the Sixth Sense* (Corgi, 1990).
Stutley, Margaret, *Hinduism* (The Aquarian Press, 1989).
Sun Bear, *The Medicine Wheel: Earth Astrology* (Prentice-Hall, 1980).
—— *The Path of Power* (Prentice-Hall, 1988).
—— *Sun Bear's Book of the Vision Quest* (Prentice-Hall, 1988).
Suzuki, D. T., *An Introduction to Zen Buddhism* (Rider, 1969).
—— *The Zen Doctrine of No Mind* (Rider, 1969).
—— *Living by Zen* (Rider, 1972).
Suzuki, Shunryu, *Zen Mind, Beginner's Mind* (Weatherhill, 1970).
Talbott, S., *Velikovsky Reconsidered* (Sidgwick & Jackson, 1977).
Tansley, David W., *Radionics and the Subtle Anatomy of Man* (Health Science Press, 1972).
Targ, Russell, and Puthoff, Harold, *Mind-Reach* (Paladin, 1978).
Tart, Charles T. (ed.), *Altered States of Consciousness* (1969).
—— *Waking Up: Overcoming the Obstacles to Human Potential* (Shambhala, 1986).
Teilhard de Chardin, *The Phenomenon of Man* (Fontana, 1968).
—— *The Future of Man* (Fontana, 1968).
—— *Human Energy* (Collins, 1969).
Temple, Robert G., *The Sirius Mystery* (Sidgwick & Jackson, 1976).

—— *Open to Suggestion: The Uses and Abuses of Hypnosis* (The Aquarian Press, 1989).

Thom, Alexander, *Megalithic Sites in Britain* (Oxford University Press, 1967).

—— *Megalithic Lunar Observatories* (Oxford University Press, 1971).

Tohei, Koichi, *Aikido* (Souvenir Press, 1966).

Tomas, Andrew, *Shambhala* (Sphere, 1977).

Tompkins, Peter, *The Secrets of the Great Pyramid* (Allen Lane, 1971).

—— and Bird, Christopher, *The Secret Life of Plants* (Viking, 1980).

Triance, Edward, *Thorsons Introductory Guide to Osteopathy* (Thorsons, 1991).

Trungpa, Chögyam, *Cutting through Spiritual Materialism* (Shambhala, 1973).

—— *The Myth of Freedom and the Way of Meditation* (Shambhala, 1976).

—— *Shambhala: The Sacred Path of the Warrior* (Shambhala, 1984).

Tweedie, Irina, *The Chasm of Fire* (Element Books, 1979).

Ullman, Montague, and Zimmerman, Nan, *Working with Dreams* (Crucible, 1989).

Underhill, E., *Mysticism* (Dutton, New York).

Velikovsky, Immanuel, *Worlds in Collision* (Abacus, 1973).

—— *Ages in Chaos* (Abacus, 1973).

—— *Earth in Upheaval* (Abacus, 1973).

Waite, A. E., *The Book of Ceremonial Magic* (University Books, 1961).

—— *The Alchemical Writings of Edward Kelley* (Robinson & Watkins, 1973).

—— *The Hermetic Museum* (2 vols) (Robinson & Watkins, 1973).

Walker, Barbara G., *The Woman's Encyclopedia of Myths and Secrets* (Harper & Row, 1983).

—— *The Woman's Dictionary of Symbols and Sacred Objects* (Harper & Row, 1988).

Walker, Benjamin, *Gnosticism* (The Aquarian Press, 1989).

Wall, Vicky, *The Miracle of Colour Healing* (The Aquarian Press, 1993).

Watkins, Alfred, *The Old Straight Track* (Garnstone Press, 1970).

Watson, Lyall, *Supernature* (Hodder & Stoughton, 1973).

Watts, Alan, *The Way of Zen* (Vintage, 1957).

—— *The Joyous Cosmology* (Random House, 1962).

—— *The Book: On the Taboo against Knowing Who You Are* (Random House, 1966).

—— *The Spirit of Zen* (The Aquarian Press, 1992).

Weeks, Nora, *Medical Discoveries of Edward Bach, Physician* (Daniel, 1940).

White, John, *The Highest State of Consciousness* (Doubleday, 1972).

—— (ed.), *What is Enlightenment?* (The Aquarian Press, 1988).

White, Ruth, *Gildas Communicates* (Spearman, 1971).

—— *The Healing Spectrum* (Spearman, 1979).

—— *A Question of Guidance* (C. W. Daniel, 1989).

Whitmont, Edward, *Return of the Goddess* (Arkana, 1983).

Wilber, Ken, *The Spectrum of Consciousness* (Theosophical Publishing House, 1977).

—— *The Atman Project* (Theosophical Publishing House, 1980).

—— (ed.), *The Holographic Paradigm* (Shambhala, 1982).

—— *Up from Eden: A Transpersonal View of Human Evolution* (Routledge & Kegan Paul, 1983).

Wilhelm, Richard (trans.), *I Ching* (Routledge & Kegan Paul, 1968).

Williamson, Marianne, *A Return to Love* (The Aquarian Press, 1992).

Wilson, Annie and Bek, Lilla, *What Colour Are You?* (The Aquarian Press, 1987).

Wilson, Colin, *The Occult* (Hodder, 1971).

—— *Mysteries* (Panther, 1978).

—— *Aleister Crowley: The Nature of the Beast* (The Aquarian Press, 1987).

—— *The Strange Life of P. D. Ouspensky* (The Aquarian Press, 1993).

Wood, Ernest, *Yoga* (Penguin, 1972).

Woodroffe, Sir John, *The Serpent Power* (Ganesh & Co., Madras, 1974).

Yates, Dame Frances, *The Art of Memory* (Routledge & Kegan Paul).

—— *Astraea* (Routledge & Kegan Paul).

—— *The Occult Philosophy in the Elizabethan Age* (Routledge & Kegan Paul).

Yogananda, Paramahansa, *Autobiography of a Yogi* (Rider, 1969).

Of further interest . . .

THE SEEKER'S GUIDE

A NEW AGE RESOURCE BOOK

Edited and with an introduction by John Button and William Bloom
Foreword by Sir George Trevelyan

This is the ultimate reference book on New Age ideas, beliefs, practices and resources. It provides

Information about the many spiritual, healing and holistic traditions which comprise the New Age movement

Descriptions of the most important ideas and practices within the spiritual, healing, therapeutic and green movements, from the Goddess to Gnosticism, Reincarnation to Rolfing, Acupuncture to Alexander, Holistic Education to Ecofeminism

A directory of resources and products including books and bookshops, courses and groups, centres and organizations

An overview of current developments in New Age thinking, from new approaches to spirituality to the frontiers of science and psychotherapy

Informative, practical and fully illustrated, The Seeker's Guide *provides both the committed New Ager and the novice with all the ingredients needed to live in harmony with the environment and to achieve their highest potential.*

A proportion of the royalties from sales of this book will go to children's and environmental charities.

THE DICTIONARY OF ALCHEMY

FROM MARIA PROPHETISSA TO ISAAC NEWTON

Mark Haeffner

Alchemy is a rich and complex esoteric tradition that has flourished world-wide since the beginning of recorded history, if not earlier. There are three main traditions: Western Christian, Indo-Tibetan and Chinese Taoist. Within this diversity there are many common features, which are analysed, organized and brought together for the first time in this comprehensive dictionary of terms, symbols and personalities.

This dictionary is the distillation of many years' research into the extensive arcane literature. It is a reference work to guide readers through the labyrinth of pre-Newtonian science and philosophy. The dictionary covers not only the materialist dimension of the search for the elixir of life and the transmutation of metals, but also the inner search for the gold of mystical illumination.

Jung called alchemy 'the projection of the drama both cosmic and spiritual in laboratory terms'. This *opus alchymicum* goes beyond the bare analysis and interpretation of terms to present a harmonic, integrated vision of man and nature, which may help to heal the fragmented world-view of modern science.

DICTIONARY FOR DREAMERS

Tom Chetwynd

Distilled from the collective wisdom of the great interpreters of dreams – Freud, Jung, Adler, Stekel and Gutheil, among others – this comprehensive key to the baffling language of dream symbolism is a thought-provoking and invaluable guide to the uncharted country of the mind. Tom Chetwynd has isolated for the first time the rich meanings of over 500 archetypal symbols from the indiscriminate mass of dream material, and rated the likelihoods of the various possible interpretations in each case. Here are the essential clues to understanding the ingeniously disguised, life-enriching, often urgent messages to be found in dreams.

DICTIONARY OF SYMBOLS

Tom Chetwynd

'Without symbols our lives would be as spiritually impoverished as sleep without dreams . . .'

Just as we dream every night without necessarily being aware of having dreamed, so our waking life is full of symbolism operating on an unconscious level. Drawn from the collective wisdom of the great psychologists, particularly Jung, this comprehensive and thought-provoking guide explains the language of symbols. Tom Chetwynd describes the major characteristics that recur in all symbolic material; identifying them can enable us to recognize the patterns and processes at work in our own minds, and to explore, develop and transform ourselves.

Tom Chetwynd studied theology at London University and wrote a number of novels and stories before turning his attention to exploring the unconscious with his *Dictionary of Dreamers*, followed by this *Dictionary of Symbols*. A third volume, *Dictionary of Sacred Myth*, completes his study of dreams, symbols and myths. He has also written *The Age of Myth*.

'A really remarkable book . . . written with a great deal of learning and good humour.'
Richard Holmes, *The Standard*

DICTIONARY OF SACRED MYTH

Tom Chetwynd

*'There is only one symbolic language – and that is used by dreams,
creative imagination and myths.'*

Myths depict the archetypal patterns in the drama of the psyche,
the universal processes of life. The language of myths and dreams
is simple and direct – but we have forgotten the art of interpreting
it. In this fascinating compilation, Tom Chetwynd explores the
oldest and most universal method of communication, drawing on
the mythologies of the ancient world, Egypt, Classical Greece and
Rome, as well as the insights of psychology and the mystical
traditions of the world's religions.

As sacred myth is an attempt on the part of the human psyche to
reflect the dynamics of nature and the universe, so working with
myths and symbols can bring renewed understanding of the ways
of the soul.

THE SEEKER'S GUIDE	1 85538 175 3	£12.99	☐
DICTIONARY OF ALCHEMY	1 85538 085 4	£12.99	☐
DICTIONARY FOR DREAMERS	1 85538 295 4	£4.99	☐
DICTIONARY OF SYMBOLS	1 85538 296 2	£6.99	☐
DICTIONARY OF SACRED MYTH	1 85538 294 6	£5.99	☐

All these books are available from your local bookseller or can be ordered direct from the publishers.

To order direct just tick the titles you want and fill in the form below:

Name: _____

Address: _____

_____

_____ Postcode: _____

Send to: Thorsons Mail Order, Dept 3, HarperCollins*Publishers*, Westerhill Road, Bishopbriggs, Glasgow G64 2QT.
Please enclose a cheque or postal order or your authority to debit your Visa/Access account —

Credit card no: _____

Expiry date: _____

Signature: _____

— up to the value of the cover price plus:
UK & BFPO: Add £1.00 for the first book and 25p for each additional book ordered.
Overseas orders including Eire: Please add £2.95 service charge. Books will be sent by surface mail but quotes for airmail despatches will be given on request.

24 HOUR TELEPHONE ORDERING SERVICE FOR ACCESS/VISA CARDHOLDERS — TEL: **041 772 2281.**